Tuning In to Young Viewers

Tuning In to Young Viewers

Social Science Perspectives on Television

Tannis M. MacBeth
Editor

SAGE Publications
International Educational and Professional Publisher
Thousand Oaks   London   New Delhi

For information address:

SAGE Publications, Inc.
2455 Teller Road
Thousand Oaks, California 91320
E-mail: order@sagepub.com

SAGE Publications Ltd.
6 Bonhill Street
London EC2A 4PU
United Kingdom

SAGE Publications India Pvt. Ltd.
M-32 Market
Greater Kailash I
New Delhi 110 048 India

Printed in the United States of America

Library of Congress Cataloging-in-Publication Data

Main entry under title:

Tuning in to young viewers: Social science perspectives on television /
   editor, Tannis M. MacBeth.
      p.   cm.
   Includes bibliographical references (p.) and index.
   ISBN 0-8039-5825-0 (cloth: acid-free paper).   ISBN 0-8039-5826-9
(pbk.: acid-free paper)
      1. Television and children—United States.   2. Television—Social
   aspects—United States.   3. Child psychology—United States.
   I. MacBeth, Tannis M.
   HQ784.T4T85   1996   95-50231
   302.23'45'083—dc20

This book is printed on acid-free paper.

            99 10 9 8 7 6 5 4 3

Sage Production Editor: Astrid Virding
Sage Typesetter: Marion S. Warren

Contents

BIZARRO

By DAN PIRARO

The *Bizarro* cartoon by Dan Piraro is reprinted courtesy of Chronicle Features, San Francisco, California. All rights reserved.

1

Introduction

Tannis M. MacBeth

A s social scientists who do research on the uses, content, and effects of television, we are often asked the following questions:

If I want to know whether and how television affects its viewers, what issues do I need to consider? How do researchers go about studying media effects, and what are the pros and cons of each approach? Is TV viewing an active or passive activity? How can I figure out whether television affects its viewers or whether viewers with different characteristics use television differently? (*Chapter 1*)

How are young children socialized to use television? What societal influences, family influences, and characteristics of the child are important in determining how much and what TV programming children watch? How do young children's patterns of viewing affect their social development and thinking? For example, can preschoolers learn vocabulary from television? (*Chapter 2*)

The multicultural nature of North American society does not seem to be reflected in its TV programming. Is this lack of diversity just an impression or has it been documented? What effect does this have on members of visible racial-ethnic groups? How are the attitudes and behavior of members of the dominant culture affected? When African American and other visible racial-ethnic groups are represented on TV do they serve as positive role models for viewers? (*Chapter 3*)

My children have nightmares about scary things they have seen on TV and in movies. Is this typical? Are parents usually aware that their children have been

1

frightened by TV? How serious and long-lasting are children's fright reactions to TV and other media? Are children at certain ages particularly vulnerable? Do the same sorts of things cause fear in young children, older children, adolescents, and adults? (*Chapter 4*)

There seems to be a lot of discussion about violence on TV, but what is the evidence that TV plays a role in the development of aggressive behavior? How—that is, through what processes—does TV violence viewing influence aggressive behavior? How can the potentially negative effects of watching violence on TV be reduced? (*Chapter 5*)

Many questions about TV effects focus on possible positive (e.g., vocabulary) and negative (e.g., aggression, fear) effects of its content. Are there other, indirect effects that seem to be due more to how TV is used, effects of the medium itself? For example, do children who are better readers, who do better in school, or both watch less TV than those who do more poorly? If so, does this mean that TV viewing causes poor school achievement? Does TV affect persistence? Does it stifle or facilitate creativity? How does TV viewing relate to participation in other activities? (*Chapter 6*)

I've read that some people are "addicted" to or psychologically dependent on television. How can people decide whether they, their children, or both are watching too much TV? How might they change their habits and use TV more constructively? What about dependence on other media, such as video games, computer games, and pornography? Is media education the answer? (*Chapter 7*)

What can parents, teachers, and others who work with families do to optimize the positive effects and minimize the negative effects of television? (*all chapters*)

There are many other important questions about TV and human behavior, but these issues are central among those most frequently raised about the role of television in the lives of children and their families. In this book, we present overviews and analyses of the evidence and prevailing wisdom that has developed through our own and others' research. We hope that this will provide students, parents, educators, mental health professionals, and others interested in media effects with the up-to-date understanding they are seeking when they ask these questions. In trying to answer such questions about media effects, we take a psychological, social science perspective in our research and in this book. Most of us are developmental or clinical psychologists, so we are primarily interested in how people respond to television and how children and adults are affected by it. Other scholars approach the topic of media effects from a variety of equally legitimate perspectives, including sociological, cultural, political, or some combination of these, but our own focus is more psychological.

After sifting and weighing the findings of the very large body of research that has been conducted over the past 40 years, we count ourselves among the majority of researchers who conclude that television does indeed have some effects. Unfortunately, the "gradual, cumulative drip-drip-drip" (Greenberg, 1988, p. 97) nature of the process through which many of these effects occur makes them difficult to measure with the methods of social science (Huston et al., 1992). Nevertheless, the hypotheses of no effects (e.g., Klapper, 1949, 1960) or "statistically trivial to practically insubstantial" effects (McGuire, 1986, p. 213) are, in our opinion, not supported by the evidence. This is not to argue that television is the most important influence and not to argue that its effects are massive or universal but to state that TV does have some effects that have been shown to be measurable on average, over and above the many other influences on its viewers and despite their many individual differences. We agree with Comstock's (1989) conclusion that television is an additional rather than primary influence and with Bandura (1986), who places television third as a source of influence, behind the family and social milieu in which a person resides.

Many different groups of experts, brought together over the years, have reached the conclusion that, although no single study can be definitive, the body of research evidence indicates that television does have some effects on some viewers under some circumstances. In the United States, these have included the Surgeon General's Scientific Advisory Committee on Television and Social Behavior (Comstock & Rubinstein, 1972a, 1972b; Comstock, Rubinstein, & Murray, 1972; Murray, Rubinstein, & Comstock, 1972; Rubinstein, Comstock, & Murray, 1972), which focused on television violence and aggressive behavior; the National Institute of Mental Health's update a decade later that reviewed a wider range of research (Pearl, Bouthilet, & Lazar, 1982); the American Psychological Association, which in 1985 adopted the position that television violence has a causal effect on aggressive behavior; and the American Psychological Association's Task Force on Television and Society (Huston et al., 1992), which focused on a wide range of positive and negative effects of TV advertising and programming on women, children, minorities, and the elderly. In Canada these groups have included the Report of the Ontario Royal Commission on Violence in the Communications Industry (1977) and, on several occasions, the Canadian Radio-Television and Telecommunications Commission, which has commissioned reports and conferences in the areas of gender role portrayals and the debate about the relationship between violence and viewers' aggressive behavior.

Children as Special

Most researchers, especially those who study human development, believe that children are a "special audience" for television (Dorr, 1986). They show interest in television as infants (Hollenbeck & Slaby, 1979; Lemish & Rice, 1986), and parents apparently often report putting their babies in front of the TV to quiet them (Huston et al., 1992). Children become regular viewers during their preschool years, and as is often pointed out, in North America they eventually spend more time with television than they do in school (Huston et al., 1992). Conservative estimates indicate that the average child in the United States watches TV between 2 and 3 hours a day (Condry, 1989), and Canadian estimates are similar. Patterns of television use, evident by age 3, tend to be maintained (Huston, Wright, Rice, Kerkman, & Peters, 1990). For a number of reasons young children are considered to be especially vulnerable to possible negative effects (Huston et al., 1992) and to be "primed" and especially open to positive effects of programming intended to be informative. They begin watching TV regularly when their knowledge of the social and physical world is very limited; it is for them an "early window" (Liebert & Sprafkin, 1988). As Dorr (1986, p. 13) points out, children's limited knowledge of the larger world has several implications for their transactions with television: (a) They may fail to understand or may misunderstand program content if they lack the necessary background knowledge (and, I would add, this may be especially true of children who are not from the dominant culture most often portrayed); (b) they may accept TV content as accurate "information" when other more knowledgeable viewers know it to be otherwise; and (c) they may evaluate content without considering the means and motives for broadcasting it.)

Several factors influence and may limit children's understanding of both real-life and media events. First, they may lack relevant background knowledge (Dorr, 1986). This includes both general knowledge and more specific knowledge.

Second, children's ability to understand various media, including television, as well as their ability to understand real-life events, is limited by their cognitive development. If they have not yet developed a full understanding of time, some techniques often used in film and television, such as flashbacks, will be incomprehensible. They will have considerable difficulty following the plot of a story or the sequence of events in a documentary. Even when their time-related knowledge is better developed, they may still lack specific knowledge, for example, about how flashbacks are used and indicated. It may be, of course, that exposure to flashbacks facilitates the development of knowledge about time and sequential events. It is more likely, however, that their knowledge of specific conventions and techniques of film and television is dependent on more general cognitive foundations.

Where Are We Coming From?
An Interactive Model of Media Influence

Saying that television does have some effects does not imply that our perspective on viewers, or the audience, is monolithic. On the contrary, we readily acknowledge that two viewers sitting side by side watching the same program will take away some different impressions, memories, and understandings. They are likely to be affected differently to some extent and could even take away completely different meanings. As is the case for any communication, the outcome results from the interaction of the characteristics of the message, in this case the television program and the nature of the television medium, and the characteristics of the receiver, in this case the viewer (e.g., Greenberg, 1974; Huston et al., 1992). In my conceptualization of this interactive process there is a continuum operating. In some cases the characteristics of the viewer will predominate, so it is less likely that different viewers will receive the same message. In other cases the characteristics of the message or content will predominate, and most viewers will receive the same message.

An illustration of the continuum in which message or viewer characteristics may predominate comes from my own studies of the content of television programming. University students who had been trained to code television programs watched a videotaped program once through without stopping or replaying the tape and then answered questions about it (Williams, Phillips, & Travis, 1985). For some questions, I was unable to train them to answer reliably—that is, to agree on the content. This is an example of such a question: "Was the political philosophy of this program—generally left, center, right, apolitical, or political but not identifiably left or right?" Students whose own views tended to the left thought the program was right-wing, whereas those with right-wing views thought it was center or left. For most of the questions, however, there was a high level of agreement among the trained coders, despite their heterogeneous class and cultural backgrounds. In a related study, the same programs were watched by university students from a wide variety of backgrounds who were not trained as television coders and didn't know the questions they would be asked until after viewing the program (Wotherspoon & Williams, 1989).[1] Like the trained coders, these untrained viewers tended to agree on most of the questions about the program's content. Moreover, these untrained viewers' answers were very similar to those of the trained coders. For most questions then, the characteristics of the content or message were apparently predominant, despite the individual differences among both the untrained viewers and trained coders. The following is an example of a question on which both trained and untrained viewers tended to agree for any given TV program: "Were the prominent characters in the program all mainstream nonethnics, mostly mainstream nonethnics with some important ethnics, an even mix, mostly ethnic with some important mainstream characters, or all ethnics?" Both the trained coders and the untrained viewers were heterogeneous and included university students from diverse racial-ethnic groups, as well as many for whom English was a second language. We might readily expect, therefore, that they would not agree when answering this question, but they did.

This interactionist model of a continuum in which the characteristics of both the viewer and the message-medium determine the effects, but to greater and lesser degrees in different cases or contexts, is consistent with Morley's (1980) conceptualization. He argues that the television message is a complex sign in which a preferred ("dominant") meaning has been inscribed but that retains the potential to be decoded in a different manner and thus to communicate a different ("oppositional") meaning. In his opinion, all meanings do not exist equally in the message. It has been structured in dominance, but its meaning can never be totally fixed or closed. Morley did not discuss the question of developmental differences in the likelihood that viewers would take away shared or different meanings from the same content. It seems plausible to me that the constraints placed by children's cognitive development, and thus their ability to understand the content of television, would result in children at similar stages of cognitive development being more likely than adults to take away shared meanings from a given program. Conversely, children at different stages of cognitive development might be more likely to take away different meanings. These hypotheses could be tested through empirical research.

Where Are We Not Coming From?

So far I have tried to make a case for the focus of this book that there is empirical evidence that television does have some psychological effects that are measurable, despite the difficulties in doing so; that children may be especially likely to be influenced by television; and that preferred or dominant messages have been inscribed in its content, structure, and forms. Readers deserve to know, and may well wish to read further, about different conceptualizations of media effects and about TV effects in particular. I have already indicated that, although the majority do not agree with their position, some reviewers of the literature on TV effects (e.g., Freedman, 1984, 1986; McGuire, 1986) contend that effects are either nonexistent or that they are so minimal as to be unimportant. Rather than presenting only their own perspective on the topics they are reviewing, the authors of chapters in this book also describe and provide references for opposing points of view so that readers can draw their own informed conclusions.

In addition to those who argue that media and television have no or only minimal effects, there are researchers who argue that there *are* effects, but these effects are so highly individualized that to conduct research that asks about general effects is to be misguided. Readers may want to read more about these latter points of view and the research it has spawned, so I shall provide a brief introduction. In Chapter 7, Robert Kubey offers some additional comments on these perspectives (see also Kubey & Csikszentmihalyi, 1990).

The "cultural studies" (e.g., Collins et al., 1986; O'Connor, 1990; Rakow, 1990) approach to media research developed as a critique of "old-style audience surveys, with their monolithic conception of 'the viewer' and simple-minded notion of message, meaning, and influence which for so long dominated media studies" (Hall, 1986, p. 7). In the cultural studies conceptualization the audience is more active and the focus is on the varied "readings" individuals construct from the content and how they "make sense" of it. The goal is to make clear how social meaning gets made. Much, if not all, of this work focuses on "the relation between cultural form and material life" with a "broad, if critical, allegiance to a Marxist problematic" (Collins et al., 1986, p. 7). Thus, the varied readings of viewers in relation to their class, gender, and status as members of a minority versus dominant cultural group are of prime interest. Most, if not all, of this research has focused on adults rather than children. This also is true of "reception analysis." "Media texts acquire meaning only at the moment of reception, that is, when they are read, viewed, listened to, or whatever. In other words, audiences are seen as *producers* of meaning, not just consumers of media content: They *decode* or *interpret* media texts in ways that are related to their social and cultural circumstances and to the way in which they subjectively experience those circumstances" (Ang, 1990, p. 160). Many reception researchers focus not on individual "readings," but on social meanings that are culturally shared by "interpretive communities" (Radway, 1987) or "subcultures" (Hebdige, 1979).

In my opinion, cultural studies and reception analysis researchers raise important and interesting questions. This does not preclude, however, as some of their adherents contend, the possibility of studying and finding effects that are sufficiently strong (in some cases because a dominant meaning has been inscribed, as Morley, 1980, argues) that they apply across individuals despite their many individual and class, race, gender, and so forth differences. For developmental psychologists, the notion that individuals, even infants, construct meaning and are active contributors to the process of their own development (as Piaget theorized) does not mean that they are not affected by aspects of their environment. Indeed, they develop through their actions on the environment (including their actions on other living things as well its nonliving aspects) in an interactive process. To say that they may be affected by media, among other influences, does not imply a passive process. Our developmental point of view was summarized well by Dorr (1986), "currently most students of children's transactions with television agree that each viewer constructs meaning from television content while simultaneously assuming that viewers on average construct the same meaning for the same content" (p. 24). She went on to argue that we need to find a middle ground that recognizes that

> meaning is constructed at several levels and that each matters for what children do with television. At the same time we need to remember that each individual constructor has access to the same television signals. When viewers share a common culture, they then also share a similar set of construction tools and processes for interpreting these signals. An understanding of the significance of television to children's lives must be built on an understanding of these processes

by which children construct both idiosyncratic and shared m
content. (p. 27)

In sum, there are many different questions researchers can as.
and their users. Those working from a cultural studies or reception u.
perspective tend to focus on the variety of adult "readings" possible, whereas
others, ourselves included, focus on a different set of questions. We want to
know whether, despite the wide variety of readings possible, there is empirical
evidence of media effects, particularly on children, and if so, how potentially
positive effects can be maximized and negative ones minimized.

Do Viewers Watch Television Actively or Passively?[2]

In popular literature and everyday conversations, phrases that refer to
television viewing as a passive activity are common: couch potato, zombie,
veg out, and so on. By striking coincidence, as I was making a pot of tea and
listening to public radio just after writing this paragraph, I heard someone who
had called in to discuss the day's topic use the phrases "blind out in front of
TV" and "get mesmerized by it." All of these phrases imply that viewers are
relatively inactive both physically and mentally. Ironically, it also is common
to hear or read phrases implying that children, in particular, are very physically active while or after watching TV: go ballistic, get hyper, frenetic, and
so on. Some phrases often used to describe TV viewing, such as mesmerized,
could imply either heightened or reduced mental activity. What perspective
on this issue do television researchers take? As is often the case, there is no
one, simple answer.

Laboratory Studies

Some of the research on the processes involved in television viewing has
been done at universities in laboratories under highly controlled conditions.
For example, Daniel Anderson and his colleagues have studied preschoolers'
attention to television in his lab (e.g., Anderson & Lorch, 1983). They find
that young children look toward the television set when they hear certain cues
(e.g., women's, children's, or puppets' voices, but not men's voices) that the
content may be interesting and understandable to young children. Once

watching, they continue until the content becomes incomprehensible, uninteresting, or both, although the longer they attend to the set the less likely they are to turn away from it. In addition, the longer they are in the room with the set but ignoring it, the less likely they are to start watching. Anderson calls this phenomenon *attentional inertia.* In part on the basis of this type of research, Aletha Huston and John Wright (Chapter 2, this volume) point out that "children are often cognitively active when watching television" (p. 38) and that "children are usually not zombies in front of the set" (p. 39). Indeed, infants and young children spend much of their waking hours trying to make sense cognitively of the world around them, so they probably do so with television as well. This may be particularly likely if the programming is planned and designed to teach and intended for young children. This is the type of programming most often studied in laboratories, but there also is evidence that children can learn from such programming when they watch at home in a more natural viewing environment. As Huston and Wright (Chapter 2, this volume) state, children do learn from such programs, although they also learn social stereotypes and antisocial behavior from other television programs not designed to teach. Evidence of the latter sort of learning also comes from both laboratory and more naturalistic studies.

Studies in Natural Settings

Other evidence about the processes involved in watching television, and whether viewers are more active or passive, comes from studies conducted with a variety of methods in homes and other natural settings. For example, in Chapter 7 (this volume), Robert Kubey describes research he has conducted with his colleagues using a technique called the "event sampling method" (ESM). ESM provides "a picture of the way people feel as they move through everyday life, from leisure to work, from eating meals to driving their cars—and of the way they feel when they watch television" (Kubey & Csikszentmihalyi, 1990, p. xiii). Each participant in their study carried a pager or beeper and a booklet of forms for one week. On a predetermined random schedule, he or she was "beeped" 7 to 9 times a day between 8 a.m. and 10 p.m. Each time they were beeped, the participants completed a brief report, which took about 2 minutes, about where they were, the main and other things they were doing, what they were thinking about, their mood, and so on. Participants did not know that the researchers were particularly interested in television viewing. As Robert Kubey describes in Chapter 7, he and his colleagues have found that for people aged 10 to 82 studied in this unobtrusive way as they conducted their daily lives in Canada, Italy, the United States, and (West) Germany, "television viewing typically involves less concentration and alertness—and is experienced more passively—than almost all other daily activities, except when people report doing nothing."

In some studies, children or adults or both have been observed while going about their daily activities. For example, Lull (1990) and his students have conducted ethnographic studies in which an observer spends all or part of a day with a family taking part in their activities. They are asked to ignore the observer's presence and carry out their routines in a normal fashion. Lull (1990) did not discuss the question of active or passive viewing using those words, but he did make a number of related points. First, attentive viewing or attention is relative, because there is no such thing as full attention to the screen. "Looking at the screen certainly does not mean that the viewer is giving full attention, and viewers do not constantly look at the screen anyway. . . . There is a wide range of activities that accompany viewing" (p. 164). Second, he underscored a distinction made by T. Lindlof and his colleagues in the United States between focused viewing, monitoring (when viewing is secondary to some other activity), and idling (when a viewer is momentarily passing time between other activities). Third, Lull (1990) emphasized that "different types of programs elicit different styles of viewing for different people at different times of the day" (p. 166).

Some observations of 191 3- and 4-year-olds (101 females; 41.4% African American, 23% Mexican American, and 35.6% Anglo American) made by Durant, Baranowski, Johnson, and Thompson (1994) in Texas are relevant to the question of the active or passive nature of television viewing. Each child was observed 6 to 12 hours per day for up to 4 days in total over 1 year. Activity level was recorded for each minute of observation. There were no gender or racial-ethnic group differences in time watching television or physical activity while watching television. Television watching was significantly negatively, but only weakly, correlated with physical activity levels, and physical activity was lower during TV-watching than nonwatching times. Television viewing behavior was not related to body composition.

Another kind of evidence relevant to the question of whether viewers are more active or passive when watching television comes from studies in which video cameras have been installed in people's homes (e.g., Anderson, Field,

Collins, Lorch, & Nathan, 1985; Bechtel, Achelpohl, & Akers, 1972). Typically, the video camera(s) turn(s) on when the TV set is switched on, producing a record of the behavior of those in the room. Sometimes a camera also records what's on the screen. For example, a recent documentary, *Does TV Kill?* (first aired January 10, 1995), that was coproduced by Oregon Public Broadcasting and the U.S. Public Broadcasting System television program *Frontline,* contained footage from cameras placed in the homes of several families. The degree and extent of the passive behavior shown in the documentary was, to me, surprising. It is crucial to remember, however, that, unlike the method used by Kubey and his colleagues, this would not be a random or representative sample of behavior but, rather, what the producers selected to show in the documentary. In the studies in which video cameras have been used by researchers to randomly sample people's behavior as they watch television in their homes (e.g., Anderson et al., 1985; Anderson, Lorch, Field, Collins, & Nathan, 1986; Bechtel et al., 1972), their behavior has varied widely and ranged from relative inaction to time-sharing TV viewing with a wide variety of other activities (e.g., dressing or undressing, reading, playing cards or other games, homework).

Who? Where? When? What? Why?

What sense can we make of the disparate evidence regarding the question of active versus passive viewing? Unfortunately, the word *versus* misleads us into thinking it must be one or the other, when, as is often the case regarding research on television, we should instead be asking the journalist's series of questions: Who? Where? When? What? Why?

With regard to "Who?" we need to consider the developmental stage of the viewers, their emotional and physical health, and so on. Those, and perhaps other individual characteristics, are probably relevant within and across subcultures. With regard to developmental level, younger children may be more mentally active or "invest more mental effort" (Salomon, 1981, 1983) in television viewing than do older children because they have more difficulty comprehending it (Field & Anderson, 1985). It also is important to ask "Who?" from a cultural perspective. As the American Psychological Association's recent task force report (Huston et al., 1992) points out, the "United States is almost alone in the world in giving preference to developing television as a commercial medium rather than as a public service" (p. 115).

In most other countries, it is "only secondarily an entertainment medium and a means of selling goods and services" (p. 115). People who grow up with a television system that emphasizes educational and informational programs likely use it and attend to it differently than do children and adults who grow up in a country or, for that matter, in a family, where the emphasis is more exclusively on its entertainment value. I review some research in Chapter 6 of this book indicating that a family's orientation toward the use of TV is related to children's school achievement.

"Where?" requires considering, at the least, whether viewing is being done in the lab or in a more naturalistic setting, such as someone's home. In addition, viewing in the kitchen or bathroom may well differ from viewing in a bedroom or living room or den, not to mention an airport, sports bar, hotel room, and so on.

"When?" prompts us to recognize that time of day, day of week, and time of year need to be considered, perhaps in conjunction with "What?" For example, although Anderson has generally emphasized the active nature of young children's viewing, he also has noted that in his own research in which video cameras were placed in homes, children seemed more focused on the set and its content when watching Saturday morning cartoons than when watching other programming at other times (D. R. Anderson, personal communication, April, 1984). Children who are studied in a laboratory setting may expect to be asked questions about the programming they are shown on TV, so they may be more attentive than they would if watching for leisure at home. As I noted earlier, in the laboratory they are often shown programming intended for children and intended to be informative, whereas much of what children watch at home is neither intended for children nor intended to be informative.

This leads us to "Why?" or motivation for viewing. Surely people are more cognitively active when viewing, for example, a program that is part of a long-distance education course that they are taking for credit through a college or university than when they are watching "to relax" or purely for entertainment. Nevertheless, I and other professors with whom I've discussed this point have noticed that when we show a videotape or film in one of our university courses, the students' behavior changes dramatically, even when they know that the material is being shown for educational purposes and that they may be examined on its content. They typically stretch their legs out, lean back, and stop taking notes, treating these times as "breaks in the class, 'opportunities to space out' " (Greenfield, 1984, p. 170).

The why of someone's television viewing, as I discussed earlier, also incorporates the question of how, and Langer and Piper (1988) have concluded that "*how* one watches TV may matter more than *what* one watches" (p. 247). Their work indicates that choice and control play a very important role in well-being, both psychologically and physiologically speaking. Television, they point out, provides the opportunity to exercise control (e.g., over program choice). The predictability provided by some characters and programs (e.g., serials) is an important component of that control. The distinction between mindlessness and mindfulness is also importantly related to control and, Langer and Piper argue, to televiewing. Mindfulness refers to

> the process of drawing distinctions, creating categories, making the unknown known, or making the novel familiar. When people are mindless, on the other hand, they are relying on rigid distinctions or on familiarity without awareness of other ways the object (person, events, idea) might exist. (Langer & Piper, 1988, p. 250)

They discuss as an example turning on a light switch. When we first learn how to turn on a light, we notice many new things about it and many aspects of our own response to it, but once it's familiar, we respond to it mindlessly and pay no attention to it. Television, they contend, may be watched mindfully or mindlessly. For example, in his research Salomon (1983) found that Israeli children tended to invest more effort and retain more information when watching an educational television program than did children in the United States who watched the same program. This may be because proportionately more Israeli television programming is intended to be informative, so more children there may have developed the habit of watching TV for information.

There is some evidence that 12-year-olds in the United States consider television to be an easier medium than printed text from which to learn and believe that they are better at learning from TV than from print (Beentjes, 1989; Salomon, 1984). As a result, as Salomon (1981, 1983) hypothesized, they may tend to invest less mental effort in watching television than in reading.

In a study of the effects of mindful versus mindless television viewing (cited in Langer & Piper, 1988) adults aged 20 to 60 were asked to watch TV one hour per day for one week at a time they chose in advance. One group was told the researchers were interested in relaxation and thought TV was often relaxing. "They were told that television is familiar, that familiarity and predictability often make people feel more secure, and that feeling secure enables one to relax" (p. 254). They were asked to watch TV in a familiar way, whereas the mindful group was told that the researchers were interested in perspective taking so they were to watch from two different perspectives each night, their own and another one the researchers would suggest (a lawyer, a child, a physician, an athlete, a psychologist, an actor, and a politician, for each respective occasion). They were to try to think and feel just like the role they were playing and to contrast that with the way they otherwise would have watched. At the end of the week, all participants were asked to watch the next episode of *Dynasty,* but no other instructions were given. They all also completed several measures. On average, the mindful group checked off more adjectives as being related to or characteristic of themselves than did the comparison group, suggesting that the mindful group had a more flexible self-image. They said they enjoyed the *Dynasty* episode more than did the comparison group. They also saw the characters as significantly more complex, whereas the comparison group saw them more stereotypically. The mindful group noticed more action and more subplots and remembered more details of the program. They more often answered "it depends," indicating greater awareness of the complexity of circumstances and thus greater mindfulness. These results suggest, therefore, that watching television in a mindful way can result in greater flexibility in thinking, but "surely, if one repeatedly looks at something the same way day in and out, even if initially the perspective is novel, eventually mindlessness will result" (Langer & Piper, 1988, p. 255). These authors suggest that one solution may be to teach people to view television programs more mindfully. Another would be to program television to be more conditional, to encourage more mindfulness.

> In any event, television need not be the medium that controls the message, and this conclusion is especially important for those who disagree with the current message. While waiting for television fare to represent one's own values better, one can still enjoy watching and learn *how* to watch television. (p. 258)

In retrospect, the question I posed at the beginning of this section, "Do viewers watch television actively or passively?" was badly stated. The best answer is probably, "It depends."

The Chicken-and-Egg and Other Methodological Issues

Whenever we ask questions about media effects or try to evaluate the evidence from studies of the effects of television and other media, we soon run into the "chicken-and-egg problem." How can we figure out whether people who differ on some dimension, for example, aggressive behavior or creativity or reading skill, use TV differently, or whether watching TV or watching certain kinds of programs affects viewers' behavior in those areas? Whether as an educator, health care worker, or other professional giving advice or as a parent, student, or a researcher, everyone trying to sift through and weigh the evidence concerning media effects must consider this question. By raising it now, I hope not only to clarify my own views on some of the methodological issues in media effects research but also to provide some relevant background for readers to use in evaluating the results they read or hear about in this book and elsewhere.

Making Causal Inferences

The chicken-and-egg problem highlights the difficulty we face in trying to make causal inferences, whatever the domain of interest. Much of the research evidence is correlational in nature, and as social science students know, it is not possible to draw causal inferences from correlational data. For example, if we measure children's use of a particular communication medium (e.g., the telephone, television) or exposure to a particular type of television content (e.g., programming for children under 12 that is intended to be informative or programming with violent content) and also measure some other aspect of their behavior (e.g., marks in school, scores on a creative problem-solving task, aggression), we cannot say whether one behavior causes the other. If we find that relative to their peers, students who obtain high scores on one measure also tend to obtain high scores on the other and that those who obtain low scores on one also do so on the other, we can say only that the two behaviors or sets of scores are related (or if we apply a statistical test, we can perhaps say that they are statistically significantly correlated). Or we could say that one measure is predictive of the other, because knowing that a student scores high on one behavior allows us to predict that she or he scores high on the other one. But we are stuck with the chicken-and-egg problem of trying to figure out whether media use causes some behavior (e.g., better performance on a creativity task), whether individuals with that characteristic (high creativity scores) use media differently than other individuals who lack that characteristic but are otherwise similar, or whether both behaviors (TV use, creativity) are caused by some other characteristic or set of characteristics (e.g., parents' attitudes regarding television viewing vs. other leisure activities). This latter possibility is sometimes referred to as a "third variable" explanation.

Sometimes we have reason to believe that a whole set of behaviors or variables is interrelated. Using certain statistical techniques we can sometimes "partial out" or "control for" the influence of a particular variable or set of variables when considering the association or correlation between the two behaviors in which we are most interested. For example, parents and teachers often ask whether reading or some other aspect of school achievement is related to TV use (see Chapter 6, this volume, for my discussion of the research findings on this issue). The results of several studies indicate that the answer may be "yes" but that several other variables or behaviors also are relevant, including performance on IQ measures, amount of reading, attitudes in the home regarding reading and TV viewing, and so on. In some studies, the statistically significant correlations between TV use and reading skill are reduced when scores on other relevant variables are statistically partialled out or controlled, but not to the point of nonsignificance. We can still say, however, only that these behaviors are related; we cannot make a causal inference about the direction of influence. In other studies, as I review in Chapter 6, controlling other relevant variables reduces the small but statistically significant correlations to nonsignificance.

Before going on to discuss other methodological issues related to causality, it should be noted that when an association is found between two behaviors, it is possible that the causal influence is not an either-or or even a third variable proposition (TV use causes other behavior, or other behavior causes TV use, or a third variable causes both), but that the relationship goes both ways and is transactional. This seems to be a more plausible hypothesis that has a better fit with the research evidence in some areas. For example, Rosengren and his colleagues (Rosengren, Roe, & Sonesson, 1983) studied 6-, 9-, and 11-year-olds in their Media Panel Program. They contended that their results fit what they called an "addiction model," in which there is a short-term effect of TV content on attitudes and related behavior, which leads to a craving for more of the same kind of content, which again has short-term effects, and so on.

In wanting to understand whether media have certain effects (or for that matter, any effects) we are asking a question that involves time: Does the content or the way it is viewed or not doing other things instead have some effect on viewers' subsequent behavior? The time lag involved will vary. At a minimum, the behavior potentially affected is measured right after viewing. In some studies the lag is much longer, for example, weeks or even years. For some behaviors it seems reasonable to expect that there might be an immediately observable effect (e.g., imitating an observed behavior), but for others (e.g., creativity), this is harder to imagine, and instead, any hypothesized effect would be expected to occur over a much longer period. In other cases both immediate and longer term effects may be imaginable (e.g., aggression). What are some of the problems we encounter when trying to determine whether viewing affects subsequent behavior, and how do we grapple with them?

The "Can" and "Does" Questions

The problem of trying to make causal inferences about the relationship between media use and some other behavior has two aspects. Some types of research design or method address what some of us call the "can" question, whereas other methods address the "does" question, but few address both. The question of whether television can affect its viewers is more strictly causal than the question of whether use of television does relate to some other behavior under real-life circumstances.

Laboratory Experiments. Under certain circumstances, when other potentially relevant factors are controlled, *can* television (or some other medium) cause a behavior or change in behavior? Studies done under very carefully controlled conditions are ideally suited to answer this question, and a laboratory provides the best situation in which to achieve that control. Content can be produced that varies in precise ways on the dimension of interest. It can then be shown under controlled conditions to participants who have been randomly assigned to view one type of content or another. Typically, the participants are interviewed or observed following exposure to that content. Sometimes they are observed or interviewed both before and after exposure so that comparisons can be made for the same individuals, whereas in other studies the responses of participants exposed to certain kinds of content are compared with the responses of others exposed to other content. The chapters in this book by Cantor (Chapter 4), by Dubow and Miller (Chapter 5), and by Graves (Chapter 3) dealing with media-induced fears, aggression, and diversity all review some results of laboratory studies. Because participants are randomly assigned to groups and other relevant factors can be carefully controlled, laboratory studies do permit us to make the causal inference that under these circumstances, viewers with these characteristics (e.g., boys aged 8-10 years) can be affected in the ways observed.

Saying that some viewers can be affected does not mean, however, that results obtained in a controlled laboratory setting do occur under more natural viewing conditions. Participants in laboratory studies may feel freer to behave antisocially, for example, than they would in the less permissive atmosphere of a home or playground. The media content to which they are exposed may be shorter and contain fewer conflicting messages than regular television or other media fare. On the other side of the coin, however, it should be noted that, for ethical reasons, the type of content to which children or adults are exposed in laboratory studies of media-induced fear or aggression are much less extreme than those to which many children and adults are exposed in real life. Hate-mongering material aimed against certain racial-ethnic groups, for example, could not ethically be used in research. Laboratory studies have shown that filmed material and televised material can have positive or prosocial effects (e.g., reducing anxiety in children facing surgery, Melamed & Siegel, 1975; reducing fear of dogs, Bandura & Menlove, 1968) as well as negative or antisocial effects (e.g., on aggressive attitudes and behavior, Bandura, Ross, & Ross, 1961, 1963; Geen, 1975).

Field Experiments. Using other methods, researchers have tried to answer the question: Does television affect its viewers, or at least some of them, in circumstances closer to those found on a day-to-day basis in our society? The term *field experiment* is used to refer to studies in which the content to which viewers are exposed is varied systematically but viewing and subsequent observation of behavior are conducted in a setting that is more natural than a laboratory. In such studies (e.g., Friedrich & Stein, 1973; Stein & Friedrich, 1972) individual children are not usually randomly assigned to groups, because intact groups are studied (e.g., a nursery or day care class), but groups are randomly assigned to watch certain kinds of content (e.g., cartoons or *Mister Rogers' Neighborhood* or children's films or nothing). Some field experiments have been conducted in institutional settings, so the viewers are less likely to be representative or typical. Thus, field experiments may provide potential answers to both the "can" and "does" questions, depending on the design of the particular study, but they also have their own set of limitations. This also applies to natural experiments.

Natural Experiments. In a natural experiment, researchers take advantage of naturally occurring events to study media effects. Studies of the effects of "media deprivation," focusing on people who had had working television sets that for one reason or another became unavailable, are an example of one type of natural experiment. Robert Kubey (Chapter 7, this volume) reviews some of the results of such studies (see also Winick, 1988). In most of these studies, the focus is on how people react to and cope with the loss of television as a leisure activity. Centerwall's (1989) work represents another type of natural experiment, one with an epidemiological focus. He studied changes in violent crime rates in Canada, the United States, and South Africa over the years and decades following the introduction of television to those countries (see Dubow & Miller, Chapter 5, this volume, for more detail). In a third type of natural experiment, before-and-after studies, researchers have studied changes in a variety of attitudes and behaviors following the initial introduction of television.

Several before-and-after studies conducted when television first became widely available in the 1950s are classic natural experiments: Himmelweit, Oppenheim, and Vince's (1958) study of the introduction of television in England; Schramm, Lyle, and Parker's (1961) study conducted in Canada and the United States; and Furu's (1962) study in Japan. These early landmarks in the study of media effects provided a wealth of important information. Some of our current hopes and concerns regarding media effects, however, were not at the forefront when television was a new technology, so the research questions asked in those studies did not speak to those hopes and concerns. Fortunately, there also have been some more recent natural experiments involving the introduction of television that fill some of the gaps: Murray and Kippax's (1977, 1978) study in Australia; a second study in Japan by Furu (1971); Brown, Cramond, and Wilde's (1974) study in Scotland; Hornik's (1978) study in El Salvador; and the study I directed (Williams, 1986, 1995) in Canada. Some of the results of these studies are described in other chapters in this book. Here, in the introduction, I will briefly introduce our natural experiment to make a few additional methodological points about studies of media effects.

In the summer of 1973, I heard about a Canadian town that did not yet have television reception even though it was not an isolated community.[3] We decided to study that town, to which we gave the pseudonym *Notel*, before and after it obtained television reception for the first time. Notel had bus and rail service and good roads linking it to the rest of the province, but because of the way in which it was located in a valley, the transmitter that was intended to provide reception of the Canadian Broadcasting Corporation's (CBC)[4] national English channel failed to do so. That same transmitter had provided CBC for about seven years to residents of a similar town, about an hour's drive away. We gave that town the pseudonym *Unitel* and studied it as a comparison or control community for Notel. We also studied a third town, which we called *Multitel*, as it had received the three national private U.S. networks, ABC, CBS, and NBC, in addition to CBC, for about 15 years. One advantage of studying this natural experiment in the 1970s rather than two decades earlier when TV was a new technology is that once reception was available, almost all Notel residents obtained it. The problem that acquisition of new technologies varies with family characteristics, especially socioeconomic status, did not apply in Notel. Indeed, as we were hurrying to collect our "before" data before the new repeating transmitter was installed in November 1973, many of the school children we interviewed said their family already had a television set hooked up and waiting.

Notel, Unitel, and Multitel were communities of similar size (about 700 in the village, which served an area about four times as large via its schools, shops, and so on) and similar diversity in cultural mix. Statistics Canada data indicated that the towns were similar on these and other dimensions, such as the type of industry in the area.

We studied all three communities just before Notel obtained television reception (Phase 1) and again 2 years later (Phase 2). In Phase 1 the median[5] number of hours of television watched by Notel school children per week was 0, whereas in Unitel it was 23.5 hours, and in Multitel, 29.3 hours. In Phase 2, the analogous figures were 20.9, 21.0, and 26.9. Unlike residents of some isolated communities, even in our "before" phase, most Notel children and adults knew what television was and watched it when they were elsewhere, but they could not watch on a regular basis. The fact that Notel residents sometimes did watch television made it less likely that we would find differences between Notel and the other towns, providing a conservative test of the effects of television. In Chapter 6 I discuss some of those effects, along with the results of other research. Some of our findings are also described in other chapters of this book.

The "natural" aspect of natural experiments such as the one we studied means that the findings can be used in trying to answer the question of whether media use, in this case television, does relate to other behaviors in real-life settings. But what about the more causal "can" question? Using the distinctions made by Cook and Campbell (1976), natural experiments such as ours are quasi experiments conducted in a field setting (defined by Cook and Campbell as "any setting which respondents do not perceive to have been set up for the primary purpose of conducting research," p. 224). They are quasi experiments because people are not randomly assigned to treatment groups by the researchers, as they would be in a true experiment. According to Cook and Campbell (1976, 1979), the extent to which causal inferences can be made for quasi experiments in field settings depends largely on whether alternative hypotheses to explain the results, which they call "threats to internal validity," can be ruled out.

In considering our results from the natural experiment in Notel, Unitel, and Multitel, we carefully considered each of the possible threats to internal validity discussed by Cook and Campbell (1979) (see Williams, 1986, pp. 28-31 for details). These included quirks of history, maturation between pretest and posttest of the people studied, repeated testing effects, instrumentation changes, selection (preexisting differences among the groups), mortality or differential dropout from the groups, interactions between selection and other threats to internal validity (especially maturation), ambiguity about the direction of causal influence, and diffusion or imitation of the treatment. The other threats they discuss (statistical regression toward the mean when groups are preselected on certain measures, compensatory equalization of treatment, compensatory rivalry, and resentful demoralization) did not apply to our particular quasi experiment. Having plausibly eliminated each of the relevant threats, we concluded that it was "possible to make confident conclusions about whether a relationship was probably causal" (Cook & Campbell, 1979, p. 55) for the results of our natural experiment.

Longitudinal Studies. Another kind of media effects study that attempts to answer the "does" question is longitudinal, meaning that the same people are studied repeatedly. Media exposure is measured at each point in terms of amount, type of content, or both, as is some other behavior of interest. In addition to asking whether the two behaviors are concurrently related at each time of measurement (e.g., ages 8, 18, and 30 years), statistical techniques can be used to determine whether behavior on one dimension predicts behavior on the other dimension, over and above any stability in the behavior being predicted.[6] For example, in our study in Notel, Unitel, and Multitel, we found that amount of TV viewing (hours per week) did contribute significantly to prediction of children's physical aggression observed in free play (Joy, Kimball, & Zabrack, 1986). The variables that significantly predicted the physical aggression observed on the school playground for boys and girls in Grades 3 and 4 were the following: first, concurrent hours of TV viewing in Grades 3 and 4 (as reported in interviews); second, ratings by the children's peers regarding aggressive behavior (e.g., who fights the most) made 2 years earlier when they were in Grades 1 and 2; and third, physical aggression observed 2 years earlier on the school playground.[7] Thus, the results indicate that children who were aggressive relative to their peers in Grades 1 and 2 were still aggressive relative to their peers 2 years later, but over and above this stability in aggressive behavior, concurrent television viewing added to the prediction of physical aggression.[8]

In Chapter 5 (this volume), Eric Dubow and Laurie Miller review longitudinal observational studies relating measures of TV use to aggressive behavior; in Chapter 2 (this volume), Aletha Huston and John Wright describe the results of their longitudinal studies relating preschool children's TV viewing to a variety of other behaviors; and in Chapter 6 (this volume), I review longitudinal studies relating TV use to school achievement.

How Is Television Viewing Measured?

When evaluating any evidence regarding the effects of television or other media it is important to ask how media use has been measured. In laboratory, field, and natural experiments, media use is defined as exposure to media of a particular nature for some specified duration. Once those parameters are spelled out, however, media use does not have to be measured. In Notel, Unitel, and Multitel, for example, exposure to television was defined as the range of regular viewing of the channels available in Unitel and Multitel in both phases of the study. In Notel it was 2 years of viewing between Phase 1 and 2 following the arrival of CBC television reception. We did obtain information from children and adults in all three towns about how much television and what programs they watched, but that information was used in secondary analyses of a correlational nature. The major analyses used to explore hypotheses about the effects of television involved comparisons for different behaviors, such as creativity and aggression among the towns and across the phases without regard to individual reports of TV use. Similarly, in laboratory and field experiments comparisons are made between groups exposed to different television content, including in some cases, comparisons of behavior before and after exposure to that content.

In much of the research aimed at untangling the nature of relationships between media use and other behavior, including any causal relationships, media use must be measured. This turns out to be more difficult than at first imagined. Even for adults it is no simple matter. For example, what do people mean when they say they watched TV for 2 hours or even a particular program? How much of the time in the room with the set qualifies as watching? How are interruptions from phone calls or the demands of children or other family members incorporated into the estimate? Even before "grazing" across several channels to follow more than one program over the same period became technologically feasible, people time-shared TV viewing with many other activities, which were sometimes primary and sometimes secondary to TV viewing. How do people who live in "constant TV households," where the set is on most of the time, determine whether a program was viewed or not? These and other issues must be addressed by companies that compile ratings based on the size of the audience with various characteristics (age, gender, socioeconomic status, and so on) that are then used to determine advertising rates, such as Nielsen in the United States and the Bureau of Broadcast Measurement (BBM) in Canada. As researchers, we also must address these issues when we conduct correlational studies.

All of the questions that complicate measurement of media use by adults also apply in an exacerbated fashion when we are interested in media use by children. The younger they are the less we feel confident in relying on their own reports and the more likely we are to obtain information from their parents or other caregivers. But just as young children cannot keep a diary of their TV viewing because they cannot read and write, so is diary keeping difficult or impossible for some parents. They may not read or write in the language(s) of the researchers, or they may be so busy with other demands that they do not reliably complete the diary for the child, or both.

The problem for correlational studies that rely on measurement of TV use and one or more other behaviors is that to the extent that measurement of any of the behaviors is unreliable, the relationship or association will be diminished. Researchers try, therefore, to improve the reliability of their measure(s) of TV use in a variety of ways. These include providing training in how to complete the diary, using time segments that reduce memory demands, and so on. Children and adults are more likely to report accurately what they watched if they are asked about this morning or yesterday rather than last week or if they are read a list of the programs aired this morning or yesterday rather than simply being asked to recall them. But as the number of programs available and the time interval increases this becomes more and more impossible. In their chapters in this book, Huston and Wright (Chapter 2) and Kubey (Chapter 7) describe methods they have used to obtain reliable information about television viewing by children and adults, respectively.

This discussion of the difficulties and complexities involved in measuring TV use is intended neither to be exhaustive (see Williams & Boyes, 1986, for further discussion) nor overly pessimistic but merely to alert those wishing to evaluate research evidence regarding the effects of television that it is dependent on the quality of the measures of use of television. My comments are intended only in a cautionary vein. Fortunately, we do have some evidence that, at least under some circumstances, researchers are succeeding in measuring TV use with considerable reliability.

Some of the best evidence on the quality of measures of TV use comes from comparisons of parental diary reports with time-lapse videotapes in the few studies in which video cameras have been installed in people's homes. For example, diary estimates of the amount of time 5-year-olds spent with TV correlated highly[9] with videotaped records (Anderson et al., 1985). In that study parents recorded their child's viewing in 15-minute blocks; for each block they indicated whether the TV was on, the program and station to which it was tuned, and who was in the room. An individual was considered present if she or he was in the viewing room for at least 6 of the 15 minutes.

In Notel, Unitel, and Multitel we were able to assess the extent to which estimates of amount of television viewing obtained by two different methods yielded similar information (Williams & Boyes, 1986). In Phase 1, there were 119 students in Grades 7 through 12 in Unitel and Multitel who on one occasion were interviewed individually and on another occasion completed a questionnaire in their classroom. The interview questions were more finely segmented (they asked, for example, about usual or typical viewing before school, after school, after supper) than those on the questionnaire (which asked, for example, about usual or typical viewing on a weekday or weekend day) but the answers were, nevertheless, very similar.[10] In Phase 2, 63 adults across the three towns completed and returned a mailed questionnaire and were also interviewed individually in their homes (Suedfeld, Little, Rank, Rank, & Ballard, 1986). Mailed questionnaires are generally considered to be a less reliable method of obtaining information than are questionnaires completed under supervision (e.g., in a classroom), but the adults in this study responded similarly in the interviews and on the mailed questionnaires.[11] Reliability was lower for estimates of hours viewed on Saturdays and Sundays than for weekdays, which could reflect either greater variability in weekend viewing, more variation in reporting for the weekend with the two methods, or both.

What Qualifies as Evidence of Media Effects?

Media researchers engage in heated debates among themselves and with their critics (e.g., representatives of the industry) about the credibility of different kinds of evidence of media effects. Some (e.g., Freedman, 1984) refuse to consider laboratory studies because of their limitations for answering the "does" question but then criticize the longitudinal studies and some of the field experiments for not being adequate to answer the "can" question. Most of us believe that no one type of study can be definitive, that all have strengths and weaknesses, and that we need to sift and weigh the evidence obtained with a wide variety of methodologies to see whether it is consistent enough to answer both the "can" and "does" questions. Nevertheless, as I pointed out earlier in this introductory chapter, some researchers, particularly those working from a reception theory or cultural studies perspective, argue that we cannot study or speak of "media effects," because every individual takes away her or his own reading of each specific medium on each specific occasion. When evaluating reviews of research evidence readers need to be alert to the kinds of evidence the writers are considering and to the perspectives they take on these issues.

Might there be other kinds of evidence of media effects—that is, other than the methodologies already discussed? I'd like to mention a couple of possibilities as food for thought.

We are taught as social scientists not to consider "anecdotal" evidence, yet it often provides hypotheses we then set out to test more rigorously. In my opinion, the line between anecdotal and scientific evidence sometimes becomes very fuzzy, particularly when we are trying to grapple with real-life issues. Some recent events surrounding the television program *Mighty Morphin Power Rangers* provide a potential case in point. The producers say this program is intended for 9- to 12-year-olds, but it is apparently very popular in North America with preschoolers, especially boys. The program features teenage boys and girls from diverse racial-ethnic groups. They have special powers to fight evil forces, which they exercise, in part, using martial arts. They sometimes say in the program that such kick and hit moves should only be used in self-defense, but such statements are unlikely to be understood by preschoolers. Parents and teachers of preschool and elementary school children in Canada, the United Kingdom, the United States, and Scandinavia have expressed considerable and widespread displeasure with the program because of the way young children behave after watching it. As nursery school and day care teachers have said to me,

> We spend a lot of time trying to socialize children not to be aggressive. We do not allow aggressive play and have time-outs for it. But our children (primarily, but not only, boys) say that they can't play *Power Rangers* without kicking and hitting; that's how you do it. The preschool boys watch it because they think it is a "big boys' " show and, of course, they want to do what big boys do.

In a recent letter to the editor, an elementary school teacher said groups of boys play *Power Rangers* on the playground, and for a while everything's fine, but then inevitably someone gets hurt and a real fight breaks out. These "anecdotal" but widespread reports could, presumably, be documented or refuted through observations. But aren't the teachers' and parents' reported concerns about the behavior they observe another kind of relevant evidence, in and of themselves? They are, but we don't know how representative they are. In this case the phenomenon seems widespread, but we would have more confidence if it were empirically documented.

In Canada, the Canadian Radio-Television and Telecommunications Commission (CRTC), the government agency that regulates the broadcast industry, approved a voluntary violence code in 1993 that bans broadcasting of programs with gratuitous violence or that glamorizes violence. For children's programming, the code requires that the consequences of violence be shown. A group of parents complained in 1994 to a provincial broadcasting standards council that *Mighty Morphin Power Rangers* violates the voluntary standards in the CRTC code. As a result, a Canadian channel that broadcasts programming intended for youths (YTV) dropped the show and another Canadian channel (Global) is running a version of the show that has been edited by its producers. The show can still be seen in its original form on U.S. stations available on cable in Canada. In part because such shows are slipping through the voluntary violence code, the CRTC announced on April 3, 1995, that it would hold public hearings on TV violence later in the year to provide parents, teachers, and others with the opportunity to express their views. The fall 1995 hearings considered the merits of a violence rating system for television shows, the possibility of blacking out shows emanating from the United States that don't meet the CRTC's voluntary violence code, and technology that would encrypt such programs so that viewers (or, presumably, their parents) would have to unscramble it using equipment supplied by their cable company. In March 1996, the CRTC ruled that cable companies must provide v-chip technology and coded programs to all subscribers.

What We Don't Know—Or Good Questions on Which There Is Little Research Evidence

This book focuses on the set of questions at the beginning of this chapter not only because we are most often asked these questions but also because there is a body of research evidence from our own and others' work on which we can draw in trying to answer them. Some parts of some chapters are more speculative than others because there has been less research. Unfortunately, we are also frequently asked many other questions for which there is even less research evidence available. For example, I was recently asked an excellent question in a radio interview that focused on the effects of televised violence: "What is the impact of 'reality shows' versus dramatic fiction?" In other words, does watching a program that purports to depict real violence and its effects, such as *Rescue 911,* affect viewers similarly or differently than watching a program such as *Hill Street Blues* or *NYPD Blue* that does not explicitly purport to depict real events? One might further ask whether the answer would differ for child and adult viewers. Unfortunately, I could not provide a direct answer, as I did not know of any research that had focused on that specific question. I could, however, discuss Joanne Cantor's work on television and children's fears (Chapter 4, this volume) as relevant. I could also discuss what we know about children's understanding of television content (MacBeth, Chapter 1, this volume; Huston & Wright, Chapter 2, this volume). Finally, I could think and talk about the processes through which media violence affects its viewers (Dubow & Miller, Chapter 5, this volume) and speculate (as is done by Kubey, Chapter 7, this volume) about the effects of purportedly real versus admittedly fictional programming. Another important question on which there has been relatively little research asks about the impact of real violence as portrayed in news and documentary programming and how that is similar to or different from the impact of violence in other programming, such as dramatic fiction or "reality shows." Chapters 1, 2, 4, and 5 discuss findings that are relevant to this question as well, although, again, there has been relatively little research that has addressed it directly.

In many cases we are unable to answer questions about media effects because new technologies are involved. For example, there has been much less research on the use and effects of video games, computer games, and the Internet than on the effects of television. Ironically, although most families in North America now have a video recording device (VCR), there has been relatively little research on how they are used and how this changes the effects of television. Even less is known at this point, of course, about the very latest technologies, such as virtual reality and interactive television.

With what seems to be an increasing pace, new technologies become available and begin to have an impact before individuals and even "professional experts" can begin to understand or envision what those effects will be in the short term, not to mention the long term. As individuals, we (parents, professionals who advise parents, and so on) have a responsibility to try to envision the possibilities and evaluate possible consequences. As researchers, we have a responsibility to communicate what we find out, not only within our academic communities but also to the larger community. The problem for all of us, as researchers or concerned individuals, is that technology is always far ahead of our awareness of the positive and negative implications of its use. While we're carefully studying one version and waiting to be confident about our results or speculations, we may find that that version is becoming obsolete and is being replaced.

We have learned in some areas of technological development that what at first seemed to be an advance turned out to have significant negative consequences that may outweigh the benefits of the new technology. For example, pesticides and chlorofluorohydrocarbons (CFCs) were developed and widely used by the countries of the north. Those same countries are now trying to regulate their use not only at home but worldwide, to the displeasure of the countries of the south who resent not being able to have the benefits earlier experienced in the north. In Canada, the CRTC has recently restricted the use of automated telephone dialing devices because of a court ruling concerning invasion of privacy. Some people grappling with the question of long-term benefits of new technologies have even questioned whether the automobile would be welcomed if introduced now, because we know so much more about the problems to which it has contributed (e.g., pollution, death and injury from accidents, and so on). Currently, considerable concern and effort is being directed toward the problems concerning privacy and confidentiality that have become widespread as computers have become widely used. Laws and other forms of regulation of access to information have lagged far behind the ingenuity of individuals to find ways to benefit from information held by others.

We all must carefully consider the evidence we do have about the positive and negative effects of television, other media, and other technologies. We also must try to understand the possible implications of that evidence not only with regard to current media available via current technology but also with regard to what might and does become available.

No Simple Answers

What is certain, whether we are discussing research evidence regarding television and other media as they were available, are now available, or will be available through current or new technologies, is that there are no simple answers. The picture, so to speak, is always complex. In this book we have tried, as social scientists doing research ourselves and evaluating the work of others, to provide you with an overview of what is currently known about how children are socialized to the world of television and some of its possible effects. We have presented the picture as we see it, with its often contradictory facets, acknowledging the views of others who disagree with our own "readings" of the evidence. We encourage you to do likewise in delving into this fascinating set of topics that touches almost all of our lives daily.

Notes

1. In this book, the Wotherspoon and Williams (1989) reference, Corteen and Williams (1986), Harrison and Wilhams (1986), Joy et al. (1986), Suedfeld et al. (1986), and all references beginning with Williams, T. M. refer to my former name, Tannis MacBeth Williams. I have recently reverted to Tannis M. MacBeth.

2. For another discussion of this topic, see Chapter 3 in Kubey and Csikszentmihalyi (1990).

3. I am grateful to Mary Morrison, a psychologist, for alerting me to this unusual research opportunity. I am also grateful to the Canada Council (later, the Social Sciences and Humanities Research Council of Canada) for funding this research and leave fellowships that enabled me to complete the data analyses and writing.

4. CBC is a public service network, publicly funded through a grant from parliament at arm's length from the government in power in Canada.

5. The median is the number above and below which 50% of the participants fall, in this case, in terms of hours of TV watched per week.

6. The use of this kind of analysis, known as regression analysis, is preferable for analyzing this type of longitudinal data. Cross-lagged panel correlations, which some researchers (e.g., Miller, 1987) have advocated for trying to make causal inferences using correlational data from longitudinal studies, are not appropriate (Rogosa, 1980). Briefly, Rogosa points out that unless the concurrent correlations are the same in both panels or phases of the study (e.g., the correlation between TV viewing and aggression at Time 1 must be the same magnitude as at Time 2) and unless the stability coefficients for both variables are also the same (i.e., in this example, the Time 1 to 2 correlation for aggression is the same magnitude as the Time 1 to 2 correlation for TV viewing in this example), then the lagged correlations (TV viewing at Time 1 to aggression at Time 2 and vice versa) cannot be compared. If the stability coefficients differ (and aggression tends to be more stable than TV viewing), then the more stable behavior will appear to be "caused" by the less stable behavior.

7. These three significant predictors, hours of TV viewing in Grades 3 and 4, peer assessment of aggression in Grades 1 and 2, and observed physical aggression in Grades 1 and 2, together accounted for 67% of the variance in the physical aggression of these same children in Grades 3 and 4.

8. It would have been helpful to know whether hours of TV viewing in Grades 1 and 2 would also have been a significant predictor of physical aggression 2 years later in Grades 3 and 4, but we could not have included Notel children in the analysis because they did not have television reception in Phase 1 of the study.

9. $r(94) = .84, p < .001$.

10. The correlations for weekend, weekday, and total weekly hours of viewing were $r = .83$, .86, and .87, respectively.

11. For total hours over the week, $r = .76$.

References

Anderson, D., Field, D., Collins, P., Lorch, E., & Nathan, J. (1985). Estimates of young children's time with television: A methodogical comparison of parent reports with time-lapse video home observation. *Child Development, 56,* 1345-1357.

Anderson, D. R., & Lorch, E. P. (1983). Looking at television: Action or reaction? In J. Bryant & D. R. Anderson (Eds.), *Children's understanding of television: Research on attention and comprehension* (pp. 1-33). New York: Academic Press.

Anderson, D. R., Lorch, E. P., Field, D. E., Collins, P. A., & Nathan, J. G. (1986). Television viewing at home: Age trends in visual attention and time with TV. *Child Development, 57,* 1024-1033.

Ang, I. (1990). The nature of the audience. In J. Downing, A. Mohammadi, & A. Sreberny-Moham-madi (Eds.), *Questioning the media: A critical introduction* (pp. 155-165). Newbury Park, CA: Sage.

Bandura, A. (1986). *Social foundations of thought and action: A social cognitive theory.* Englewood Cliffs, NJ: Prentice Hall.

Bandura, A., & Menlove, F. L. (1968). Factors determining vicarious extinction of avoidance behavior through symbolic modeling. *Journal of Personality and Social Psychology, 8*(2), 99-108.

Bandura, A., Ross, D., & Ross, S. (1961). Transmission of aggression through imitation of aggressive models. *Journal of Abnormal and Social Psychology, 63,* 575-582.

Bandura, A., Ross, D., & Ross, S. (1963). Imitation of film-mediated aggressive models. *Journal of Abnormal and Social Psychology, 66,* 3-11.

Bechtel, R., Achelpohl, C., & Akers, R. (1972). Correlates between observed behavior and questionnaire responses on television viewing. In E. A. Rubinstein, G. Comstock, & J. Murray (Eds.), *Television and social behavior, Vol. 4. Television in day-to-day life: Patterns of use* (pp. 274-344). Washington, DC: Government Printing Office.

Beentjes, J. W. J. (1989). Learning from television and books: A Dutch replication study based on Salomon's model. *Educational Technology Research and Development, 37*(2), 47-58.

Brown, J., Cramond, D. J., & Wilde, R. (1974). Displacement effects of television and the child's functional orientation to media. In J. G. Blumler & E. Katz (Eds.), *The uses of mass communications* (pp. 93-112). Beverly Hills, CA: Sage.

Centerwall, B. S. (1989). Exposure to television as a cause of violence. In G. Comstock (Ed.), *Public communication and behavior* (Vol. 2, pp. 1-59). San Diego, CA: Academic Press.

Collins, R., Curran, N., Garnham, P., Scannell, P., Schlesinger, P., & Sparks, C. (1986). *Media, culture, and society: A critical reader.* Newbury Park, CA: Sage.

Comstock, G. (1989). *The evolution of American television.* Newbury Park, CA: Sage.

Comstock, G. A., & Rubinstein, E. A. (Eds.). (1972a). *Television and social behavior (Vol. 1), Media content and control.* Washington, DC: Government Printing Office.

Comstock, G. A., & Rubinstein, E. A. (Eds.). (1972b). *Television and social behavior (Vol. 3), television and adolescent aggressiveness.* Washington, DC: Government Printing Office.

Comstock, G. A., Rubinstein, E. A., & Murray, J. P. (Eds.). (1972). *Television and social behavior (Vol. 5), Television's effects: Further explorations.* Washington, DC: Government Printing Office.

Condry, J. (1989). *The psychology of television.* Hillsdale, NJ: Lawrence Erlbaum.

Cook, T. D., & Campbell, D. T. (1976). The design and conduct of quasi-experiments and true experiments in field settings. In M. D. Dunette (Ed.), *Handbook of industrial and organizational psychology.* Chicago: Rand McNally.

Cook, T. D., & Campbell, D. T. (1979). *Quasi-experimentation: Design and analysis issues for field settings.* Boston: Houghton Mifflin.

Dorr, A. (1986). *Television and children: A special medium for a special audience.* Newbury Park, CA: Sage.

Durant, R. H., Baranowski, T., Johnson, M., & Thompson, W. O. (1994). The relationship among television watching, physical activity, and body composition of young children. *Pediatrics, 4*(1), 449-455.

Field, D., & Anderson, D. (1985). Instruction and modality effects of children's television attention and comprehension. *Journal of Educational Psychology, 77*(1), 91-100.

Freedman, J. L. (1984). Effect of television violence on aggressiveness. *Psychological Bulletin, 96*(2), 227-246.

Freedman, J. L. (1986). Television violence and aggression: A rejoinder. *Psychological Bulletin, 100,* 372-378.

Friedrich, L. K., & Stein, A. H. (1973). Aggressive and prosocial television programs and the natural behavior of preschool children. *Monographs of the Society for Research in Child Development, 38*(Serial No. 151).

Furu, T. (1962). *Television and children's life: A before-after study.* Tokyo: Japan Broadcasting Corporation.

Furu, T. (1971). *The functions of television for children and adolescents.* Tokyo: Sophia University.

Geen, R. G. (1975). The meaning of observed violence: Real versus fictional violence and consequent effects on aggression and emotional arousal. *Journal of Research in Personality, 9,* 270-281.

Greenberg, B. S. (1974). Gratifications of television viewing and their correlates for British children. In J. G. Blumler & E. Katz (Eds.), *The uses of mass communications: Current perspectives on gratifications research* (pp. 72-92). Newbury Park, CA: Sage.

Greenberg, B. S. (1988). Some uncommon television images and the drench hypothesis. In S. Oskamp (Ed.), *Applied social psychology annual: Television as a social issue* (Vol. 8, pp. 88-102). Newbury Park, CA: Sage.

Greenfield, P. M. (1984). *Mind and media: The effects of television, video games, and computers.* Cambridge, MA: Harvard University Press.

Hall, S. (1986). Introduction. In D. Morley (Ed.), *Family television: Cultural power and domestic leisure* (pp. 7-10). London: Comedia.

Hebdige, D. (1979). *Subculture: The meaning of style.* London: Methuen.

Himmelweit, H. T., Oppenheim, A. N., & Vince, P. (1958). *Television and the child.* London: Oxford University Press.

Hollenbeck, A. R., & Slaby, R. G. (1979). Infant visual and vocal responses to television. *Child Development, 50*(1), 41-45.

Hornik, R. (1978). Television access and the slowing of cognitive growth. *American Educational Research Journal, 15*(1), 1-15.

Huston, A. C., Donnerstein, E., Fairchild, H., Feshbach, N. D., Katz, P. A., Murray, J. P., Rubinstein, E. A., Wilcox, B. L., & Zuckerman, D. (1992). *Big world, small screen: The role of television in American society.* Lincoln: University of Nebraska Press.

Huston, A. C., Wright, J. C., Rice, M. L., Kerkman, D., & St. Peters, M. (1990). The development of television viewing patterns in early childhood: A longitudinal investigation. *Developmental Psychology, 26,* 409-420.

Joy, L. A., Kimball, M. M., & Zabrack, M. L. (1986). Television and children's aggressive behavior. In T. M. Williams (Ed.), *The impact of television: A natural experiment in three communities* (pp. 303-360). Orlando, FL: Academic Press.

Klapper, J. T. (1949). *The effects of the mass media.* New York: Columbia University, Bureau of Applied Social Research.

Klapper, J. T. (1960). *The effects of mass communications.* Glencoe, IL: Free Press.

Kubey, R., & Csikszentmihalyi, M. (1990). *Television and the quality of life: How viewing shapes everyday experience.* Hillsdale, NJ: Lawrence Erlbaum.

Langer, E. J., & Piper, A. (1988). Television from a mindful/mindless perspective. In S. Oskamp (Ed.), *Applied social psychology annual: Television as a social issue* (Vol. 8, pp. 247-260). Beverly Hills, CA: Sage.

Lemish, D., & Rice, M. L. (1986). Television as a talking picture book: A prop for language acquisition. *Journal of Child Language, 13,* 251-274.

Liebert, R. M., & Sprafkin, J. (1988). *The early window: Effects of television on children and youth* (3rd ed.). Elmsford, NY: Pergamon.

Lull, J. (1990). *Inside family viewing: Ethnographic research on television's audiences.* London: Routledge.

McGuire, W. J. (1986). The myth of massive media impact: Savagings and salvagings. In G. Comstock (Ed.), *Public communication and behavior* (Vol. 1, pp. 175-257). Orlando, FL: Academic Press.

Melamed, B. G., & Siegel, L. (1975). Reduction of anxiety in children facing hospitalization and surgery by use of film modeling. *Journal of Consulting and Clinical Psychology, 43,* 511-521.

Miller, S. A. (1987). *Developmental research methods.* Englewood Cliffs, NJ: Prentice Hall.

Morley, D. (1980). *The "nationwide" audience: Structure and decoding.* London: British Film Institute.

Murray, J. P., & Kippax, S. (1977). Television diffusion and social behavior in three communities: A field experiment. *Australian Journal of Psychology, 29*(1), 31-43.

Murray, J. P., & Kippax, S. (1978). Children's social behavior in three towns with differing television experience. *Journal of Communication, 30*(4), 19-29.

Murray, J. P., Rubinstein, E. A., & Comstock, G. A. (Eds.). (1972). *Television and social behavior (Vol. 2), Television and learning.* Washington, DC: Government Printing Office.

O'Connor, A. (1990). Culture and communication. In J. Downing, A. Mohammadi, & A. Sreberny-Mohammadi (Eds.), *Questioning the media: A critical introduction* (pp. 27-41). Newbury Park, CA: Sage.

Pearl, D., Bouthilet, L., & Lazar, J. (1982). *Television and behavior: Ten years of scientific progress and implications for the 80s: Vols. 1 and 2.* Rockville, MD: National Institute of Mental Health.

Radway, J. (1987). Interpretive communities and variable literacies (commentary on T. Lindlof, media audiences as interpretive communities). In J. Anderson (Ed.), *Communication yearbook II.* Newbury Park, CA: Sage.

Rakow, L. (1990). Feminist perspectives on popular culture. In J. Downing, A. Mohammadi, & A. Sreberny-Mohammadi (Eds.), *Questioning the media: A critical introduction* (pp. 231-241). Newbury Park, CA: Sage.

Report of the Ontario Royal Commission on Violence in the Communications Industry. (1977). Volumes 1 through 5. Toronto, Ontario: Queen's Printer.

Rogosa, D. (1980). A critique of cross-lagged correlation. *Psychological Bulletin, 88,* 245-258.

Rosengren, K. E., Roe, K., & Sonesson, E. (1983). *Finality and causality in adolescents' mass media use* (Media Panel Report No. 24 [Mimeo]). Lund, Sweden: University of Lund, Department of Sociology.

Rubinstein, E. A., Comstock, G. A., & Murray, J. P. (Eds.). (1972). *Television and social behavior (Vol. 4), Television in day-to-day life: Patterns of use.* Washington, DC: Government Printing Office.

Salomon, G. (1981). Introducing AIME: The assessment of children's mental involvement with television. In H. Kelley & H. Gardner (Eds.), *New directions for child development: Viewing children through television* (No. 13, pp. 89-112). San Francisco, CA: Jossey-Bass.

Salomon, G. (1983). Television watching and mental effort: A social psychological view. In J. Bryant & D. R. Anderson (Eds.), *Children's understanding of television: Research on attention and comprehension* (pp. 181-198). New York: Academic Press.

Salomon, G. (1984). Television is "easy" and print is "tough": The differential investment of mental effort as a function of perceptions and attributions. *Journal of Educational Psychology, 76,* 647-658.

Schramm, W., Lyle, J., & Parker, E. B. (1961). *Television in the lives of our children.* Stanford, CA: Stanford University Press.

Stein, A. H., & Friedrich, L. K. (1972). Television content and young children's behavior. In J. P. Murray, E. A. Rubinstein, & G. A. Comstock (Eds.), *Television and social behavior, Vol. 2. Television and social learning* (pp. 202-317). Washington, DC: Government Printing Office.

Suedfeld, P., Little, B. R., Rank, A. D., Rank, D. S., & Ballard, E. J. (1986). Television and adults: Thinking, personality, and attitudes. In T. M. Williams (Ed.), *The impact of television: A natural experiment in three communities* (pp. 361-393). Orlando, FL: Academic Press.

Williams, T. M. (1986). *The impact of television: A natural experiment in three communities.* Orlando, FL: Academic Press.

Williams, T. M. (1995). The impact of television: A longitudinal Canadian study. In B. D. Singer (Ed.), *Communications in Canadian society* (4th ed., pp. 172-200). Scarborough, Ontario: Nelson Canada.

Williams, T. M., & Boyes, M. C. (1986). Television-viewing patterns and use of other media. In T. M. Williams (Ed.), *The impact of television: A natural experiment in three communities* (pp. 215-264). Orlando, FL: Academic Press.

Williams, T. M., Phillips, S., & Travis, L. (1985). *The University of British Columbia TV content coding system (UBCCS) and manual.* (Available from Tannis M. MacBeth, Department of Psychology, University of British Columbia, Vancouver, B.C. Canada V6T 1Z4)

Winick, C. (1988). The functions of television: Life without the big box. In S. Oskamp (Ed.), *Applied social psychology annual: Television as a social issue* (Vol. 8, pp. 217-237). Newbury Park, CA: Sage.

Wotherspoon, D., & Williams, T. M. (1989, May). *Television content analysis: Agreement between expert and naive coders.* Paper presented at the annual meeting of the International Communication Association, San Francisco.

BIZARRO

By DAN PIRARO

Television and Socialization
of Young Children

Aletha C. Huston
John C. Wright

Background

Public figures, the popular press, and many individuals believe that television is the root of almost every social evil from declining test scores to the loss of "family values." "I don't let my children watch television on weekdays." "We don't have a television set" (said with pride). Advice from a former President of the United States to school children: "Don't watch so much television." Some educators have attacked the medium of television as fundamentally superficial and have argued that it encourages short attention spans and superficial thinking.

At the same time, the public relies on television for its news, its political information, its entertainment. People believe television news more than they believe newspapers. With the advent of home videocassette recorders,

AUTHORS' NOTE: The research described in this chapter was supported by grants to the authors from the Spencer Foundation, the National Institute of Mental Health (MH 39595), and the Children's Television Workshop.

videotapes of real events have become a new source of "truth" as in the beating of Rodney King by Los Angeles police officers.

The one thing on which the critics and defenders of television agree is that it is a central and pervasive part of modern life. Children spend more time watching television than in any other activity except sleep. The television set is turned on for several hours a day in the average household. Children are exposed to television from birth onward. It reaches children at a younger age and for more time than any other socializing institution except the family.

Parents often have a lot of questions about how they should deal with this attractive and seductive medium. How much television should children be allowed to watch? Should parents restrict the programs children are allowed to watch? If they don't allow their children to watch popular programs, will the children be ostracized or excluded from the peer group? Should they get rid of the television set altogether? How can they find out about good programs? Is watching television a passive activity?

In this chapter, we address two major questions. First, how are young children socialized to use the television medium? What influences in the larger society, the family, and the child are important in determining the amount and type of television viewing the child does? Second, how do early patterns of viewing affect some aspects of children's cognitive and social development?

Assumptions

We begin with some assumptions. First, television as a medium is neither good nor bad for children. Television is not monolithic but pluralistic. Programming can be stimulating, creative, and of high quality or it can be dull and badly produced; it can display prosocial interactions between people, or it can portray violence and cruelty. We would not condemn the medium of newspapers simply because some are tabloid publications featuring the lives of show business stars. It does not make sense, therefore, to discuss the effects of "television"; we prefer to discuss the effects of different kinds of television.

Our second assumption is that children are often cognitively active when watching television. There is now a solid base of data showing that even very young children watch television actively. They attend when the content is comprehensible and interesting; they do something else when it is incomprehensible or uninteresting (Anderson & Lorch, 1983). They learn from television. When programs are planned and designed to teach, children can learn academic skills, information, and social values (Huston et al., 1992). Even when programs are not designed to teach, children learn from them, and sometimes what they learn is antisocial aggression or social stereotypes. But children are usually not zombies in front of the set, and there is no evidence that television as a medium leads to problems of poor attention or learning (Anderson & Collins, 1988).

Our third assumption is that the family is the core socializing force influencing children's use of television and what they learn from it. Most television is viewed at home. Children's early exposure to television occurs largely through the viewing choices of other members of their families, and viewing is often a family affair. Families are in turn affected by the social institutions and culture in which they live.

Center for Research on the Influences of Television on Children (CRITC) Longitudinal Studies

Although this chapter is informed by the work of other researchers, much of what is presented is based on our own investigations of young children's media use. We begin with a brief summary of those investigations.

Topeka Study. From 1981 through 1983, we followed two cohorts or age groups of children for 2 years; one group from ages 3 to 5 and the other from ages 5 to 7. The major purposes of the study were to identify patterns of developmental continuity and change in children's early television viewing and to investigate how those patterns are related to family environmental influences and to children's cognitive skills and social behavior. The families represented a wide range of educational and occupational levels, but they were predominantly white with two parents in the home. Every 6 months during the 2-year period, parents completed a 1-week television diary describing all viewing by all members of the household (a total of five diaries). Parents were interviewed and children were tested before and after the 2-year period. Details of the method are available in Huston, Wright, Rice, Kerkman, and St. Peters (1990); Pinon, Huston, and Wright (1989).

To find out whether different types of programs have different effects, all television programs viewed were classified according to intended audience (child or adult) and informative purpose (yes or no). Children's viewing was also analyzed for the presence of one or both parents, siblings, and other people.

Interviews at the beginning and end of the 2-year period covered parental attitudes toward TV and their reports of their children's use of it, as well as parental regulation and encouragement of viewing. Children's vocabulary was tested at the beginning and the end of the study. At the end, children's attention to television, reading skills, short-term memory skills, and ability to solve a logical reasoning problem were measured.

Early Window Study. In 1990, we began a new longitudinal study following two cohorts of children who were age 2 and 4 at the beginning of the study. The families of these approximately 240 children were primarily urban and low to moderate income. There was a fairly even mix of European American, African American, and Hispanic families. Each year for 4 years, parents were interviewed, and children were given tests of vocabulary, school-related skills, knowledge about emotions, attention to television, and expectancies of success. As a part of the interview, parents filled out a checklist of what their children watched on television. Viewing information was also collected several times a year by telephone using a daily time use interview (Wright & Huston, 1995).

Young Children's Viewing Patterns

How Much Children Watch

Between ages 3 and 5, children in the Topeka study watched an average of 19 to 20 hours of television per week. The total amount of viewing dropped to 15.5 hours per week by age 7, largely because the children entered school (Huston et al., 1990). Using similar methods, Anderson, Field, Collins, Lorch, and Nathan (1985) found that 5-year-old children in Massachusetts watched an average of about 15 hours per week.

In the Early Window study, we asked parents to indicate whether watching television was the child's primary activity or whether it was secondary to another activity. Both 2- and 4-year-olds watched television as a primary activity slightly more than 14 hours per week. For 2-year-olds, television was secondary for another 12 hours per week; their total viewing, therefore, was slightly over 26 hours per week. For 4-year-olds, secondary viewing occupied slightly over 8 hours a week for a total of 22.5. All of these figures are somewhat lower than frequently cited Nielsen estimates (cf. Comstock & Paik, 1991); we think they are more accurate than Nielsen ratings for young children because the methods are more sophisticated and precise.

What Children Watch

In keeping with the assumption that what children watch is more important than total time with television, we have analyzed the types of programs viewed. The distribution of viewing across different types of programs for children in the Topeka study is shown in Figures 2.1a and 2.1b. Although children watched a good deal of programming designed for child audiences, their viewing of informational programs for children declined with age. The majority of time devoted to child informative programming was spent with one program, *Sesame Street.* As children grew beyond its target age (3 to 5), there was nothing with the same popularity to replace it. One characteristic of educational programming is the need to be more age-specific than most programs designed primarily for entertainment.

Viewing in different program categories for the Early Window children at age 2 and 4 is shown in Figure 2.2. The patterns are similar to those already described. The younger children watched more child informative programs than older children. They were also exposed to considerably more adult programs (secondary viewing), presumably because they were at home or in home-based child care while adults were viewing. The patterns of primary viewing were similar for the 2- and 4-year-olds.

Although a fair amount of the programming viewed by both groups was designed for child audiences, a large amount was not. From an early age, children were watching or at least exposed to a wide range of programming. There are several reasons to think that much of this "viewing" is a result of the viewing choices of parents and other family members, a point to which we shall return later.

Stability of Viewing Over Time

The averages can disguise the wide range of individual differences in total amount of viewing and viewing patterns. Our studies and one other longitudinal investigation have shown that these individual differences are quite

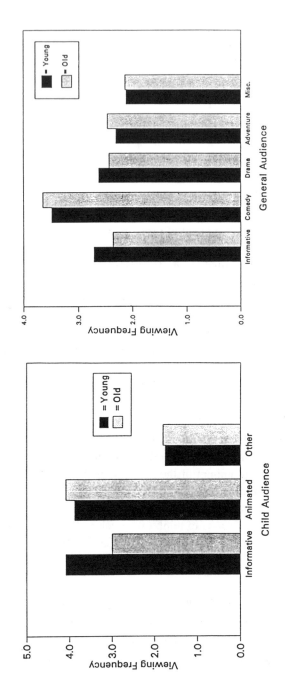

Figures 2.1a and 2.1b. Time That Children in the Topeka Longitudinal Study Watched Different Types of Programs

NOTE: Viewing was originally recorded in 15-minute intervals. The numbers shown here are the number of 15-minute intervals per week; converted to a square root to normalize the distribution for statistical analysis. An average of 1 = 15 minutes/week; 2 = 1 hour/week; 3 = 2.25 hours/week; 4 = 4 hours/week; 5 = 6.25 hours/week.

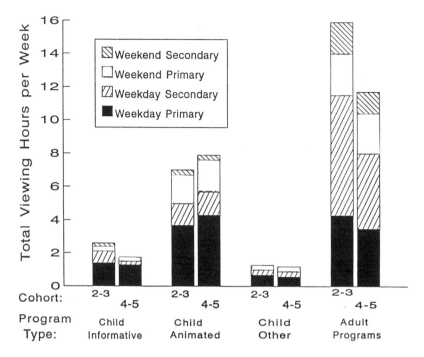

Figure 2.2. Minutes Per Week That Children in the Early Window Study Watched Different Types of Programs
NOTE: Primary viewing is child's primary activity; secondary is viewing that is secondary to another activity.

stable over time. Children who watch a lot of television at one age are likely to be frequent viewers at later ages, and infrequent viewers tend to remain low viewers. Moreover, there is stability within program types (Huston & Wright, 1993; Huston et al., 1990; Singer & Singer, 1981). That is, heavy cartoon viewers at one age remain relatively heavy cartoon viewers 1 to 2 years later.

What Affects Young Children's Media Use

Because television is such a pervasive and complex part of children's lives, many factors affect how much and what they view. A model we have used for organizing these factors is shown in Figure 2.3. In this model, there are four

LEVEL OF ANALYSIS   IMPORTANT INFLUENCES

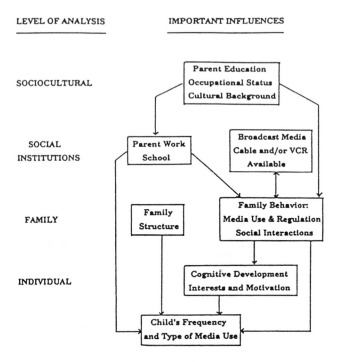

Figure 2.3. A Model for the Determinants of Children's Media Use
SOURCE: Wright, St. Peters, and Huston (1990). Reprinted by permission of Lawrence Erlbaum & Associates, Inc.

levels of analysis—sociocultural, social institutions, family, and individual (Wright, St. Peters, & Huston, 1990). For young children, the family is probably central to the process, in part because influences from the larger society are often filtered through the family. In this discussion, we begin with the most specific level, the individual child, then turn to sociocultural factors and social institutions. Finally, we will discuss the way in which families socialize and affect their children's use of television.

Individual Factors

In the 1970s a "new wave" of research on children and television was guided by the premise that children *use* television, that they are active viewers employing their cognitive resources and social knowledge to select and interpret television content. It is now well documented that children's attention to television is guided by their judgments about the comprehensibility and interest value of program content; by age 2 or 3, their attention is not controlled primarily by such perceptually demanding audiovisual events as animation, high action, sound effects, and visual special effects (Anderson & Lorch, 1983; Huston & Wright, 1989). Collins's (1983) studies demonstrated that children in middle childhood increasingly comprehend temporal relationships between plot events, motives and intentions of characters, as well as implied content that is not explicitly shown. A group of researchers studying the "uses and gratifications" of television have demonstrated that children and adults use television for many purposes, including entertainment, information, and filling time; they are not simple receptacles for its content (e.g., Rosengren, Wenner, & Palmgreen, 1985).

In the Topeka study, developmental changes in viewing were related to the cognitive demands of programs. Children moved from programs that were fairly redundant and did not require them to integrate plot events over a long time span to programs that were less redundant and had longer or more complex plots. Children appeared to be choosing programs that were consistent with their ability to understand and interpret the content (Huston et al., 1990).

Other individual characteristics contribute to the kind and amount of programming they watch. By age 4 or 5, for example, sex differences in viewing emerge (Huston et al., 1990; Singer & Singer, 1981). On the average, boys watch more television than girls, but that difference occurs primarily for programs with masculine sex-typed content and form, cartoons, action adventure shows, and sports (Alvarez, Huston, Wright, & Kerkman, 1988).

In the Topeka study, children's overall interest and involvement in television content predicted the amount of viewing. Children who talked about television characters and events, used such events in their play and asked questions of their parents about television were apt to watch a lot of television. Obviously, there could be two directions of causation, exposure to television could lead to involvement as well as involvement leading to viewing. In our opinion, both processes probably occur.

Although age-related cognitive abilities and interests are related to children's viewing, they do not explain individual variation as much as we had expected. Instead, environmental forces acting on the child and family have a major influence on what and when children view.

Sociocultural Factors

For adults, advanced education, high occupational status, and high income are associated with relatively low television use (Condry, 1989; Huston et al., 1992). It is not surprising, therefore, that parents' education and occupational status predict children's viewing. Children view most in families with parents who have little education or low occupational status.

Parents' education also predicts what kinds of programming children watch. Programs aimed at a child audience can be divided into three groups: educational or informative, nonanimated entertainment, and animated entertainment. Children of better-educated parents (compared to less well-educated parents) watch an equal or greater amount of educational programming, an equal amount of nonanimated entertainment, and less animated entertainment. They also spend a lot less time viewing adult entertainment programs (situation comedies, soap operas, action adventure, and variety game programs). Well-educated parents also more often encourage their children to use books and print media, and time use diaries show that the children spend more time reading. When parent education is statistically controlled, family income does not predict viewing; that is, income differences are accounted for by differences in parents' educational levels.

These demographic variables appear to affect the child through the parent and the kind of environment the parent supplies for the young child (Huston et al., 1990). Within demographic groups, variations in the quality of affection and stimulation provided by the parents also predict viewing. In the Early Window Project, we collected the Home Observational Measure of the Environment (HOME) (Caldwell & Bradley, 1984), a general measure of the quality of the home environment. Parents with high HOME scores had children who watched more educational programming and less child animated and adult programming than those with low HOME scores.

Social Institutions

Families are part of larger social systems that shape their lives and govern the range of choices they can make. Parents' jobs require their presence at certain hours; when there are young children, they must be cared for if no parent is available for some portion of the day. Schools require children's attendance and participation during certain time periods. Both parents' jobs and schools, therefore, set the boundaries for opportunities to watch television, primarily because they impose constraints on time at home. We have already noted, for example, that children's total viewing time declines when they enter school, a well-documented phenomenon in other investigations (Comstock & Paik, 1991).

Maternal Employment. The popular press and social critics often say or imply that problem television viewing results from mothers working outside the home. They convey images of latchkey children watching television by the hour when no parent is at home or of busy, uncaring parents using television as a "baby-sitter." In fact, preschool children of employed mothers in both of our studies watched less television than children whose mothers were full-time homemakers (Pinon et al., 1989; Huston & Wright, 1993). The primary reason was that many of those children were in organized child care settings that showed little or no television during the day.

Before applauding this pattern, however, it might be well to note that some of the television those children were missing was educational programming for children. As more children enter child care, and at younger ages, fewer of them have opportunities to see some of the quality programs available for preschoolers on weekdays. In response to this trend, the producers of both *Sesame Street* and *Mister Rogers' Neighborhood* are now distributing curriculum materials that include television and print for use in child care settings. The Public Broadcasting Service has launched a Ready to Learn initiative combining educational programming with community outreach to caregivers for young children.

School-age children with employed mothers are more apt than preschoolers to be without adult supervision after school, but most investigations show no differences in television viewing associated with maternal employment in that age group (Messaris & Hornik, 1983). Unfortunately, the reason appears to be that parents do not limit television viewing even when they are home. In one recent study, children in organized after school programs watched less television than those who were at home with their mothers or in other informal after school care settings (Posner & Vandell, 1994).

Television Programs Available. The social institutions that produce and distribute television programs and video technology also define the range of opportunities for viewing available to individuals and families. In the United States, most television is commercial; it is financed primarily by advertisers. Producers, broadcasters, and advertisers decide what programs will be produced and how they will be distributed on the basis of anticipated profits. In Canada and many European countries, publicly financed television is relatively more important than it is in the United States; decisions about programming are based on a range of criteria that are distinctly different from those guiding commercial systems (Huston et al., 1992).

Technological changes also affect the options available to families. Cable systems with many channels are now available in much of North America. About half of the households in the United States and three quarters in Canada (74% in 1994; Frank, 1995) subscribe to cable. Videotape recorders (VCRs) are owned by a majority of U.S. households (Dorr & Kunkel, 1990). By 1993, for example, over 90% of the low- to moderate-income families in the Early Window study owned a VCR. In 1994, 79% of all Canadian households, but 92% of those with children under 18, had a VCR (Frank, 1995).

Cable and Videotapes. Both the amount and type of television viewed are related to program availability, cable, and video technology. From the 1960s on, there has been a secular trend in the United States toward more hours of viewing in large-scale surveys by Nielsen and others (Condry, 1989). As television broadcasts more hours with more options, people watch more. The total time devoted to television by both children and adults in the mid-1970s in a Canadian town with one channel (CBC) was considerably less than that in a comparable town with four channels (CBC and three U.S. networks) (Williams & Boyes, 1986). Recently, however, Statistics Canada's national surveys indicate a downward trend in time spent with television, despite its increased availability. In 1994, Canadian children 12 and under spent 17.7 hours a week watching television and movie videos, 90 minutes less than 5 years earlier (Frank, 1995).

In our Topeka study, the amount of time children spent viewing certain types of programs (e.g., action adventure) varied with the amount of such programming available over the course of 2 years. Introduction of the Disney channel on cable led to a large increase in watching children's entertainment programs. But there were few overall differences in viewing between children who had cable and those who did not. Children with cable watched more cartoons and fewer child informative programs, probably because cable supplied cartoons on weekdays during hours when they were not on broadcast stations. For households without cable, cartoons were available primarily on weekends. In the Early Window study, where several independent channels were received without cable, cartoons were available to all viewers, and there were no viewing differences associated with cable subscription.

In Early Window, there were no overall differences in viewing time between children whose families owned VCRs and those without home VCRs, but there were some differences in the types of programs viewed (St. Peters, Oppenheimer, Eakins, Wright, & Huston, 1991). Children with VCRs watched more child-audience programs and fewer adult-audience programs than did those without a VCR. It appears that VCRs permit parents to supply programming that is better suited to their children's interests and levels of understanding than that provided by broadcast television. For the most part, however, videotapes watched by children are light entertainment; parents and children do not select informative or educational tapes very often (Huston & Wright, 1993; Wartella, Heintz, Aidman, & Mazzarella, 1990).

The social institutions of work, school, and broadcasting affect viewing largely by shaping and delimiting the opportunities for viewing and the selections available. The context established by work and school routines and by the television industry have important effects on viewing. They account for many of the viewing differences among children. Nevertheless, there is still considerable latitude for individuals and families to watch or not to watch within these constraints, and there is a wide range of content from which to choose. For the young child, the family plays a major role in deciding what and how much to watch.

Family

Parents affect children's media use by setting an example, by exposing children to television, by watching with their children (or not doing so), and by encouraging or regulating their children's viewing.

Coviewing. Because television sets are located in the common living areas of most homes, young children are often present and exposed to the programming watched by their parents. Among the 3- to 7-year-olds in the Topeka study, for instance, a parent was present during the majority of time children watched general audience programs. By contrast, parents were present for about 25% of the time that children viewed child audience programs (see Figure 2.4). Other investigations using diaries confirm the finding that much

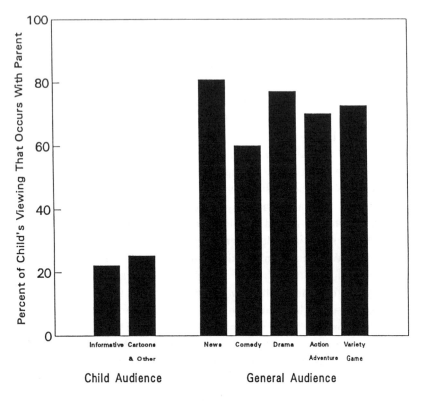

Figure 2.4. Percentage of Children's Viewing That Occurred With Parents in the Topeka Study for Different Categories of Television Programs

of children's television viewing occurs in the company of their parent(s) (Carpenter, Huston, & Spera, 1989; Field, 1989). Surveys provide lower estimates, especially for older children. In one investigation, parents of 2nd-, 6th-, and 10th-grade students said they watched popular family programs only a few times a year with their children (Dorr, Kovaric, & Doubleday, 1989).

Analyses of the types of programs that parents and children viewed together suggested that the choices were guided by the parents' tastes, not those of the children (St. Peters, Fitch, Huston, Wright, & Eakins, 1991). The programs coviewed were similar to those that parents watched when children were not present; they were not similar to those that children watched without their parents.

Taken together, these findings suggest that parents' own viewing habits and preferences are a powerful source of modeling and early exposure to television for young children. The amount and kind of television that young children "see" depends considerably on the amount and kind of viewing parents do. This seemingly obvious conclusion is often overlooked in discussions that focus on parental neglect and absence as the source of "too much" television viewing. At least for young children, exposure to adult programs occurs with parents more than without them.

Children also watch a lot of television with their sisters and brothers, and these siblings influence program choices. Children with older siblings move away from educational programs such as *Sesame Street* and toward cartoons and situation comedies at an earlier age than do those without older siblings. Conversely, children with younger siblings watch more programs designed for preschoolers than do those who have no younger siblings (Pinon et al., 1989).

Parents or older siblings who coview television with children can make the experience worthwhile. Several investigations have demonstrated that adults who watch with children and offer comments and interpretations of content improve the amount that children learn from educational programs (Friedrich & Stein, 1975; Salomon, 1977; Watkins, Calvert, Huston-Stein, & Wright, 1980). Adult explanation also improves children's understanding of plots, characters, and events in dramatic programs (Collins, Sobol, & Westby, 1981). Many authors have pointed out that television can provide an occasion for parents to discuss values, beliefs, and moral issues (Messaris & Sarett, 1981).

Unfortunately, it appears that most parents do not use coviewing opportunities for these purposes. Some parents use educational programs for children as "talking picture books" (Lemish & Rice, 1986), but most of the time, they absent themselves while children are watching such programs. Observations of parents and children in a playroom containing toys in the laboratory showed considerably less conversation when the television was turned on than when it was not (St. Peters, 1993). One reason may be that it is difficult to converse during a program without losing the thread of the program; broadcast television is not well suited to interaction. Newer technologies, including videotapes and interactive media, may lend themselves to interaction more readily.

For young children, coviewing appears to be a function of circumstances. The fact that the programs coviewed are those that fit the parents' tastes rather than the children's tastes suggests that coviewing is often not motivated by a parent's desire to share a learning experience with the child. Children in some families spend a lot of time in the room with programming they do not understand or find interesting (e.g., news). As soon as they are old enough to be away from immediate adult supervision, they tend to leave the television area when parents are watching these adult-oriented programs (St. Peters, Fitch, et al., 1991).

Encouragement and Regulation. Numerous investigations show that North American parents impose relatively little regulation on the amount of time their children watch television. They more often regulate the kinds of programs children are allowed to watch. Many parents of young children try to prohibit exposure to graphic violence, sexuality, frightening content, and bad language (Wright et al., 1990), but their definitions of negative content do not necessarily match those of experts. Most parents in our Topeka study did not object to many programs with demonstrated violence, for example, cartoons, action adventure programs. They seemed most concerned about explicit violence, sexuality, and improper language on such movie channels as HBO.

Parents also encourage children to watch television programs that they consider educational or entertaining for children. Parental encouragement is distinct from nonregulation. In the Topeka study, we classified parents in four groups on the basis of their regulation and encouragement of television. These are shown in Figure 2.5.

Children's viewing over 2 years was related to parents' patterns of encouragement and regulation. Children in Restrictive families (low encouragement and high regulation) watched less of every type of television than other groups. Their parents succeeded in limiting viewing, particularly of cartoons and adult programming, but these blanket limitations resulted in relatively low viewing of educational programming as well. Moreover, when these children did watch television, they were more likely to watch without their parents than children in Selective and Promotive families.

Laissez-faire families (low encouragement and low restriction) had children with the least beneficial patterns of viewing. They watched a fair amount of entertainment programming but relatively little child informative

PARENT REGULATION AND ENCOURAGEMENT

REGULATION	ENCOURAGEMENT	
	LOW	HIGH
HIGH	Restrictive	Selective
LOW	Laissez Faire	Promotive

Figure 2.5. A Typology of Parent Practices With Respect to Their Children's Television Use—Topeka Study

programming. Like children in Restrictive families, these children did a lot of their viewing without parents. Hence, the content they viewed was not the most beneficial, and they often did not have parents available to mediate what they viewed.

Children in Promotive families (high encouragement, low restriction) also watched a lot of television, but their viewing included high amounts of child informative programming, and they often watched with their parents. These families seemed to be positive about television, to view as a family activity, and to use television for a wide range of purposes.

Selective families, who both encouraged and regulated television, also watched a lot of television, although not quite as much as Promotive families. Their children were heavy viewers of child informative programs and watched slightly fewer child entertainment programs than children of Promotive or Laissez-faire families. These families were also positive about television and viewed as families, but they appeared to be somewhat more discriminating than Promotive families in their choices of programs for their children (St. Peters, Fitch, et al., 1991).

As children get older, parental regulation and encouragement probably becomes less effective as an influence on viewing. It appears, however, that many television viewing habits are established early, so the experiences of children during the first 5 or 6 years of their lives may indeed have long-term consequences for the ways in which they use the medium.

Outcomes of Television Viewing

Television and Intellectual skills

A hypothetical case can be made for both positive and negative influences of television on children's intellectual development, but careful evaluation of the evidence leads to the conclusion that television as a medium does not have clear effects on patterns of cognition or achievement (Anderson & Collins, 1988; see also MacBeth, Chapter 1, this volume). The effects depend on the nature of the programming. Television can be a rich source of stimulating, entertaining learning opportunities, or it can be a mind-numbing waste of time.

Since the evaluations of *Sesame Street* in its first 2 years of broadcasting, there has been good evidence that children can gain knowledge and cognitive skills from well-designed television programs. Low-income children who were encouraged to view *Sesame Street* at home gained in understanding letters, words, numbers, classification, and other skills considered important for school success (Ball & Bogatz, 1970; Bogatz & Ball, 1971). These early evaluations were criticized, however, because they did not sample "normal" home viewing without intervention (Cook et al., 1975).

Our longitudinal data from the Topeka study provided evidence that natural home viewing of children's informative programming contributes to children's intellectual skills. Children who viewed *Sesame Street* often between ages 3 and 5 showed more improvement in vocabulary than did infrequent viewers. This difference remained even when parent education and other social environmental variables were taken into account and controlled statistically (Rice, Huston, Truglio, & Wright, 1990). Children who were heavy viewers of informational programs designed for children or for general audiences also performed better on prereading skills at age 5 (Truglio, Huston, & Wright, 1986).

The Early Window study contained measures of school readiness, letter, and number skills, and vocabulary. When performance on these measures at age 5 was analyzed in relation to viewing between ages 2 and 4, *Sesame Street* viewers had higher scores than children who rarely or never viewed. This pattern occurred when controls were imposed for children's initial language competency, parent education, family income, primary language spoken in the home, and the HOME score (Wright & Huston, 1995). These and other findings support the value of educational television, particularly for very young children who do not attend preschool or educational child care.

By contrast, heavy viewing of programs for children and adults that were not intended to be informative was associated with poor reading skills and lowered attention. In the Early Window study, frequent cartoon viewing was associated with poor performance on school readiness and related skills (Wright & Huston, 1995). In the Topeka study, 5-year-olds who had been exposed to a lot of general audience entertainment programs showed poorer prereading skills than did low viewers. Ironically, they were also less attentive to televised stimuli shown in the laboratory and performed less well on tests of short-term memory (Huston, 1993). We think that, for these young viewers, "exposure" to general audience programs occurred primarily as a result of parents' and siblings' viewing choices; in effect, they had spent a lot of time in the room with television programs that they probably did not understand and in which they were not interested. The large amount of "secondary viewing" of adult programs reported for children in the Early Window study supports this interpretation. The older children and adults around them were engrossed in these programs, at least part of the time. Hence, television displaced more stimulating interactions with adults, and children learned to treat television as a background while they engaged in other activities.

By age 7, when children had entered school, their earlier television viewing did not predict reading skill. Instead, reading skill was associated with earlier vocabulary scores and with early experience with using books, being read to, and using print media. The amount of time that children spent in leisure reading was also measured; some educators believe that leisure reading is at least as important as early technical skill for long-term educational attainment. Children who were heavy viewers of cartoons and other children's entertainment programs in the prior 2 years were unlikely to spend much leisure time with books and print materials at age 7 (Truglio et al., 1986).

In the Early Window study, the time use diaries provided direct information about how children spent their nontelevision viewing time. Children who spent more time looking at books and being read to also spent more time watching educational programs and less time watching cartoons and adult programs than did children with little involvement in print media (Wright & Huston, 1995). It appears that the positive effects of educational television on reading skill and interest in reading can be amplified by experience with print materials, but books and other print sources may be a less important part of children's everyday leisure activities when they watch a lot of cartoons and adult entertainment television.

In summary, both longitudinal and experimental studies provide evidence that children can learn school-related skills from educational programs and that heavy viewing of cartoons and adult programming may detract from some aspects of intellectual development. These findings are not solely a function of parent education, social class, or quality of the home environment; they appear even when those variables are controlled.

Social Development

The effects of television on aggression (Dubow & Miller, Chapter 5) and fear (Cantor, Chapter 4) are discussed elsewhere in this book. Just as violence and horror can stimulate aggression and fear, portrayals of helpful, sympathetic, cooperative interactions can instigate socially positive attitudes and behavior. In a recent review of a large number of studies, the author concluded that prosocial television had at least as much if not more effect than violent television (Hearold, 1986). *Chosing to watch tv tv instead of their friends*

In the 1970s, several studies investigated children's responses to seeing *Mister Rogers' Neighborhood,* a program that portrays positive interactions and adaptive ways of dealing with emotion. Preschoolers who watched the program showed increases in cooperation, helpfulness, ability to verbalize feelings, task persistence, and imagination (Friedrich & Stein, 1973; Singer & Singer, 1981). *Fat Albert and the Cosby Kids* was designed to deal with difficult issues such as gender identity, divorce, and alcohol. Children enjoyed the program and learned important messages from it (Calvert, Huston, Watkins, & Wright, 1982; Calvert, Huston, & Wright, 1987; CBS Broadcast Group, 1974).

Television has also been used successfully to counteract ethnic and gender stereotyping. *Freestyle* was a series designed to reduce gender stereotyped occupational interests among children. It succeeded in changing children's attitudes about what boys and girls could and should do, and it had some modest effects on their behavior (Johnston & Ettema, 1982).

Although television can counteract stereotypes, the predominant content may serve to reinforce and maintain views that women are helpless and incompetent; men are aggressive; most people are white, affluent Americans;

and the principal racial-ethnic group members are African Americans residing in situation comedies. The "social reality" typically shown on broadcast television is not representative; it is a prism concentrating certain images and eliminating others rather than being a mirror of the social world in North America (Huston et al., 1992).

Conclusion

Television as a medium is neither good nor bad; its effects and value depend on the types of programs broadcast and the ways in which they are used by viewers. Television viewing is not inherently passive. Children are often cognitively active while they view; they make choices about when and what to watch that depend on their understanding and interests. Nevertheless, and most important, in their early years, children's exposure to television depends on their families. In turn, family patterns are partly governed by the social institutions and conditions in which they live.

The early years are a critical time for the socialization of television viewing habits. Children learn about what to watch and how much to watch through the example set by parents and siblings. Much of their exposure to adult programs is a direct result of viewing choices made by others in their families. Parents who are selective or restrictive influence their children's viewing patterns, but their own viewing serves as a powerful model for their children. The popular belief that heavy viewing results from parental absence or neglect seems to be misguided. Young children with employed mothers do not watch more than those whose mothers are at home full-time, and the majority of adult programming that young children watch is in the company of their parents.

Although families are crucial mediators of their children's exposure to television, their choices are constrained by decisions in the broadcasting industry about what to produce and broadcast and by the time requirements of jobs and schools. If television is to become a more positive force for children's development, the industry has a responsibility for supplying varied, well-designed, creative programming rather than using children's programs primarily as marketing devices for advertisers' products. Schools and child care settings can also use television in positive ways to enhance development rather than ignoring television altogether or using it primarily for entertainment.

References

Alvarez, M., Huston, A. C., Wright, J. C., & Kerkman, D. (1988). Gender differences in visual attention to television form and content. *Journal of Applied Developmental Psychology, 9,* 459-476.

Anderson, D. R., & Collins, P. A. (1988). *The impact on children's education: Television's influence on cognitive development.* Washington, DC: U.S. Department of Education.

Anderson, D. R., Field, D. E., Collins, P. A., Lorch, E. P., & Nathan, J. G. (1985). Estimates of young children's time with television: A methodological comparison of parent reports with time-lapse video home observation. *Child Development, 56,* 1345-1357.

Anderson, D. R., & Lorch, E. P. (1983). Looking at television: Action or reaction? In J. Bryant & D. R. Anderson (Eds.), *Children's understanding of television: Research on attention and comprehension* (pp. 1-33). New York: Academic Press.

Ball, S., & Bogatz, G. (1970). *The first year of* Sesame Street. Princeton, NJ: Educational Testing Service.

Bogatz, G., & Ball, S. (1971). *The second year of* Sesame Street. Princeton, NJ: Educational Testing Service.

Caldwell, B. M., & Bradley, R. H. (1984). *Home observation for measurement of the environment.* Little Rock: University of Arkansas.

Calvert, S. L., Huston, A. C., Watkins, B. A., & Wright, J. C. (1982). The relation between selective attention to television forms and children's comprehension of content. *Child Development, 53,* 601-610.

Calvert, S. L., Huston, A. C., & Wright, J. C. (1987). Effects of television preplay formats on children's attention and story comprehension. *Journal of Applied Developmental Psychology, 8,* 329-342.

Carpenter, C. J., Huston, A. C., & Spera, L. (1989). Children's use of time in their everyday activities during middle childhood. In M. Bloch & A. Pellegrini (Eds.), *The ecological context of children's play* (pp. 165-190). Norwood, NJ: Ablex.

CBS Broadcast Group. (1974). *A study of messages received by children who viewed an episode of* Fat Albert and the Cosby Kids. New York: CBS Broadcast Group, Office of Social Research, Department of Economics and Research.

Collins, W. A. (1983). Social antecedents, cognitive processing, and comprehension of social portrayals on television. In E. T. Higgins, D. N. Ruble, & W. W. Hartup (Eds.), *Social cognition and social development* (pp. 110-133). Cambridge: Cambridge University Press.

Collins, W. A., Sobol, B. L., & Westby, S. (1981). Effects of adult commentary on children's comprehension and inferences about a televised aggressive portrayal. *Child Development, 52,* 158-163.

Comstock, G., & Paik, H. (1991). *Television and the American child.* San Diego: Academic Press.

Condry, J. (1989). *The psychology of television.* Hillsdale, NJ: Lawrence Erlbaum.

Cook, T. D., Appleton, H., Conner, R. F., Shaffer, A., Tamkin, G., & Weber, S. J. (1975). Sesame Street *revisited.* New York: Russell Sage.

Dorr, A., Kovaric, P., & Doubleday, C. (1989). Parent-child coviewing of television. *Journal of Broadcasting and Electronic Media, 33,* 35-51.

Dorr, A., & Kunkel, D. (1990). Children and the media environment: Change and constancy amid change. *Communication Research, 17,* 5-25.

Field, D. E. (1989). *Television coviewing related to family characteristics and cognitive performance.* Unpublished doctoral dissertation, University of Massachusetts, Amherst.

Frank, J. (1995). Preparing for the information highway. *Canadian Social Trends, 38*(Autumn), Catalogue 11-008.

Friedrich, L. K., & Stein, A. H. (1973). Aggressive and prosocial television programs and the natural behavior of preschool children. *Monographs of the Society for Research in Child Development, 38*(No. 4, Whole No. 151).

Friedrich, L. K., & Stein, A. H. (1975). Prosocial television and young children: The effects of verbal labeling and role playing on learning and behavior. *Child Development, 46,* 27-38.

Hearold, S. (1986). A synthesis of 1043 effects of television on social behavior. In G. Comstock (Ed.), *Public communication and behavior: Vol. 1* (pp. 65-130). Orlando, FL: Academic Press.

Huston, A. C. (1993, February). *Family and environmental antecedents of intellectual ability in early childhood: Longitudinal analyses.* Paper presented at the Esther Katz Rosen Symposium on the Psychological Development of Gifted Children, Lawrence, KS.

Huston, A. C., Donnerstein, E., Fairchild, H., Feshbach, N., Katz, P., Murray, J., Rubinstein, E., Wilcox, B., & Zuckerman, D. (1992). *Big world, small screen: The role of television in American society.* Lincoln: University of Nebraska Press.

Huston, A. C., & Wright, J. C. (1989). The forms of television and the child viewer. In G. Comstock (Ed.), *Public communication and behavior* (Vol. 2, pp. 103-159). Orlando, FL: Academic Press.

Huston, A. C., & Wright, J. C. (1993, September). *Television viewing from age 2 to 5: What children watch and how they spend time when they are not watching TV* (Report to Children's Television Workshop). Lawrence: University of Kansas, Center for Research on the Influences of Television on Children.

Huston, A. C., Wright, J. C., Rice, M. L., Kerkman, D., & St. Peters, M. (1990). The development of television viewing patterns in early childhood: A longitudinal investigation. *Developmental Psychology, 26,* 409-420.

Johnston, J., & Ettema, J. S. (1982). *Positive images: Breaking stereotypes with children's television.* Beverly Hills, CA: Sage.

Lemish, D., & Rice, M. L. (1986). Television as a talking picture book: A prop for language acquisition. *Journal of Child Language, 13,* 251-274.

Messaris, P., & Hornik, R. C. (1983). Work status, television exposure, and educational outcomes. In C. Hayes & S. B. Kamerman (Eds.), *Children of working parents: Experiences and outcomes* (pp. 44-72). Washington, DC: National Academy Press.

Messaris, P., & Sarett, C. (1981). On the consequences of television-related parent-child interaction. *Human Communication Research, 7,* 226-244.

Pinon, M. F., Huston, A. C., & Wright, J. C. (1989). Family ecology and child characteristics that predict young children's educational television viewing. *Child Development, 60,* 846-856.

Posner, J. K., & Vandell, D. L. (1994). Low-income children's after-school care: Are there beneficial effects of after-school programs? *Child Development, 65,* 440-456.

Rice, M. L., Huston, A. C., Truglio, R., & Wright, J. C. (1990). Words from *Sesame Street*: Learning vocabulary while viewing. *Developmental Psychology, 26,* 421-428.

Rosengren, K. E., Wenner, L. A., & Palmgreen, P. (Eds.) (1985). *Media gratification research: Current perspectives.* Beverly Hills, CA: Sage.

Salomon, G. (1977). Effects of encouraging Israeli mothers to co-observe *Sesame Street* with their five-year-olds. *Child Development, 48,* 1146-1151.

Singer, J. L., & Singer, D. G. (1981). *Television, imagination and aggression: A study of preschoolers.* Hillsdale, NJ: Lawrence Erlbaum.

St. Peters, M. (1993). *The ecology of mother child interaction.* Unpublished doctoral dissertation, University of Kansas, Lawrence.

St. Peters, M., Fitch, M., Huston, A. C., Wright, J. C., & Eakins, D. (1991). Television and families: What do young children watch with their parents? *Child Development, 62,* 1409-1423.

St. Peters, M., Oppenheimer, S., Eakins, D. J., Wright, J. C., & Huston, A. C. (1991, April). *Media use among preschool children as a function of income and media options.* Paper presented at the biennial meeting of the Society for Research in Child Development, Seattle.

Truglio, R., Huston, A. C., & Wright, J. C. (1986, August). *The relation between types of television viewing and young children's reading abilities.* Paper presented at the annual meeting of the American Psychological Association, Washington, DC.

Wartella, E., Heintz, K. E., Aidman, A. J., & Mazzarella, S. R. (1990). Television and beyond: Children's video media in one community. *Communication Research, 17,* 45-64.

Watkins, B., Calvert, S. L., Huston-Stein, A., & Wright, J. C. (1980). Children's recall of television material: Effects of presentation mode and adult labeling. *Developmental Psychology, 16,* 672-674.

Williams, T. M., & Boyes, M. C. (1986). Television-viewing patterns and use of other media. In T. M. Williams (Ed.), *The impact of television: A natural experiment in three communities* (pp. 215-264). Orlando, FL: Academic Press.

Wright, J. C., & Huston, A. C. (1995, June). *Effects of educational TV viewing of lower-income preschoolers on academic skills, school readiness, and school adjustment one to three years later* (Report to Children's Television Workshop). Lawrence: University of Kansas, Center for Research on the Influences of Television on Children.

Wright, J. C., St. Peters, M., & Huston, A. C. (1990). Family television use and its relation to children's cognitive skills and social behavior. In J. Bryant (Ed.), *Television and the American family* (pp. 227-252). Hillsdale, NJ: Lawrence Erlbaum.

3

Diversity on Television

Sherryl Browne Graves

Television provides children with a world populated by people or symbolic representations of people such as puppets and cartoon characters. This is true no matter what the program genre, the nature of the program content, the time of broadcast, the type of broadcasting system delivering the programs, or the production unit creating the content. Who are the people populating this television world? The focus of this chapter is on one particular aspect of that question—namely, whether and how the diverse population of North America[1] is portrayed on television. Through TV, our society could provide children with effective positive models of race, gender, and intergroup interaction. This is a potentially important role for television because at the end of the 20th century we still need help in learning how to live, work, and play together with people of diverse racial, ethnic, and religious groups who differ in ability, class, gender, and sexual orientation. In this chapter I will focus on racial and ethnic diversity.

Before proceeding, it is critical to understand the framework from which this chapter emerges. First, I want to define some terms that I will use. The word *race* is used in its sociological or socially constructed sense of five color groupings, despite the fact that from the biological perspective humans represent a single race, the human race. Furthermore, members of *racial groups* are referred to by continental identifiers rather than by color terms. Using this terminology, Marian Wright Edelman, head of the Children's Defense Fund in the United States, for example, is called African American because a significant number of her ancestors came from the African continent, whereas Meryl Streep, the actress, is called European American because the majority of her ancestors came from Europe. Moreover, the term *visible racial-ethnic group* is used instead of the term *minority,* because the latter designation is relative and varies according to the context within which a group is located. Thus, for example, African Americans are a numerical minority within the context of the population of the United States, but they are a numerical majority within the context of the city of East St. Louis.

The richness of diversity of the population of the United States is readily apparent. Current statistics indicate that of the approximately 250 million residents, 51.3% are female and 48.7% are male. The distribution of the population by age is such that 7.6% are below 5 years of age, 12.9% are between 5 and 13 years, 15.8% are between 14 and 24 years, and 12.6% are over 65 years. Racially, 80.3 % are European American, 12.1% are of African descent, 0.8% are Native American, 2.9% are Pacific Islander or Asian, and 2.9% are other. According to U.S. census data (U.S. Bureau of the Census, 1991), people of Hispanic origin can be of any race; 9% are of Hispanic origin and 91% are not. Economic data indicate that 13.1% of all U.S. residents live below the poverty line, whereas 2% have household incomes of $150,000 or more. It is expected that by the year 2020 demographic changes will result in visible racial-ethnic groups comprising an even larger proportion of the U.S. population.

Given the demography of diversity and given the desire to understand the role of television in teaching children how to live and work effectively with others who may appear to be different, what is the relevant television content? Who is exposed to it? What sense do they make of that content? What is its impact? Diversity can be understood along a wide range of important variables, including sexual orientation, religion, and physical and mental ability. For this chapter I am focusing on racial and ethnic groups.

Diversity and Television Presentations: Frequency and Quantity

Diversity in Programs

As is often pointed out, the social world of television is predominantly European American, middle-class, and male, regardless of the type of programming examined. This statement, however, is too broad and general; it fails to provide the detail necessary to understand how and which visible racial-ethnic groups are portrayed. Statements about visible racial-ethnic group portrayals refer mainly to African Americans, because Asian Americans, Latino(a) Americans, and Native Americans have been even more marginal and remained so through the fall 1994 season (Berry, 1988; Graves, 1980, 1993; Graves & Ottaviani, 1995; Greenberg, Simmons, Hogan, & Atkins, 1980; Huston et al., 1992; Williams & Condry, 1989). This marginality is readily apparent in the publicity surrounding an ethnic situation comedy series that debuted in fall, 1994. The show, *All-American Girl,* a comedy featuring three generations of Korean Americans, was touted as the very first series on U.S. television to feature an Asian American cast.

In their study of programming and commercials from 1987, Williams and Condry (1989) found that of the total television population, 7.7% were African Americans, 1.3% Asian Americans, and 0.6% Hispanic Americans. Native American Indians were so rare that they were not counted. Asian Americans were more likely to be seen on television than were Latino Americans, despite the fact that Asian Americans were one third as likely as Latino Americans to be found in the U.S. population. In another study of commercial entertainment television (Subervi-Velez, 1990) Hispanics represented only 1% of prime-time television families over a 10-year period. In our study of prime-time series shown over the 1993-1994 television season we found that the relative percentages of the various visible racial-ethnic groups had not changed significantly from the 1987 figures I've just cited (Graves & Ottaviani, 1995).

The presentation of diversity on television, although limited overall, does vary by channel. Four hours of Saturday morning programming on the three major private networks (ABC, CBS, NBC) and four hours of children's programming on public television were analyzed in a recent study (Greenberg & Brand, 1993). On the sample Saturday, a child watching CBS would not have seen a single visible racial-ethnic group member in a regular or major role. A child watching NBC at the same time would have had a somewhat different experience, because NBC featured visible racial-ethnic groups in public service announcements and in starring roles in two shows. Of the total of 20 programs shown by all four networks, 3 had regularly appearing visible racial-ethnic groups, and all were African Americans. Only one Latino(a) was shown and there were no Asian or Native Americans featured during the sample Saturday.

Public and private television networks provide different pictures of diversity. Public television programming for children regularly presents people of different visible racial-ethnic and economic groups. People on public television sometimes have physical disabilities or communicate in languages other than English (Greenberg & Brand, 1993). This difference in the presentation of diversity comes about because many children's programs on public television are developed with explicit educational goals. For many of these programs one of the goals is to show diverse people living, working, learning, and playing together.

Diversity in Commercials

How is diversity represented in televised advertising? African American characters in 1987 were as likely to be included in commercials as in programs, but Asian and Hispanic Americans were only one third as likely to be seen in commercials as in programs and thus were even more underrepresented in commercials (Williams & Condry, 1989). In another study comparing African and Hispanic American representation in commercials, Hispanics appeared in 4.5% of the ads whereas African Americans appeared in 17% (Wilkes & Valencia, 1989). Both Hispanic and African Americans tended to be assigned minor and background roles when they did appear in commercials (Wilkes & Valencia, 1989). Hispanics were also more likely to appear in large groups. Such portrayals are sometimes referred to as blinkers—that is, roles so minor you would miss them if you blinked at that point in the commercial (Greenberg & Brand, 1993). Other researchers (Palmer, Smith, & Strawser, 1993) have found that 100% of the commercials they analyzed portrayed European Americans. They concluded that whereas European Americans often appear as the only group in a commercial, visible racial-ethnic groups are practically never found as the sole group endorsing a product. They are almost always shown as a numerical minority, with European Americans dominant. In advertising inserted in programming directed at niche audiences, however, such as the Fox network series, *Martin,* one may find members from a single visible racial-ethnic group presenting a product (e.g., a Coke ad featuring hip-hop music and African American basketball players).

Some commercials directed at children are very different from the programming that surrounds them. Some companies, such as McDonald's, Reebok, Lego, and Kelloggs, provide highly diverse casts in their commercials (Greenberg & Brand, 1993). Whereas these advertisers offer the diverse North American child audience a multicultural set of models, others who advertise during children's programs are not as inclusive. For example, advertisements for nonfood items directed at girls (e.g., Barbie dolls) almost never show girls from visible racial-ethnic groups and European American girls playing together with the advertised toy. Such portrayals implicitly suggest that positive relations between girls of diverse groups are unlikely, even when they have identical toy preferences.

In sum, visible racial-ethnic groups are numerically underrepresented in the world of both television programs and commercials. Generally speaking, advertising directed toward children is more inclusive than the children's programs in which it appears. Programming for children on public television is the exception to this rule, providing viewers with racial and ethnic diversity among the cast members of its shows.

Diversity in Role Portrayals

Role portrayals encompass the level of characters' participation in a television program (starring, supporting, and background roles), the nature of the portrayal (positive, negative, neutral), and other role characteristics, including occupation, age, gender, and scope of action of the character. How diverse are the role portrayals of visible racial-ethnic groups? In a study of television characters from 1955 to 1986 (Lichter, Lichter, Rothman, & Amundson, 1987), African and European Americans on television were assigned to starring roles in proportion to their representation on television, but Latinos(as) were rarely stars; the latter were almost always in supporting roles. Most television characters were portrayed positively, but Latinos(as) were almost twice as likely as African Americans to be portrayed negatively.

Latinos(as) were also twice as likely as European Americans and four times as likely as African Americans to be portrayed as lawbreakers. Even in local news presentations, African Americans were more likely than European Americans to be presented as physically threatening and demanding (Entman, 1990). This pattern that Latinos(as) were most likely to have roles as criminals or delinquents has been confirmed by other researchers (Williams & Condry, 1989). Compared with European Americans, Latinos(as) were three times as likely and African Americans and Asian Americans were two times as likely to be cast as lawbreakers. This greater likelihood of visible racial-ethnic groups being depicted as criminals in turn dictates the likelihood and the nature of their intergroup interactions, making them infrequent, mainly formal, and nonfriendly.

Another less positive type of portrayal assigned more frequently to visible racial-ethnic groups, as well as to women and the elderly, is that of victim (Gerbner & Signorelli, 1990). Hispanic Americans were four times as likely as African and European Americans to be portrayed in the role of victim (Williams & Condry, 1989). In the area of victimization on television, Gerbner (1994) suggests that when some women and members of visible racial-ethnic groups are portrayed as being as powerful and assertive as European American males, other members of their racial-ethnic and gender groups are more likely to be presented as victims. For example, for every 100 powerful and assertive Asian television characters, 400 other Asians are portrayed as being victims of violence.

Although the picture for African, Asian, and Hispanic Americans is bleak, for Native North Americans the picture has been even more desolate, with highly stereotyped presentations shrouded in distortions of Native North American culture. The dearth of Native North Americans involved in the creative side of television may partly explain why their portrayals have been sporadic and isolated (Geiogamah & Pavel, 1993). More detailed analyses of television content about Native North Americans are difficult to conduct, as there have been so few regularly featured Native characters since the demise of the western. Over the last two decades, only five series and two commercials featuring regularly occurring Native American characters were identified on U.S. channels by Geiogamah and Pavel (1993). *Northern Exposure,* produced in the United States, and *North of Sixty,* produced in Canada, are recent examples of popular programs featuring Native North Americans. In the 1994 season, Turner Broadcasting presented a three-part, historical series on Native Americans with the majority of the creative and production staff being Native American.

Occupational portrayals on television also vary by racial-ethnic group. In one study, 50% of African American characters had white-collar jobs and 30% had blue-collar jobs, whereas 50% of Asian Americans were in blue-collar and only 18% in white-collar jobs (Williams & Condry, 1989). The jobs of Latinos(as) were 40% white collar and 35% blue collar. In all three groups, public safety jobs accounted for 15% to 20% of the occupational roles. In another study of Saturday morning programming, African American males were more likely to appear in service occupations, such as mailman, fireman, policeman, and electrician as opposed to professional, managerial, or laborer roles (Greenberg & Brand, 1993). Thus, visible racial-ethnic groups on television are more likely to be in blue-collar jobs than are European American characters. One important consequence of these structural constraints is that they may restrict how often intergroup interaction, of any type, takes place between characters from diverse groups. Moreover, these occupational assignments may also affect the nature of the interactions that do take place. The different occupational status profiles of the different groups suggest that relations between people of diverse groups will be less frequent, more formal, and less egalitarian than their interactions would be if they were in the same occupational status. As a consequence, racial homogeneity within an occupation status is more likely to be presented.

The genre or type of television programming tends to be linked systematically to the numerical minority status of visible racial-ethnic groups, resulting in "restricted scope of action, stereotyped roles, diminished life chances and undervaluation" (Signorelli, 1981, p. 99). Thus, for example, during prime time, African American television characters were largely restricted to appearances in the half-hour situation comedies broadcast between 8 and 9 p.m. Moreover, these situation comedies were racially segregated, thereby, once again providing little modeling of positive intergroup interaction.

There are other ways in which televised role portrayals are restricted by race and ethnicity. In 1987 programming, Asian Americans were one half as likely as African and European Americans and one fourth as likely as Hispanic Americans to have roles as a parent or a spouse, familiar and commonplace roles on television and in society (Williams & Condry, 1989). Hispanic Americans were four times as likely as African and European Americans to be portrayed in the role of medical patient, a positive but subordinate role.

African and Asian Americans were equally likely to be portrayed as a friend or neighbor, but no Latinos(as) were seen in these prevalent roles. For children of all backgrounds who watch television, the reduced chance of Asian American, Hispanic American, and African American characters being portrayed in common, familiar, and positive roles may increase the viewers' sense of unfamiliarity and discomfort with these groups.

Age and gender differences are evident in portrayals of diverse racial-ethnic groups. In one study (Palmer, Smith, & Strawser, 1993), African Americans and European Americans were equally likely to be portrayed as children, whereas Latinos(as) were least likely to be in these roles despite the actual younger median age of this group in the United States. Among all visible racial-ethnic groups, female characters were one third to one half as likely as male characters to be included (Baptista-Fernandez & Greenberg, 1980; Berry, 1980; Graves & Ottaviani, 1995; Greenberg, 1986). Interestingly, although the proportion of televised females in general increased from 1970 through the 1980s, the proportion of African American female characters decreased (Seggar, Hafen, & Hannonen-Gladden, 1981). This same trend was evident in Saturday morning children's programming, in which not a single African American adult female was shown in any commercial and the regularly featured visible racial-ethnic group characters were almost always African American males (Greenberg & Brand, 1993). In another study of Hispanic prime-time characters, males were three times as likely as Hispanic females to be portrayed (Wilkes & Valencia, 1989). These age and gender differences serve to further limit plot opportunities for positive interaction between males and females and between members of diverse groups.

The racial and ethnic identity of televised characters also varies with respect to the assignment of family roles. Dorr and her colleagues (Dorr, Rabin, Kovaric, Doubleday, & Brannon, 1991) found that only 4 of 40 family series shown between 1983 and 1987 featured African American families. None featured Asian American, Latino(a), or Native North American families. Seven of the family series included at least one family member from a visible racial-ethnic group. In families that included members from more than one racial group, all were headed by European Americans without the benefit of an interracial marriage, interethnic marriage, or both. These television shows suggest that marriage between diverse people is rarer than the data provided by the U.S. Bureau of the Census (U.S. Bureau of the Census, 1991) (2% of all marriages). Moreover, these series suggest that family life is rarer for visible racial-ethnic group members than it is in the mainstream.

Diverse families on television differ in other important ways. Dorr and her colleagues (1991) found that, overwhelmingly, whereas African American families were urban, European American families were suburban. European American families were presented as solidly middle-class, whereas African American families generally were skewed toward the lower class. Those families with members from more than one race, however, were skewed to upper-class status. In television, as in life, segregated residential living patterns restrict the possibility of intergroup interaction and the nature of that interaction. Social class differences permit unusual intergroup interaction patterns: African American children are allowed to interact with European American adults and children only when they have the benefit of family member status.

Family structure on television also varies by race (Dorr et al., 1991). African American families were most likely to be two-parent families with related children. European American families with African American children were most likely to be single-parent families. Other European American families displayed a wide range of family structures, the most common being based on biological relationships between parents and children.

In sum, visible racial-ethnic groups are not only underrepresented in the social world of television, but they are segregated by the type of show and portrayed in limited roles. Their victim status, family group configuration, and occupational level vary with their specific racial-ethnic group. Such racial patterns structurally limit the possibilities for relationships between diverse television characters (Huston et al., 1992) and thereby reduce television's positive role in educating children.

What does intergroup interaction look like when it does occur on television? When there is intergroup interaction, there is little explicit discussion of race relations (Greenberg, 1986; Lovelace, Freund, & Graves, in press; Pierce, 1980; Williams, & Condry, 1989). Intergroup interaction, although generally portrayed as neutral or positive, is more likely to occur in the context of job-related activities rather than in social or recreational activities (Williams & Condry, 1989). This follows logically from the residential segregation on television and the ways in which the work worlds of white- and blue-collar employees intersect. Among youths of visible racial-ethnic groups there is a greater likelihood of positive interaction with characters of other ethnic groups than with members of the same racial-ethnic group (Williams & Condry, 1989). On television this pattern of intergroup interaction between young people suggests that there is greater intragroup conflict within visible racial-ethnic groups. Such interaction patterns reinforce negative stereotypes about higher levels of deviance in visible racial-ethic communities than in mainstream ones. Within the limited opportunities for relationships between diverse people on television, the likelihood of greater positive interaction across racial-ethnic groups than within, particularly for African Americans, reflects more formal interracial interaction patterns (e.g., the relationship between police officers and victims of violence). In addition, these patterns imply that a European American presence is needed to decrease conflict or violence and to increase civility and decorum in groups.

Other features of intergroup behavior on television could be further examined. Behavior among people from the same racial-ethnic group on television generally features interdependent communication patterns. These interdependent patterns stress understanding, self-disclosure, confirmation of the other, collaboration, and empathic listening (Auletta & Hammerback, 1985). In contrast, intergroup relations, generally speaking, feature independent communication patterns. This type of communication emphasizes judgmental feedback, lack of self-disclosure, and unwillingness to collaborate, along with rejection and neglect of the other. Unfortunately, there have been very few studies of television content at this behavioral level. Further study of these patterns might provide producers with specific guidelines about how to create more authentic, positive, and interesting intergroup interactions.

Racial-ethnic portrayals endow characters with specific behaviors and personality characteristics. Some features are influenced by the presence of other ethnic group members. For example, during the 1970s African Americans were permitted to dominate European Americans in situation comedies, but the reverse was true in crime dramas (Lemon, 1977). There is some evidence that lesser identification with one's ethnicity may be valued in the television world. In a study of prime-time programs on Canadian and U.S. channels, visible racial-ethnic group members with strong ethnic identities were more likely to be negatively portrayed than were more assimilated racial-ethnic characters (Jackson, Travis, Williams, & Phillips, 1986). In another study, African Americans in segregated shows were more likely to display stereotyped behaviors than were those in integrated shows (Banks, 1975). In commercial children's television, racial or ethnic messages were rare in programs that featured African American and other visible racial-ethnic groups in integrated programming (Barcus, 1983). On the other hand, cartoon comedies avoided African American portrayals but employed the most blatant other ethnic stereotyping (e.g., the use of foreigners as bad guys).

It should be remembered that the media convey messages about visible racial-ethnic groups through both what is presented and what is omitted. Clark (1972) suggests that social groups are legitimized by the media by "recognition and respect." Visible racial-ethnic groups who are underrepresented are invisible because they lack recognition by the larger society. Television treats visible racial-ethnic groups in a perverse way, paying attention to them when it does not matter and failing to shine the spotlight on them when it is important. This nonrecognition carries as much weight, if not more, than the plethora of stereotypic presentations. The use of stereotypes is evidence of the lack of respect afforded visible racial-ethnic groups on television. Greater familiarity and sensitivity could be generated in the audience if diverse groups were presented in positive and supportive roles. The research I've reviewed suggests that neither recognition nor respect have been the predominant processes directing commercial television's inclusion of visible racial-ethnic group members.

Unlike the relationships portrayed on commercial television, interracial interaction regularly occurs on educational and public television programs such as *Sesame Street, 3-2-1 Contact, Barney and Friends,* and *Reading Rainbow.* From the onset of *Sesame Street,* positive intergroup interaction has been presented. Moreover, within the last few years *Sesame Street* has developed a "race relations" curriculum that presents children from different racial-ethnic groups in situations in which their racial-ethnic identity is an integral feature of their portrayals. These new presentations are replete with children who have identifiable racial-ethnic features and who express cultural characteristics through their behaviors, values, and attitudes. In addition, the race relations curriculum directly acknowledges differences among people that children notice. Differences in skin color, hair textures, eye shapes, and languages are presented and discussed. Simultaneously, this curriculum emphasizes that diversity is good while helping preschoolers look for similarities among the members of the various groups (Children's Television Workshop, Sesame Street Research [CTW], 1992).

In sum, with exceptions notable by their rarity, television presents limited diversity. Diverse characters that are shown are restricted to specific content ghettos. When visible racial-ethnic groups are portrayed, they are restricted in terms of their roles, occupations, and personality characteristics. The limited roles and scope of action assigned to visible racial-ethnic groups reduces chances for diverse people to encounter one another. A commercial television series that did make a point of having diverse people encounter each other in their social worlds is *Northern Exposure*. Educational television for children is at the forefront of programming making specific efforts to expand the range of portrayals for visible racial-ethnic groups and to increase examples of positive intergroup interaction.

Diversity and Television: Who's Watching?

Diversity in television portrayals would not be important if no one were watching. Viewing patterns can be examined in different ways. One way is to start with diverse groups and track what they watch. Another is to start with programming that includes visible racial-ethnic groups and ask who is viewing this content.

Racial-ethnic viewing patterns suggest that African Americans watch more television than do other racial-ethnic groups. African American households watched 48% more than all other racial groups during the 1989 November sweeps month (Baseline [BSL], 1991). Similarly, African American children watch more TV than do European American children (Blosser, 1988; Brown, Childers, Bauman, & Koch, 1990; Stroman, 1984; Tangney & Feshbach, 1988). There is less research evidence about the viewing habits of Asian American and Hispanic American children. In some areas of North America, Asian and Hispanic youngsters and adults can choose from programming that features members of their racial-ethnic groups in their own languages.

There is strong evidence that African American children and adolescents are more likely to view programs featuring African Americans (Anderson & Merritt, 1978; Liss, 1981). BSL (1991) revealed that, according to Nielsen, the top five television programs in African American households all featured same-race performers (*A Different World, The Cosby Show, Fresh Prince of Bel-Air, In Living Color,* and *In the Heat of the Night*). For the same period, only one or two of these programs were as high in Nielsen ratings for the general audience. Unfortunately, there is little known about the viewing preferences of Asian American, Hispanic American, and Native North American children for the same content.

Looking at diversity and television from the perspective of programming, the popularity of African American situation comedies attests to the fact that children of all groups watch these programs. They are, nevertheless, viewed by proportionately more African American than European American children. Because the European American population is so much larger, they must, in absolute numbers, watch more. Thus, most children are exposed to portrayals of African Americans under conditions of limited intergroup interaction and little discussion of racial-ethnic issues because of the segregated nature of these programs. What needs to be investigated is how children of other visible racial-ethnic groups relate to programming featuring members of different groups or featuring intergroup interaction. Do they seek out programming that features a member of any visible racial-ethnic group as an alternative to mainstream stars? Or do they avoid such programming to be more knowledgeable about mainstream society? Again, these processes may be different for groups for whom language, length of residence in North America, and social class diversity varies from that of African Americans.

Research conducted with Anglo, African, and Hispanic American adults sheds some light on these issues (Faber, O'Guinn, & Meyer, 1987). All three groups stated that there were too few African Americans on television, but this belief was more common among African Americans. Both the Hispanic American and African American groups felt that there were too few Hispanics on television. These two groups were significantly more likely to believe this than were Anglos, even though half the Anglo sample did endorse this statement. More Hispanics than Anglos strongly endorsed the statement that Hispanics were underrepresented, and more Hispanics endorsed the latter statement than endorsed the statement that African Americans were underrepresented. African Americans were equally likely to endorse both statements. Thus, the findings of this study suggest that members of visible racial-ethnic groups may be more sensitive to issues of minority representation on television than are European Americans, whether or not their own visible racial-ethnic group is involved.

In sum, children do watch programming including members from diverse groups. There is some evidence to suggest that program preferences may be stronger among African Americans for shows featuring African American characters. More information is needed about the viewing habits and program preferences of Asian American, Hispanic American, and Native American children.

Can We All Just Get Along?:
The Television Version

What type of impact could one reasonably expect from exposure to televised portrayals of positive or negative race relations? Much of the research has assumed that the direction of the effect is from the content to passive child viewers. As has been emphasized by Aletha Huston and John Wright in their chapter in this book (Chapter 2), children can be active viewers of television. They come to television with varied needs and with different purposes for viewing (Blumler & Katz, 1974). Children are more responsive to information that aids their comprehension of the world and their experiences (Anderson, 1981, 1983). It may also be the case, as Greenberg (1988) suggests, that unusual or distinct television portrayals have far greater impact than those that are commonplace. Thus, his "drench hypothesis" implies potentially greater impact for a very popular program such as *The Cosby Show* than for a plethora of more neutral or negative portrayals of African American family and group interactions in situation comedies, which merely "drip" their effects slowly and in much smaller amounts.

Is the impact of television in the area of race relations simply the direct result of specific content messages? Perhaps not. The messages of invisible minority groups, racial-ethnic stereotypes, minorities as social problems, minorities as tokens, or all of these are noticed, understood, and remembered through the viewer's prior knowledge and experience. Exposure to, for example, fictional, highly attractive, middle-class African Americans supporting the validity of the "American dream," and exposure to news broadcasts of handcuffed, hooded, African American male suspects from the underclass may interact to create a set of ideas about African Americans and about the nature of interactions with this group (Fleras, 1995; Gray, 1989). These two extreme presentations, one fictional and one nonfictional, help maintain stereotypic ideas about African Americans in our society. The nonfictional presentations confirm the stereotype of African American sloth, aggression, and deviance, whereas the fictional portrayals reinforce for the viewers that they can have positive responses to members of different racial-ethnic groups. In addition, stereotypic presentations do not force the viewer to confront the contradictions that may exist in race relations. These contradictory portrayals allow the viewer to believe the following: (a) racism is not a factor in our society; (b) regardless of race or ethnicity, the American dream is accessible to all Americans; and (c) society is basically functioning well.

Unfortunately, fictional African American characters often are depicted in situations in which their racial identity does not matter (Gray, 1989) and in which there is little intergroup interaction. Moreover, examples of middle-class African Americans of the type that dominate fictional presentations are largely absent from television news (Fleras, 1995; Goodman, 1990). Even local television news programs tend to be devoid of males from visible racial-ethnic groups; instead, African American, Asian American, and Latina American females are more likely to be found at the anchor or co-anchor spot. Thus, viewers learn to respond positively to fictional visible racial-ethnic group members while also learning to be wary and fearful of real visible racial-ethnic group members, particularly if they are male. This television lesson on intergroup interaction stimulates positive feelings for unavailable types of visible, racial-ethnic group members—that is, fictional middle-class ones—and reinforces negative sentiments toward real and presumably more accessible visible, racial-ethnic group members—that is, real and suspected criminals.

Portrayals of race relations on television may influence children in a number of different ways. Emotional responses can be affected. Knowledge about intergroup interaction can be acquired. Attitudes toward working and playing with people from different groups can be altered. Finally, there is the possibility that actual behavior under conditions of intergroup interaction can be affected. The major impediment to television having a greater impact on race relations may be the limited extent to which interracial interaction is shown and the limited extent to which racial and ethnic group relations are discussed on television. Moreover, the sharp contrast between highly negative presentations of real African American criminal types and positive portrayals of fictional African Americans characters may further cloud perceptions about the possibility or even the desirability of positive intergroup interaction.

Race Relations and Affect

Research with preschoolers suggests that European American children can acquire information about emotions better from human portrayals, even African American ones, than from nonhuman portrayals (Hayes & Casey, 1992). Research conducted by the *Sesame Street* research group on the program's race relations curriculum (Lovelace & Freund, 1992; Lovelace et al., in press) found that 3-, 4-, and 5-year-old African American, Hispanic American, and European American children knew that televised African American and European American children were positive or happy about their visits with each other. Moreover, almost all of these preschoolers (81%-94%) were attentive to the examples of interracial interaction and were able to report what happened in the story. After viewing these segments more African American children were able to name similarities between the racially dissimilar children than could do so before exposure to these segments. Thus, exposure to mutually beneficial interracial and intergroup interaction can positively affect children's emotions. In general, when the relations are portrayed positively, children are able to recognize these affirmative emotions.

Race Relations: Perceptions and Comprehension of Portrayals

Most television viewers respond to diverse portrayals in predictable ways. They are more critical of portrayals of their own group than they are of portrayals of other groups (Dorr, Graves, & Phelps, 1980; Faber et al., 1987; Lichter & Lichter, 1988). Presumably, they are more critical of portrayals of their own group because they can compare the television presentations with direct experience. Their more positive evaluations of the portrayals of other groups may be the result of viewers' lack of experience with diverse groups and with notions that television is an important source of information about other people. Their positive evaluation of other group portrayals also may be related to viewer attitudes about the credibility of television in general (Comstock & Cobbey, 1982; Greenberg & Reeves, 1976). That is, those who believe that television is a more credible source may attribute greater believability to its portrayal of diverse groups.

An understanding of the portrayals of African Americans by children of other racial groups is influenced by a number of variables. For example, using drawings, Lawrence (1991) found that European American children interpreted the behavior of African American, nontelevision, characters less positively than that of their own group when the behavior occurred in socially ambiguous situations. Recourse to negative stereotypes as explanatory frames may have been used by the children when there were no clear cues from the story. Similarly, 10- to 12-year-old European American children from segregated schools were more likely to use personal and situational attributions for the behavior of European American characters than for African American ones (Williams, Collins, & Cornelius, 1991). Again, the children used explanations that reflected a perception of similarity between themselves and the European American characters. Their attempts to understand the African American characters reflected their perception of them as different, foreign, and unfamiliar. These two studies suggest that stereotypes of African Americans may influence the perception and understanding of African American portrayals for European American child viewers.

Viewing interactions between children, adults, or both from different racial-ethnic groups provides an opportunity for acquisition of racial knowledge and information. From the work with *Sesame Street,* it was clear that the race relations segments provided opportunities for viewers to acquire information about home life, cultural celebrations, crafts, language, food, and music. Perhaps not surprisingly, however, retention of names for specific cultural features were more difficult for children unfamiliar with the activities. So, for example, more African American children remembered the name Aiesha, whereas more European American children remembered the name of the white child, Olivia. Similarly, more African than European American children knew that grits were served (Lovelace & Freund, 1992).

Children can acquire information and knowledge about diverse racial and ethnic groups from exposure to positive television portrayals. Under other conditions, children may use prior attitudes and knowledge of stereotypes to assist in their understanding and appreciation of television presentations of visible racial-ethnic groups. Thus, positive presentations of diverse groups on television may not be effective if they fail to directly address children's knowledge of negative stereotypes.

Televised Race Relations and Racial Attitudes and Knowledge

Viewers from different cultural or social backgrounds may interpret the same program content or character portrayals differently. Content that can be interpreted differently can therefore have different effects (Livingstone, 1990). Research on the impact of such portrayals on attitudes supports this idea. The nature or type of African American portrayal predicts the impact on the racial attitudes of European American children (Dorr et al., 1980; Graves, 1975), but the relationship between type of portrayal and impact on racial attitudes of African American children is less clear (Graves, 1980). In one instance mere exposure to same-race characters, regardless of the nature of the portrayal, had a positive impact on African American child viewers (Graves, 1975), but in another study, exposure led to more negative same-race attitudes (Dorr et al., 1980). The difference between the findings for these two studies must surely lie in the distinct and varied experiences of African American youth in general and with television in particular (Ogbu, 1978; Stroman, 1984). That is, some of the characters in the first study were based on real African Americans (e.g., the Harlem Globetrotters and Bill Cosby) and these African American portrayals were animated. In the second study, none of the presentations were animated and none included or were based on real African Americans. Thus, type of television format (animation vs. live action) and knowledge of African American experience (celebrities vs. fictional people) may have a greater influence on the African American child viewer than on the European American child viewer.

For European American viewers, parental and child viewing habits and racial attitudes may be intertwined (Zuckerman, Singer, & Singer, 1980). European American children who watched more programs with African American characters and who watched more violent programming described African Americans as less competent and obedient than did children who watched a less violent diet of television. European American children whose mothers watched less violent programming were more likely to describe African Americans as superior athletes, a more positive, although still stereotypical, attribute. Thus, the mothers' lesser exposure to negative portrayals of African Americans may have had an indirect influence on the children's racial attitudes separate from the direct effect of the television diets of the children.

Because much of television does not involve intergroup interactions, most of what we know about their impact focuses on how programs specifically designed to present positive racial portrayals influence child viewers. There is some indication that African American characters involved in intergroup interaction are more powerful influences than are similar characters in segregated settings (Graves, 1975; Kraus, 1972). These shows can positively affect racial attitudes (Bogatz & Ball, 1971) and they can increase acceptance of members of other visible racial-ethnic groups (Mays, Henderson, Seidman, & Steiner, 1975). Our recent research on the race relations curriculum of *Sesame Street* indicates that children will attend to positive intergroup interaction, recognize emotional reactions of characters and be positively disposed to such interaction (Lovelace et al., in press). Children of different racial-ethnic groups may vary, however, in their attention to portrayals in which someone is rejected because of skin color (Lovelace & Freund, 1992). These differences in attention may be related to children's different prior experiences and therefore may lead to differences in perceptions and in the effects of those perceptions on outcomes.

In sum, television can influence children's attitudes toward, knowledge about, and perceptions of members of visible racial-ethnic groups. The amount and nature of the impact varies with the child's racial-ethnic background and the nature of the presentation. Television presentations of visible racial-ethnic groups can affect children indirectly through their impact on parental attitudes.

Conclusions and Suggestions for Future Research

What conclusions can been drawn from this review of research? North American television provides limited diversity both numerically and qualitatively—that is, in the nature of the portrayals. Most U.S. programming is dominated by European Americans who are middle-class and are more likely to be male. Diverse portrayals, when included, are predominantly presentations of African Americans. Portrayals of diverse groups are restricted by the types of roles, occupations, and personality characteristics that are assigned. Even social roles, including family membership, location of residence, and community roles, vary as a function of visible racial-ethnic group membership. The structural features of the portrayals, in terms of both frequency of appearance and quality of characterization, dictate the nature and possibility for intergroup interaction and for discussion of race relations.

Research on viewing patterns and program preferences indicates that children from all racial-ethnic groups watch programs that include members of visible racial-ethnic groups. Indeed, they watch these programs to such an extent that some shows featuring visible racial-ethnic group members have been among the top Nielsen-rated shows. There is also evidence that African Americans tend to have a stronger preference for programs featuring African Americans. There is insufficient research to shed light on the program preferences of other visible racial-ethnic group members.

Television could present more interracial or other intergroup interactions. Not surprisingly, given what is known about the frequency and quality of portrayals of diverse individuals, intergroup interaction on North American television has been very limited. When it does occur, it is usually presented within the context of work. Only on children's programming on public television are viewers likely to regularly encounter positive social relationships between members of diverse groups.

For children, exposure to members of diverse groups interacting can influence their feelings about working and playing with others. From watching diverse portrayals children can acquire general information about people, as well as specific cultural information about the groups presented. Finally, exposure to presentations of visible racial-ethnic groups can affect children's attitudes toward those groups. The direction of the attitude change is the result of characteristics of the child, characteristics of the television content, and features of the social context.

When intergroup interactions are portrayed on television they often are limited, simplistic, and unrealistic. Most are limited to the workplace, and despite political preoccupations with issues such as affirmative action and minority set-aside programs, there is almost no discussion of race relations, racism, prejudice, or discrimination. Although it is true that these topics are controversial and difficult to present, it is my experience, as an African American, that such topics are talked about in "mixed company," particularly within the safety of the work environment. Discussion of issues such as prejudice or racism would require television to take a more critical view of society and the establishment. This is a difficult role for television organizations to play because, despite their protestations to the contrary, media corporations are an integral part of the economic and political establishment in North America. Acknowledgment of the existence of racism and prejudice might involve the presentation of unpleasant attitudes, beliefs, and behaviors on television, for example, as was shown in the 1970s on *Archie Bunker* and *The Jeffersons*. Portraying negative attitudes and behaviors and discussing stereotypes risks the possibility of reinforcing these ideas in the minds of children. But avoiding these issues has made groups outside the mainstream invisible, implying that they are irrelevant and unimportant. Flight from these issues also has led to an overreliance on stereotypes that leaves the audience with a sense of familiarity with those diverse people they do, albeit infrequently, encounter on television. Avoidance of these issues has, in addition, led to the presentation of most visible racial-ethnic groups as people with social problems and people without solutions for those problems. Finally, retreat from these issues has permitted the use of visible racial-ethnic group members as peripheral, as accessory, as minor, as unimportant, and as dispensable. Thus, if there has been a concerted effort to protect the child audience, it seems unlikely that much more would be lost if the difficult issues were faced directly. Good examples do exist. Commercial and cable television might look to public television to see how visible racial-ethnic groups can be portrayed in nonstereotypical ways and with more complex, three-dimensional characteristics.

Television rarely shows intergroup interaction in a social context. Under conditions of friendship and mutual interest it is possible not only to show positive interaction but also to present positive discussion of difficult issues. This, however, is not easy. It is very difficult to think about how to present positive interracial or intergroup interaction on television because of the powerful nature of stereotyping. I remember watching television and seeing a commercial for an automobile. In the ad there are two young women, one European American and one African American, who are both accountants. The owner of the car is the European American and she drives her African American friend around. My first reaction was this: Of course the advertiser had the European American as the car owner because that was compatible with the stereotype that African Americans are lazy and could not afford a new car or the stereotype that African Americans would not have the competence and disposition to buy a car that was such good value. Then I tried to imagine a bias-free or nonstereotyped version of this ad. If the African American woman were the car owner and she drove her European American friend, the viewer might think that this was natural and compatible with the stereotype of African Americans as servants or service personnel, à la *Driving Miss Daisy*. I have since spent some time thinking about how to improve the ad. Acknowledging that I am not a Madison Avenue ad executive, I add more dialogue to establish clearly the egalitarian nature of the relationship. Or I imagine multiple versions of the commercial where the roles are reversed. Or I add additional groups of car owners and drivers who vary by race to establish a sense that lots of different types of people can own and drive the product. Stereotypes are difficult to eradicate both on the screen and in the mind of the viewers.

Unfortunately, the research on diversity on television is very limited. Most of it has focused on African American portrayals and the impact of these portrayals on African American and European American audiences. We need to move beyond comparisons of African and European American groups to include the many other visible racial-ethnic groups in North American society.

We still need content analysis research to permit us to track changes or the maintenance of the status quo in the presentation of visible racial-ethnic groups. As researchers we also need, however, to move beyond simplistic enumeration of visible racial-ethnic representation and beyond the description of limited role portrayals. Finally, we should move beyond the description of visible racial-ethnic group portrayals in isolation. Content analyses could include more complex analyses of the nature of intergroup communication patterns and dominance relationships. Analyses should be conducted to reveal the unique ways in which television skews the assignment of age, occupation, family, socioeconomic status, and residential patterns among groups. Greater attention should be given to the nature of intergroup interaction and the discussion of racial-ethnic relations between diverse people. Finally, researchers could relate their content analysis findings to data on viewer preferences and viewing habits. For example, we could ask, "If children watch television every weekday evening from 8 p.m. to 9 p.m., how frequently are they likely to encounter portrayals of diverse groups?" Moreover, "What conclusions will these viewers draw about the life experiences of the members of visible racial-ethnic groups they see?"

In the same way that we need to expand our knowledge of how portrayals are changing, so too should our knowledge about viewing habits and program preferences be expanded. Particular focus should be given to the preferences of groups other than African and European Americans for viewing television programs featuring mainstream groups, their own group, and diverse casts. It is also important to assess the extent to which new television options (new networks, cable, satellite TV, and computer-based multimedia presentations) differ in their offerings and thus may be associated with different program preferences. This research on preferences should be coupled with increased information about children's knowledge, perceptions, attitudes, and emotions after watching various presentations.

Finally, we need to know more not only about the impact of a single type of portrayal but also about the impact of the interaction of multiple portrayals of visible racial-ethnic groups. For example, how do positive fictional portrayals interact with negative real life portrayals? And conversely, how do positive real-life portrayals interact with negative fictional ones?

There is much to be learned about the nature of diversity in North American television. Currently, the public is expressing renewed interest in this topic. There also is renewed interest at the policy level, with a number of different funding sources providing resources for the creation of programs featuring diverse casts and the inclusion of issues involving intergroup interactions. As the global village shrinks through the use of technological advances, it is important to ensure that children can benefit from exposure to diverse groups on television as well as in their own multicultural society.

Note

1. Most of the research discussed in this chapter was conducted in the United States, so that is its primary focus. The diversity of portrayals in programming produced in the United States is also highly relevant in Canada, however, because most Canadians have access to numerous U.S. television channels as well as to programming produced in the United States that is shown on Canadian channels.

References

Anderson, J. A. (1981). Research on children and television: A critique. *Journal of Broadcasting, 25*(4), 395-400.

Anderson, J. A. (1983). Television literacy and critical viewer. In J. Bryant & D. R. Anderson (Eds.), *Children's understanding of television: Research on attention and comprehension* (pp. 297-330). New York: Academic Press.

Anderson, W. H., & Merritt, B. (1978). *Using television to enhance the self-esteem of black children.* Paper presented at the annual meeting of the Association of Black Psychologists, St. Louis, MO.

Auletta, G. S., & Hammerback, J. C. (1985). A relational model for interracial interactions on television. *Western Journal of Speech Communication, 49*(4), 301-321.

Banks, C. (1975). *A content analysis of the treatment of black Americans on television.* (ERIC Document Reproduction Service No. 115)

Baptista-Fernandez, P., & Greenberg, B. S. (1980). The context, characteristics, and communication of blacks on television. In B. S. Greenberg (Ed.), *Life on television* (pp. 13-21). Norwood, NJ: Ablex.

Barcus, F. E. (1983). *Images of life on children's television.* New York: Praeger.

Baseline, Inc. (1991, September 24). TV viewing by blacks declining. *The Hollywood Reporter.*

Berry, G. L. (1980). Television and Afro-Americans: Past legacy and present portrayals. In S. B. Withey & R. P. Abeles (Eds.), *Television and social behavior: Beyond violence toward children.* Hillsdale, NJ: Lawrence Erlbaum.

Berry, G. L. (1988). Multicultural role portrayals on television as a social psychological issue. In S. Oskamp (Ed.), *Applied social psychology annual: Television as a social issue* (Vol. 8, pp. 118-129). Newbury Park, CA: Sage.

Blosser, B. J. (1988). Ethnic differences in children's media use. *Journal of Broadcasting and Electronic Media, 32*(4), 453-470.

Blumler, J. G., & Katz, E. (1974). *The uses of mass communications.* Beverly Hills, CA: Sage.

Bogatz, G. A., & Ball, S. (1971). *The second year of Sesame Street: A continuing evaluation* (Vols. 1 & 2). Princeton, NJ: Educational Testing Service.

Brown, J. D., Childers, K. W., Bauman, K. E., & Koch, G. G. (1990). The influence of new media and family structure on young adolescents' television and radio use. *Communication Research, 17*(1), 65-82.

Children's Television Workshop, Sesame Street Research. (1992). *New race relations goals for season 24.* New York: Children's Television Workshop.

Clark, C. (1972). Race, identification, and television violence. In G. A. Comstock, E. A. Rubinstein, & J. P. Murray (Eds.), *Television and social behavior. Vol. 5: Television's effects: Further explorations* (pp. 120-184). Washington, DC: Government Printing Office.

Comstock, G., & Cobbey, R. E. (1982). Television and the children of ethnic minorities: Perspectives from research. In G. L. Berry, & C. Mitchell- Kiernan (Eds.), *Television and the socialization of the minority child* (pp. 245-260). New York: Academic Press.

Dorr, A., Graves, S. B., & Phelps, E. (1980). Television literacy for young children. *Journal of Communication, 30*(3), 71-83.

Dorr, A., Rabin, B. E., Kovaric, P., Doubleday, C., & Brannon, C. (1991). Racial and ethnic diversity in television series featuring families. In *Ethnicity and diversity: Implications for research and policy.* Hillsdale, NJ: Lawrence Erlbaum.

Entman, R. M. (1990). Modern racism and the images of blacks in local television news. *Critical Studies in Mass Communication, 7,* 332-345.

Faber, R. J., O'Guinn, T. C., & Meyer, T. P. (1987). Televised portrayals of Hispanics: A comparison of ethnic perceptions. *International Journal of Intercultural Relations, 11,* 155-169.

Fleras, A. (1995). "Please adjust your set": Media and minorities in a multicultural society. In B. D. Singer (Ed.) *Communications in Canadian society* (4th ed., pp. 406-431). Toronto: Nelson Canada.

Geiogamah, H., & Pavel, D. M. (1993). Developing television for American Indian and Alaska Native children in the late 20th century. In G. L. Berry & J. K. Asamen (Eds.), *Children and television: Images in a changing sociocultural world* (pp. 191-204). Newbury Park, CA: Sage.

Gerbner, G. (1994). Keynote speech presented at the Television Violence in the Media Conference, New York, NY.

Gerbner, G., & Signorelli, N. (1990). *Violence profile 1967 through 1988-89: Enduring patterns.* Unpublished manuscript

Goodman, W. (1990, May 20). Missing middle-class blacks in TV news. *New York Times.*

Graves, S. B. (1975). *Racial diversity in children's television: Its impact on racial attitudes and stated program preferences.* Unpublished doctoral dissertation, Harvard University, Cambridge, MA.

Graves, S. B. (1980). Psychological effects of black portrayals on television. In S. B. Withey & R. P. Abeles (Eds.), *Television and the socialization of the ethnic minority child* (pp. 259-289). New York: Academic Press.

Graves, S. B. (1993). Television, the portrayal of African Americans and the development of children's attitudes. In G. L. Berry & J. K. Asamen (Eds.), *Children and television: Images in a changing sociocultural world* (pp. 179-190). Newbury Park, CA: Sage.

Graves, S. B., & Ottaviani, B. F. (1995). *The Hunter College Television and Diversity Project.* New York: Hunter College.

Gray, H. (1989). Television, black Americans, and the American dream. *Critical Studies in Mass Communication, 6,* 376-386.

Greenberg, B. S. (1986). Minorities and the mass media. In J. Bryant, & D. Zillmann (Eds.), *Perspectives on media effects* (pp. 165-188). Hillsdale, NJ: Lawrence Erlbaum.

Greenberg, B. S. (1988). Some uncommon television images and the drench hypothesis. In S. Oskamp (Ed.), *Applied social psychology annual: Television as a social issue* (Vol. 8, pp. 88-102). Newbury Park, CA: Sage.

Greenberg, B. S., & Brand, J. E. (1993). Cultural diversity on Saturday morning television. In G. L. Berry & J. K. Asamen (Eds.), *Children and television: Images in a changing sociocultural world* (pp. 132-142). Newbury Park, CA: Sage.

Greenberg, B. S., & Reeves, B. (1976). Children and the perceived reality of television. *Journal of Social Issues, 32,* 86-97.

Greenberg, B. S., Simmons, K., Hogan, L., & Atkins, C. (1980). Three seasons of television characters: A demographic analysis. *Journal of Broadcasting, 24,* 49-60.

Hayes, D. S., & Casey, D. M. (1992). Young children and television: The retention of emotional reactions. *Child Development, 63*(6), 1423-1436.

Huston, A. C., Donnerstein, E., Fairchild, H., Feshbach, N. D., Katz, P. A., Murray, J. P., Rubinstein, E. A., Wilcox, B. L., & Zuckerman, D. (1992). *Big world, small screen: The role of television in American society.* Lincoln, NE: University of Nebraska Press.

Jackson, D., Travis, L., Williams, T. M., & Phillips, S. (1986). *Ethnic minorities in Canada: TV's roles in the development of attitudes and stereotypes.* Paper presented at the annual meeting of the Canadian Psychological Association, Vancouver.

Kraus, S. (1972). Modifying prejudice: Attitude change as a function of the race of the communicator. *Audiovisual Communication Review, 10*(1).

Lawrence, V. W. (1991). Effect of socially ambiguous information on white and black children's behavioral and trait perceptions. *Merrill-Palmer Quarterly, 37*(4), 619-630.

Lemon, J. (1977). Women and blacks on prime-time television. *Journal of Communication, 27*(1), 70-74.

Lichter, S. R., & Lichter, L. (1988). *Television's impact on ethnic and racial images: A study of Howard Beach adolescents.* New York: Institute of Human Relations, American Jewish Committee.

Lichter, S. R., Lichter, L. S., Rothman, S., & Amundson, D. (1987, July/August). Prime-time prejudice: TV's images of blacks and Hispanics. *Public Opinion, pp. 13-16.*

Liss, M. B. (1981). Children's television selections: A study of indicators of same-race preferences. *Journal of Cross-Cultural Psychology, 12*(1), 103-110.

Livingstone, S. M. (1990). Interpreting a television narrative: How different viewers see a story. *Journal of Communication, 40*(1), 72-85.

Lovelace, V., & Freund, S. (1992, October 19). *Race relations revisited.* Presentation at the Children's Television Workshop, New York.

Lovelace, V., Freund, S., & Graves, S. B. (in press). Role relations and *Sesame Street*: Racial knowledge, attitudes, and understanding in preschool children. In M. B. Spencer & G. K. Brookins (Eds.), *Research in minority children's development.* Hillsdale, NJ: Lawrence Erlbaum.

Mays, L., Henderson, E. H., Seidman, S. K., & Steiner, V. S. (1975). *An evaluation report on Vegetable Soup: The effects of a multiethnic children's television series on intergroup attitudes of children.* Unpublished manuscript, Department of Education, State of New York.

Ogbu, J. U. (1978). *Minority education and caste.* New York: Academic Press.

Palmer, E., Smith, K. T., & Strawser, K. S. (1993). Rubik's tube: Developing a child's television worldview. In B. L. Berry & J. K. Asamen (Eds.), *Children and television: Images in a changing sociocultural world* (pp. 143-154). Newbury Park, CA: Sage.

Pierce, C. M. (1980). Social trace contaminants: Subtle indicators of racism in TV. In S. B. Withey & R. P. Abeles (Eds.), *Television and social behavior: Beyond violence toward children* (pp. 249-259). Hillsdale, NJ: Lawrence Erlbaum.

Seggar, J. F., Hafen, J. K., & Hannonen-Gladden, H. (1981). Television's portrayals of minorities and women in drama and comedy drama, 1971-1988. *Journal of Broadcasting, 25*(3), 277-288.

Signorelli, N. (1981). Content analysis: More than just counting minorities. In H. Myrick, & C. Keegan (Eds.), *In search of diversity* (pp. 97-109). Washington, DC: Corporation for Public Broadcasting.

Stroman, C. A. (1984). The socialization influence of television on black children. *Journal of Black Studies, 15*(1), 79-100.

Subervi-Velez, F. A. (1990). Interactions between Latinos and Anglos on prime-time television: A case study of "Condo." In S. Chan (Ed.), *Income and status differences between white and minority Americans: A persistent equality* (pp. 306-336). Lewiston, NY: Edwin Mellen.

Tangney, J. P., & Feshbach, S. (1988). Children's television viewing frequency: Individual differences and demographic correlates. *Personality and Social Psychology Bulletin, 14*(1), 145-158.

Wilkes, R. E., & Valencia, H. (1989). Hispanics and blacks in television commercials. *Journal of Advertising, 18*(1), 19-25.

Williams, M. E., Collins, W. A., & Cornelius, S. W. (1991, April). *The salience of race and role of intergroup conflict in white children's understanding of fictional television characters.* Paper presented at the biennial meeting of the Society for Research in Child Development, Seattle, WA.

Williams, M. E., & Condry, J. C. (1989). *Living color: Minority portrayals and cross-racial interactions on television.* Paper presented at the biennial meeting of the Society for Research in Child Development, Kansas City, MO.

Zuckerman, D. M., Singer, D. G., & Singer, J. L. (1980). Children's television viewing, racial, and sex-role attitudes. *Journal of Applied Social Psychology, 10*(4), 281-294.

4

Television and Children's Fear

Joanne Cantor

The music sounded interesting, I wasn't sleepy, and besides, our babysitter was watching it. . . . I was about 6 years old. . . . The late movie was on and I think it was titled *The Tingler*—at least that was what everyone called it.

One scene I remember occurred in a bathroom. A man, I think, was going to take a shower. When he turned on the faucet, the water was discolored. I think that then blood began to pour out of the faucet and the man could not turn it off. Then panicked, he ran for the door, which was locked. Suddenly, the sink faucets had blood flowing from them, too. I remember all the horror and how freaked out the man was because he knew that it was the Tingler.

After that night I was afraid to take a bath alone. I had to have someone in the room with me. I had a fear that blood would start pouring from the faucets and I would be locked inside. I was afraid that if I left the door open and I was alone that the Tingler would slam the door shut. I was told over and over that there was no such thing as the Tingler, but I always thought, "What if?"

These fears persisted for about 3 or 4 years and then disappeared. I still liked to watch frightening movies, although I wasn't allowed to for obvious reasons. (L. T., female college student)

AUTHOR'S NOTE: Much of the research reported in this chapter was supported by Grant 1 R01 MH 35320 from the National Institute of Mental Health, by support from the A. C. Nielsen Foundation, and by grants from the Graduate School of the University of Wisconsin.

This quote from a student's retrospective report of an early fright reaction produced by television illustrates the type of response that is quite prevalent among those who have grown up with television. Although the specific details are unique to a particular individual, recollections of such intense responses with long-term emotional effects are not uncommon.

Research on fright reactions to mass media goes back long before the advent of television. Several investigators in the 1930s and 1940s focused on fear reactions to mass media (Blumer, 1933; Cantril, 1940; Dysinger & Ruckmick, 1933; Eisenberg, 1936; Preston, 1941). In addition, some major volumes reporting research conducted in the 1950s addressed this issue seriously (Himmelweit, Oppenheim, & Vince, 1958; Schramm, Lyle, & Parker, 1961; Wertham, 1953). But fright responses to mass media were largely ignored in the 1960s and 1970s. There were only passing references to them in the Surgeon General's Report (Comstock & Rubinstein, 1972), and in the Surgeon General's Update (Pearl, Bouthilet, & Lazar, 1982), fear was addressed in terms of the long-term effects of media exposure on perceptions of danger but, for the most part, not in terms of the transitory or more enduring emotional effects of particular programs or films.

One reason for the resurgence of interest in fright responses may be that mass media content has become increasingly graphic and horror filled (see Stein, 1982). As anecdotal reports of intense emotional responses to popular films such as *Jaws* and *The Exorcist* proliferated in the press, public attention became more focused on the phenomenon. Although many adults experience such reactions, the major share of public concern has been over children's responses. The furor over children's reactions to especially intense scenes in *Indiana Jones and the Temple of Doom* and *Gremlins* prompted the Motion Picture Association of America (MPAA) to add "PG-13" to its rating system, to caution parents that, for whatever reason, a film might be inappropriate for children under the age of 13 (Zoglin, 1984). In addition, the rapid expansion in the number of cable channels has meant that most films produced for theatrical distribution, no matter how brutal or bizarre, eventually end up on television and consequently become accessible to large numbers of children, often without their parents' knowledge. Finally, the widespread prior speculation about children's potential emotional responses to the broadcast of the nuclear holocaust film *The Day After* seems to have been unprecedented (see Schofield & Pavelchak, 1985), and similar intense concerns surfaced regarding media coverage of the 1991 war in the Middle East (Greenberg & Gantz, 1993; Taylor, 1991).

Although some psychoanalytically oriented observers would disagree (e.g., Bettelheim, 1975; Smetak, 1986), many researchers who have interviewed children on the topic of exposure to frightening media fare have speculated on its potential negative effects on children. Blumer (1933) argued that "emotional possession" could occur and cause children to lose ordinary control over their feelings and perceptions. Preston (1941) contended that exposure to media horrors could become an "addiction" with profound negative effects on children's physical and psychological health. More recently, Singer (1975) argued that children who are exposed to frightening movies may be haunted for years by night terrors and bizarre and weird fantasies. Sarafino (1986) has placed a great deal of blame on scary television shows and films for inducing and exacerbating children's fears. His book on children's fears contains countless anecdotes involving the media's negative impact and he contends that exposure to "scary portrayals of animals, violence, and monsters on TV and in the movies can impair children's psychological development" (p. 56). He also argues that such fears need to be addressed before they become unreasonably debilitating or develop into phobias.

Research into potential negative effects on children has unique problems, however, in that it is not feasible, for ethical reasons, to demonstrate harmful effects in the experimental laboratory. Thus, what evidence there is for intense emotional disturbances in children comes from anecdotes, retrospective reports, case studies, and surveys. In these studies, effects observed in the "real world" are reported, but control over variables is impossible, and causal conclusions remain highly tentative. The laboratory research that has been conducted on fright responses to mass media, in contrast, has not been designed to demonstrate longer term negative effects but, rather, to determine the variables that contribute to immediate and short-lived fright responses and those that prevent or mitigate them.

Review of Research on Media-Induced Fright

Prevalence and Intensity of Media-Induced Fright Reactions

Many researchers, myself included, have found that a substantial proportion of children and adolescents have experienced fright while watching mass media productions (e.g., Blumer, 1933; Himmelweit et al., 1958; Lyle &

Hoffman, 1972; Wilson, Hoffner, & Cantor, 1987). Moreover, most researchers who have studied the issue have observed that intense reactions lasting beyond the time of exposure are quite common. Although von Feilitzen (1975), in summarizing the results of Danish research, concluded that few children have suffered severe effects in the form of anxiety, nightmares, or lost sleep, other researchers have reported that enduring and intense responses are more pervasive. Eisenberg (1936), for example, found that more than 40% of a sample of children had recently dreamed about things they had heard on the radio and that approximately half of these children said that their dreams had involved witches, murders, crimes, nightmares, and the like. Himmelweit et al. (1958) reported that almost one fifth of the adolescents they questioned following the introduction of television in England reported having said they had seen something on TV that they "couldn't get out of their mind." In a study by Hess and Goldman (1962), three fourths of the parents interviewed agreed that children sometimes get nightmares from watching television programs; most of them agreed "strongly."

More recently, one fourth of a group of adolescents we studied said that they experienced enduring fright "sometimes" or "often" after watching television shows (Cantor & Reilly, 1982). Furthermore, almost as many children said they sometimes or often regretted having seen a scary program because of how much it had upset them. Finally, about half the sample of elementary school children questioned by Palmer, Hockett, and Dean (1983) reported that they experienced enduring fright reactions to television programs "sometimes" or "frequently," and over a third said that they sometimes or frequently were sorry they had seen such programs.

To explore children's fright reactions to media coverage of real-world events, we recently conducted a survey to determine the prevalence of emotional disturbances produced by televised coverage of the war in the Persian Gulf (Cantor, Mares, & Oliver, 1993). Of a random sample of parents of children in the public schools in Madison, Wisconsin, a sizable proportion reported that their child had been upset by the televised war coverage. Approximately one fourth mentioned the coverage spontaneously when asked to name something on television that had upset their child recently, and when asked directly about the war coverage, 45% said that their child had been upset.

In a study designed to assess the severity of typical enduring fright reactions to mass media, Johnson (1980) asked a random sample of adults whether they had ever seen a motion picture that had disturbed them "a great deal." Of this sample, 40% replied that they had, with the disturbance lasting, on average, 3 days. Respondents also reported on the type, intensity, and duration of symptoms such as nervousness, depression, fear of specific things, and recurring thoughts and images. On the basis of these reports, Johnson judged that almost half of these adults (one fifth of the total sample) had experienced, for at least 2 days, a "significant stress reaction" of the type identified by Horowitz (1976) and Lazarus (1966) as constituting a "stress response syndrome." Johnson argued that these reactions are severe and should be taken seriously:

> It is one thing to walk away from a frightening or disturbing event with mild residue of the images and quite another thing to ruminate about it, feel anxious or depressed for days, and/or to avoid anything that might create the same unpleasant experience. (p. 786)

On the basis of his data, Johnson concluded that such reactions were more prevalent and more severe than had previously been assumed. Anecdotal reports of such intense reactions involving obsessive thoughts, the inability to sleep, avoidance of common activities, and recurrent nightmares are abundant (see Cantor & Oliver, 1996).

The most extreme reactions reported in the literature come from psychiatric case studies in which acute and disabling anxiety states, sometimes requiring hospitalization and often lasting several days to several weeks or more, are said to have been precipitated by the viewing of horror movies such as *The Exorcist* and *Invasion of the Body Snatchers* (Buzzuto, 1975; Mathai, 1983). Most of the patients in the cases reported had not had previously diagnosed psychiatric problems, but the viewing of the film was seen as exacerbating other stressors in the patients' lives. Most recently, a 10-year-old's extreme reaction to a program with the title *Ghostwatch* was reported in the *British Medical Journal* (Simons & Silveira, 1994). The child was diagnosed as suffering from television-induced posttraumatic stress disorder and was hospitalized for 8 weeks.

In summary, the research literature indicates that transitory fright responses to mass media stimuli are quite typical, that enduring and intense emotional disturbances occur in a substantial proportion of children and adolescents, and that severe and debilitating reactions affect a small minority of particularly susceptible individuals of all ages.

Parental Awareness

Parents typically underestimate their children's fright reactions to media. Preston (1941) found that for the most part, the parents of the children she studied either were unaware of their children's fright responses to mass media horrors or minimized their significance. More recent findings are in accord with this generalization. We found that parents' estimates of how often their children were frightened by mass media were significantly lower than their children's self-reports (Cantor & Reilly, 1982). They were not, however, merely systematically lower; generally speaking, the parents' estimates were not significantly correlated with those of their children.

We also found that parents' estimates of their children's exposure to frightening media were also significantly lower than their children's own reports (Cantor & Reilly, 1982). The difference between parents' and children's estimates of exposure is difficult to interpret because it may reflect either the parent's ignorance of what the child has seen or a difference between the parent's and the child's expectation of what would be frightening to a child. Data to be reported later in this chapter suggest that children often experience fright reactions to programs that most parents would not expect to be scary. Nevertheless, there is evidence that children are widely exposed to televised stimuli that were originally intended for adults and that are considered frightening by a large proportion of adult moviegoers. For example, Sparks (1986) reported that almost half of the 4- to 10-year-olds he interviewed had seen *Poltergeist* and *Jaws,* and substantial proportions of his sample had seen *Halloween* and *Friday the 13th.* Most of this viewing was done in the home, on cable television.

Reasons for Children's Exposure to Frightening Media

Given the data just cited on the prevalence of immediate fright and other more enduring emotional disturbances produced by exposure to frightening productions, the question obviously arises as to why children are subjected to the risk of such unpleasant experiences. There are several possible answers. Preston (1941) argued that children cannot avoid being exposed to such programs if their parents insist on watching them. She also maintained that children choose such fare themselves so that they can talk about the "hair-raising details" with their friends at school. But in speaking of the habitual consumption of media horrors as "addiction," Preston implicitly endorsed the notion that such exposure produces intrinsic rewards as well. In fact, most researchers who have asked the question have discovered that many children enjoy frightening media presentations, despite the negative emotional reactions that sometimes occur. Blumer (1933) reported that in a third-grade class he interviewed, 86% of the children gave instances of being frightened, on occasion severely, by motion pictures; yet most of those who had been frightened said that they liked to be frightened by movies. More than half of the elementary school children interviewed by Palmer et al. (1983), and 80% of the adolescents we interviewed in one of our studies (Cantor & Reilly, 1982) said they liked scary television and films "somewhat" or a "lot." Sparks (1986) found that more than a third of the elementary school children he interviewed said they enjoyed scary programs, and an additional one fourth said they both enjoyed and disliked them. Finally, in a study we conducted on children's perceptions of fear-reducing techniques, almost two thirds of the children in one sample replied "yes" when asked whether they liked scary programs; about three fourths of the children in another sample stated that they liked them, with about half of that sample saying they liked them "a lot" (Wilson et al., 1987).

Several researchers (e.g., Blumer, 1933) have noted that many children enjoy being frightened while viewing scary presentations, even though they suffer unwanted effects afterward. Himmelweit and her associates (1958) argued that the child "enjoys being frightened just a little, but not too much," and that the child "likes the suspense for the pleasure of the relief that follows it" (p. 210). Zillmann (1980) has proposed an explanation for the pleasure produced by the resolution of suspense. He has argued that physiological arousal is produced by the anticipation of threatened negative outcomes and that, through the process of excitation transfer (e.g., Zillmann, 1978), this arousal intensifies the enjoyment of the "happy endings" that such presentations usually provide. Moreover, Zillmann has argued that the enjoyment of suspenseful presentations does not necessarily hinge on the final outcome but may occur throughout the presentation as various episodes within a plot induce and then reduce suspense (Zillmann, Hay, & Bryant, 1975).

Consistent with Zillmann's reasoning, we have argued that undergoing fright reactions to scary presentations does not necessarily reduce the enjoyment of such presentations, and that fright may even be positively associated with liking (Cantor & Reilly, 1982). In a sixth-grade sample, children who reported experiencing enduring fright reactions "sometimes" or "often," did not differ from less reactive children in their liking for scary media. Moreover, in a 10th-grade sample, highly reactive adolescents tended to like scary programs more than their less reactive peers did. Furthermore, adolescents who were highly reactive did not avoid scary programs; they did not differ from those who were less reactive in their reports of frequency of exposure to scary presentations.

Developmental Considerations in Fear Effects

In a recent chapter (Cantor, 1994), I proposed an explanation for the fact that media depictions often induce anxiety and fear when the viewer, objectively speaking, is in no immediate danger. It was argued that there are categories of stimuli that humans either are predisposed to fear spontaneously or come to fear through experience. Through the process of stimulus generalization, stimuli and events that would evoke fear if encountered in reality produce fear when witnessed in the media. Major fear-producing media stimuli were categorized as depictions of danger and injuries, distortions of natural forms, and the experience of endangerment and fear by others.

Although it is useful to categorize the types of stimuli that typically produce fright, it is clear that responses to the depiction of frightening stimuli and events depend to a great extent on characteristics of the viewer. Perhaps the most important viewer attribute that has been identified to predict fright reactions to media is chronological age or developmental level.

The expectation that developmental level will affect fright reactions is based on several factors. First, research shows that there are consistent developmental trends in the real-world stimuli and issues that evoke fear (e.g., Angelino, Dollins, & Mech, 1956; Maurer, 1965), and these differences should be reflected in responses to mediated depictions. Second, perceptions of danger will depend in some cases on world knowledge or experience. Although an attacking animal might be feared automatically because it provides what Bowlby (1973) refers to as "natural cues" to danger, such as rapid approach, sudden or strange movement, and loud noise, a certain degree of knowledge is necessary to fear such awesome threats as nuclear weapons or AIDS.

A third reason to expect age and developmental differences derives from the fact that the perception of stimuli and the comprehension of event sequences are involved, in varying degrees, in the viewer's response to television productions. Therefore, developmental differences in information-processing tendencies related to media viewing (see Collins, 1983; Wartella, 1979) should affect the nature and intensity of fright responses to specific depictions. Finally, it will be argued here that certain complex cognitive operations or thinking abilities are involved in fright reactions to some types of media stimuli. The ability to perform such operations is limited in very young viewers and improves throughout childhood.

For more than a decade, my collaborators and I have conducted a program of research to explore two major developmental issues in fright reactions to media: (a) specifying the types of mass media stimuli and events that frighten children at different ages and (b) determining the strategies that are most effective for different age groups in preventing or reducing unwanted fear reactions. Using observations and theories from developmental psychology as guidelines, particularly theories of cognitive development, we have conducted a series of experiments and surveys. The experiments have had the advantage of testing rigorously controlled variations in program content and viewing conditions, using various combinations of self-reports, physiological responses, the coding of facial expressions of emotion, and behavioral measures. In a complementary fashion, the surveys have investigated the responses of children who had voluntarily exposed themselves to a particular mass media offering in their natural environment, without any researcher intervention (see Cantor, 1989).

Developmental Differences in the Media Stimuli That Produce Fright

Although one might expect otherwise, it is not true that as children get older they become less and less susceptible to media-produced emotional disturbances. As children mature cognitively, some things become less likely to disturb them, whereas other things become potentially more upsetting. This generalization is consistent with developmental differences in children's fears in general. According to a variety of studies using diverse methodologies, children from approximately 3 to 8 years of age are frightened primarily by animals; the dark; supernatural beings, such as ghosts, monsters, and witches; and by anything that looks strange or moves suddenly. The fears of 9- to 12-year-olds are more often related to personal injury and physical destruction and the injury and death of relatives. Adolescents continue to fear personal injury and physical destruction, but school fears and social fears arise at this age, as do fears regarding political, economic, and global issues (see Cantor, Wilson, & Hoffner, 1986, for review).

A review of these developmental trends suggests that fears in young children derive largely from the direct or mediated experience of perceptually salient stimuli that are either real or fantastic (e.g., animals, monsters). The fears of older elementary school children are characterized by objectively dangerous events that have strong perceptual components when they occur (e.g., kidnapping, accidents, natural disasters), but the fears seem to derive from the anticipation that the events might occur more often than from the perceptual experience of the dangers themselves. The fears of adolescents become even more abstract and diverse (exams, dating, war) and involve the threat of psychological as well as physical harm.

Our findings regarding the media stimuli that frighten children at different ages are consistent with observed changes in children's fears in general. Broad generalizations from our research are summarized here. The first generalization is that the relative importance of the immediately perceptible components of a fear-inducing media stimulus decreases as a child's age increases. Research on cognitive development indicates that, in general, very young children react to stimuli predominantly in terms of their perceptible characteristics and that with increasing maturity, they respond more and more to the conceptual aspects of stimuli. Piaget referred to young children's tendency to react to things as they appear in immediate, egocentric perception as "concreteness" of thought (see Flavell, 1963); Bruner (1966) characterized the thought of preschool children as "perceptually dominated." A variety of studies have shown that young children tend to sort, match, and remember items in terms of their perceptible attributes and that between the ages of about 5 and 8 years, this tendency is increasingly replaced by the tendency to use functional or conceptual groupings (e.g., Birch & Bortner, 1966; Melkman, Tversky, & Baratz, 1981). For example, when asked to sort pictures into piles of similar objects, younger children will tend to use similarity of color or shape as a criterion; older children will increasingly group items together that have a similar function or belong in the same category.

The notion of a developmental shift from perceptual to conceptual processing has been tested in terms of the impact of visual features of a stimulus. Our research findings support the generalization that preschool children (approximately 3 to 5 years old) are more likely to be frightened by something that looks scary but that is actually harmless, than by something that looks attractive but that is actually harmful; for older elementary school children (approximately 9 to 11 years), appearance carries much less weight, relative to the behavior or destructive potential of a character, animal or object.

One set of data that supports this generalization comes from a survey (Cantor & Sparks, 1984) in which we asked parents to name the programs and films that had frightened their children the most. In this survey, parents of preschool children most often mentioned offerings with grotesque-looking, unreal characters, such as the television series *The Incredible Hulk* and the feature film *The Wizard of Oz*; parents of older elementary school children more often mentioned movies (such as *The Amityville Horror*) that involved threats without a strong visual component and that required a good deal of imagination to comprehend. Sparks (1986) replicated this study, using children's own reports rather than parents' observations and reported similar findings. Both surveys included controls for possible differences in exposure patterns in the different age groups.

A second investigation that supports this generalization was a laboratory study involving an episode of *The Incredible Hulk* series (Sparks & Cantor, 1986). This study helps explain the unexpected finding that 40% of the parents of preschool children in our survey (Cantor & Sparks, 1984) spontaneously mentioned this program as one that had scared their child. When we tracked children's levels of fear during different parts of the program, we found that preschool children experienced the most fear after the attractive, mild-mannered hero was transformed into the monstrous-looking Hulk, and we concluded that their reactions were partially due to their overresponse to the grotesque visual image of the Hulk character. Older elementary school children, in contrast, reported the least fear when the Hulk was present, because they understood that the Hulk was really the benevolent hero in another physical form and that he was using his superhuman powers on the side of "law and order" and against threats to the well-being of sympathetic characters. Figure 4.1 presents the data from this study.

In another study (Hoffner & Cantor, 1985), we tested the effect of appearance more directly by creating a video in four versions so that a major character was either attractive and grandmotherly looking or ugly and grotesque. The character's appearance was systematically varied with her behavior. Both the attractive and ugly characters were depicted as behaving either kindly or cruelly toward a cat who had wandered into their home. Figure 4.2 illustrates the manipulation of the character's appearance and behavior. Each child in the study saw only one of these four versions of the video. In judging how nice or mean the character was and in predicting what she would do to

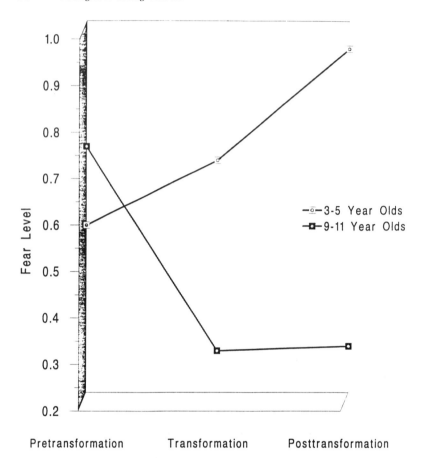

Figure 4.1. Children's Self-Reports of Fear in Response to the Television Program *The Incredible Hulk* Before, During, and After the Transformation of the Main Character Into the Hulk Figure
SOURCE: Adapted from Sparks and Cantor (1986).
NOTE: Younger children's fear increased as a function of exposure to the transformation, whereas the fear of older children decreased.

two children she was about to discover hiding in her house, preschool children were more influenced than older children (6-7 years and 9-10 years) by the character's looks and less influenced than older children by her kind or cruel behavior. As the age of the child increased, the character's looks became less important and her behavior carried increasing weight. Figure 4.3 illustrates the effects of the character's appearance and behavior on children's evaluations of her. A follow-up study revealed that children in the three age groups

Figure 4.2. Manipulation of Character's Appearance and Behavior in the Experiment by Hoffner and Cantor (1985)
SOURCE: Reprinted from Hoffner, C., & Cantor, J. (1985). Developmental differences in responses to a television character's appearance and behavior. *Developmental Psychology, 21,* 1065-1074. (Copyright 1985, American Psychological Association.)
NOTE: Upper left: attractive-kind; upper right: ugly-kind; lower left: attractive-cruel; lower right: ugly-cruel.

engaged in similar levels of physical appearance stereotyping in the absence of information about the character's behavior. In other words, without any knowledge of her behavior, children at all three ages expected the ugly woman to be cruel and the attractive woman to be kind.

A second generalization that emerges from our studies is that as children mature, they become more responsive to realistic dangers and less responsive to fantastic dangers depicted in the media. The data on trends in children's fears suggest that very young children are more likely than older children and adolescents to fear things that are not real, in the sense that their occurrence in the real world is impossible (e.g., monsters). The development of more "mature" fears seems to presuppose the acquisition of knowledge regarding the objective dangers posed by different situations. One important component of this knowledge includes an understanding of the distinction between reality

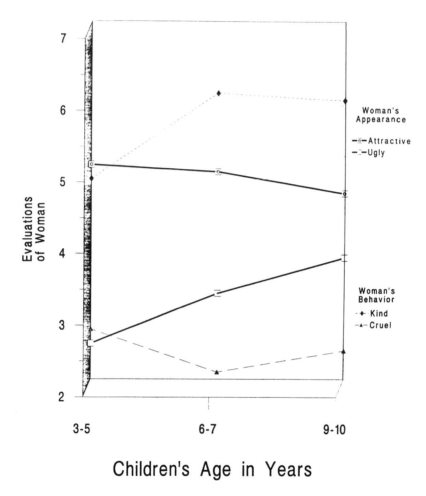

Children's Age in Years

Figure 4.3. Effect of Manipulation of Character's Appearance and Behavior on Children's Perceptions of Woman's Personality

SOURCE: Adapted from Hoffner and Cantor (1985).

NOTE: Solid lines indicate that the effect of her appearance decreased as the child's age increased. Broken lines indicate that the effect of her behavior increased as the child's age increased.

and fantasy. Much research has been conducted on the child's gradual acquisition of the various components of the fantasy-reality distinction (see Flavell, 1963; Kelly, 1981; Morison & Gardner, 1978). Until a child understands the distinction, he or she will be unable to understand that something that is not real cannot pose a threat; thus, for young children, the reality or fantasy status of a media depiction should have little effect on the fear it evokes. As the child comes increasingly to understand this distinction and increasingly appreciates the implications of real-world threats, depictions of real dangers should gain in fear-evoking potential relative to depictions of fantasy dangers.

This generalization is supported by our survey of parents, mentioned earlier, on the sources of their children's fear (Cantor & Sparks, 1984). In general, the tendency to mention fantasy offerings, depicting events that could not possibly occur in the real world, decreased as the child's age increased, and the tendency to mention fictional offerings, depicting events that might possibly occur, increased with age. Again, Sparks (1986) replicated these findings using children's self-reports rather than parents' perceptions.

Our third generalization is that as children mature, they become frightened by media depictions involving increasingly abstract concepts. This generalization is clearly consistent with the general sources of children's fears cited earlier. It is also consistent with theories of cognitive development (e.g., Flavell, 1963), which indicate that the ability to think abstractly emerges relatively late.

Data supporting this generalization come from a survey we conducted on children's responses to the television movie *The Day After* (Cantor et al., 1986). Many people were concerned about young children's reactions to this movie, which depicted the devastation of a Kansas community by a nuclear attack, but our research led us to predict that the youngest children would be the least affected by it. We conducted a telephone survey (using random sampling) the night after the broadcast of this movie. As we predicted, children under age 12 were much less disturbed by the film than were teenagers, and parents were the most disturbed. The very youngest children apparently were not upset or frightened at all. Most of the parents of the younger children who had seen the film could think of other shows that had frightened their child more during the preceding year. Most of the parents of the teenagers could not. We concluded that the strongest emotional impact of the film comes from the contemplation of the potential annihilation of the earth as we know it, a concept that is beyond the grasp of the young child. The visual depictions of injury in this movie were quite mild compared to what most children have become used to seeing on television. The increase in fear reactions with increasing age was not expected by organizations such as Educators for Social Responsibility and by many school systems, which urged that children under the age of 12 not be permitted to watch the movie (Schofield & Pavelchak, 1985).

These developmental generalizations apply to children's responses to news reports as well as to dramatizations. In the survey of parents that we conducted during the war in the Persian Gulf (Cantor et al., 1993), there were no significant differences between 1st, 4th, 7th, and 11th graders in the reported prevalence or intensity of negative emotional reactions to television coverage of the war. Children in different grades were upset by different aspects of the coverage, however. Parents of younger children, but not of older children, stressed the visual aspects of the coverage and the direct, concrete consequences of combat in their descriptions of the elements that had disturbed their child the most. As the child's age increased, the more abstract, conceptual aspects of the coverage and of the war in general (e.g., the threat of a global war) were cited by parents as the most disturbing.

The series of studies just described supports the contention that developmental issues in perception, comprehension, and interpretation must be taken into account in understanding and predicting children's media-induced fright reactions. Quite frequently, children respond with fear to depictions that their parents would not have the least qualms about showing them. For example, in our survey of responses to *The Day After* (Cantor et al., 1986), apparently benign offerings such as *Captain Kangaroo* and *Charlotte's Web* were reported to have caused greater levels of disturbance in young children than the nuclear holocaust movie. Developmental considerations could no doubt illuminate the threatening aspects of these programs as well as young children's relative insensitivity to *The Day After*.

Developmental Differences in the Effectiveness of Coping Strategies

There are strong developmental differences in the effectiveness of strategies to prevent or reduce media-induced fears, and these differences are consistent with developmental differences in children's information-processing abilities (Cantor & Wilson, 1988). The findings of our research on coping strategies can be summarized as follows: In general, preschool children benefit more from *noncognitive* than from *cognitive strategies;* both cognitive and noncognitive strategies can be effective for older elementary school children, although this older group tends to prefer cognitive strategies.

Noncognitive Strategies. We have categorized as "noncognitive" those strategies that do not involve the processing of verbal information and that appear to be relatively automatic. The process of visual desensitization is one such strategy that has been shown to be effective for both preschool and older elementary school children in five separate experiments. In one experiment, gradual visual exposure to filmed footage of snakes tended to reduce fear reactions to the snake-pit scene from the action-adventure film *Raiders of the Lost Ark* (Wilson & Cantor, 1987). In a second experiment (Wilson, 1987), prior exposure to a realistic rubber replica of a tarantula reduced the emotional impact of a scene involving tarantulas from *Kingdom of the Spiders*. In a third experiment (Wilson, 1989a), prior exposure to a live lizard reduced children's expressions of fear while watching a scene involving deadly lizards in *Frogs*. In a fourth experiment (Weiss, Imrich, & Wilson, 1993), prior exposure to graphic photographs of worms taken from the horror film *Squirm* reduced children's self-reports of fear during a scene from that movie. Finally, fear reactions to the Hulk character in *The Incredible Hulk* were reduced by exposure to footage of Lou Ferrigno, the actor who plays the character, having his makeup applied so that he gradually took on the menacing appearance of the character (Cantor, Sparks, & Hoffner, 1988). None of these experiments revealed developmental differences in the technique's effectiveness.

Other noncognitive strategies involve physical activities, such as clinging to an attachment object or having something to eat or drink. Although these techniques are available to viewers of all ages, there is reason to believe they are more effective for younger than for older children. First, it has been argued that the effectiveness of such techniques is likely to diminish as the infant's tendency to grasp and suck objects for comfort and exploration decreases (Bowlby, 1973). Second, it seems likely that the effectiveness of such techniques is partially attributable to distraction, and distraction techniques should be more effective in younger children, who have greater difficulty allocating cognitive processing to two simultaneous activities (e.g., Manis, Keating, & Morison, 1980).

There is no experimental evidence of the effectiveness of physical coping strategies in the mass media situation. However, in a study of children's perceptions of the effectiveness of strategies for coping with media-induced fright, we found that preschool children's evaluations of "holding onto a blanket or a toy" and "getting something to eat or drink" were significantly more favorable than those of older elementary school children (Wilson et al., 1987).

Another noncognitive strategy that has been shown to have more appeal and more effectiveness for younger than older children is covering one's eyes during frightening portions of a presentation. In an experiment by Wilson (1989b), when covering the eyes was suggested as an option, younger children used this strategy more often than did older children. Moreover, the suggestion that this strategy was available reduced the fear of younger children but actually increased the fear of older children. Perhaps younger children were reassured by the implication that covering their eyes would give them control over their exposure to the stimulus. Older children may have sensed that this technique would not alter the threatening nature of the film, nor would it block out the auditory aspects of the threat. Wilson argued that the provision of a strategy that older children expected to be ineffective may have caused them to feel a lack of control, which would increase their negative expectations of the movie and produce more fear.

Cognitive Strategies. In contrast to noncognitive strategies, cognitive strategies involve verbal explanations or instructions that encourage the child to think about the fear stimulus in a way that casts the threat in a different light. The strategies involve relatively complex cognitive operations or thinking skills, and our research consistently finds such strategies to be more effective for older than for younger children.

When dealing with fantasy depictions, the most typically used cognitive strategy seems to be to provide an explanation focusing on the unreality of the situation. This strategy should be especially difficult for preschool children, who do not have a full grasp of the implications of the fantasy-reality distinction. In one of our studies (Cantor & Wilson, 1984), we found that older elementary school children who were told to remember that the events they were seeing (in *The Wizard of Oz*) were not real showed less fear than their classmates who received no instructions. The same instructions had no effect on the fear of preschoolers, however. Similarly, in a more recent study (Wilson & Weiss, 1991), a verbal explanation of how visual special effects such as makeup are used to make things look scary was effective in reducing the fear of 7- to 9-year-olds while watching a movie scene involving vampires. This explanation did not reduce the fear of 5- to 6-year-olds.

Children's own beliefs about the effectiveness of focusing on the unreality of the stimulus have been shown to be consistent with these experimental findings. In our study of perceptions of techniques to reduce fear, preschool children evaluated "tell yourself it's not real" as significantly less effective than did older elementary school children (Wilson et al., 1987). In contrast to children, who apparently have an accurate view of this strategy's effectiveness, parents do not seem to appreciate the inadequacy of this technique for young children. Of the parents of both the preschool and elementary school children who participated in another of our studies (Wilson & Cantor, 1987), 80% reported that they employed a "tell them it's not real" coping strategy to reduce their child's media-induced fear. An early study by Jersild and Holmes (1935) suggests that even as children begin to be able to classify things as either real or make-believe, they may not yet be able to use this strategy effectively. One child in their study, who was afraid of animals that appeared in his nightmares, was quoted as saying, "I told them they were a dream, but they wouldn't go away." Another child reported attempts to reduce his fear by classifying fairy tale characters as real or unreal. Nevertheless, he remained afraid of them regardless of their classification.

Reality explanations that are too abstract and are not specifically tied to the program content to be viewed have been shown to be ineffective for even older elementary school children. In the study by Wilson and Weiss (1991) involving an explanation of special effects such as scary makeup, other children of the same ages heard a general explanation that things sometimes occur on television that cannot actually occur in real life. This explanation did not reduce the fear of either 5- to 6-year-olds or 7- to 9-year-olds to the vampire scene.

For media depictions involving realistic threats, the most prevalent cognitive strategy seems to be to provide an explanation that minimizes the perceived severity or likelihood of the depicted danger. Not only is this type of strategy more effective with older than with younger children, in certain situations it has been shown to have a fear-enhancing rather than anxiety-reducing effect with younger children. In our experiment involving the snake-pit scene from *Raiders of the Lost Ark,* mentioned earlier (Wilson & Cantor, 1987), a second experimental variation involved the presence or absence of reassuring information about snakes (for example, the statement that most snakes are not poisonous). Although this information tended to reduce the fear of older elementary school children, kindergarten and first-grade children seem to have only partially understood the information, and for them, negative emotional reactions were more likely if they had heard the information than if they had not. Perhaps bringing up the topic of poisonousness made that aspect of snakes more salient, without effectively communicating to the younger children that poisonous snakes are rare. Figure 4.4 presents the data from this study.

Older children use cognitive coping strategies more frequently than do preschool children. In our survey of reactions to *The Day After* (Cantor et al., 1986), we found that the tendency to discuss the movie with parents after viewing increased with the age of the child. In a recent laboratory experiment (Hoffner & Cantor, 1990), we found that significantly more 9- to 11-year-olds than 5- to 7-year-olds reported spontaneously employing cognitive coping strategies (thinking about the expected happy outcome or thinking about the fact that what was happening was not real). Moreover, in our study of

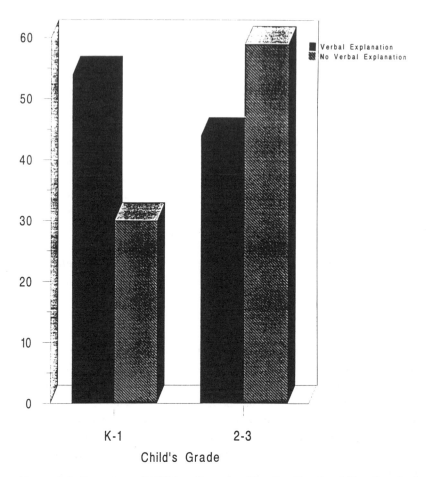

Figure 4.4. Percentage of Children Reporting Negative Emotional Reactions to the Snake Pit Scene in the Movie *Raiders of the Lost Ark*
SOURCE: Adapted from Wilson and Cantor (1987).
NOTE: Among older children, hearing verbal information involving the concept that most snakes are not poisonous tended to reduce negative emotional reactions to the scene. Among younger children, however, those who heard this supposedly reassuring information experienced more emotional disturbances than those who did not.

perceptions of techniques for coping with media-induced fear (Wilson et al., 1987), the perceived effectiveness of "talk to your mom or dad about the program" increased with age, although nonsignificantly.

We have also determined ways of improving the effectiveness of cognitive strategies for young children. Because of our recognition that young children's inability to benefit from cognitive strategies is due in part to poor comprehension and inadequate storage and retrieval of the information presented, we have identified techniques to tailor the explanations to young children's abilities. In one study involving *The Incredible Hulk* program (Cantor et al., 1988), we not only explained that the Hulk, like his human counterpart David, likes to help people, we visually illustrated this concept by showing scenes in which the Hulk came to the rescue of people in distress. In another study, by Wilson (1987), the researcher provided simplified, unequivocal statements regarding the fact that tarantulas do not pose a threat to humans ("Tarantulas cannot hurt people") and had the child repeat the statements out loud before viewing a scene involving tarantulas. In both of these experiments, the enhanced verbal explanations were effective in reducing the fear of younger, as well as older children.

Evidence of Long-Term Impact

One question that arises out of the research on children's fright reactions regards the degree to which fright responses produced by the media are actually detrimental to a child's development. Although many of the researchers cited at the beginning of this chapter have assumed the potential for long-term negative effects, no systematic research has documented the pervasiveness of such reactions. The absence of this type of data is no doubt attributable, in part, to ethical considerations. It simply is not possible nor would it be desirable to carry out an experiment to demonstrate the ability of media horrors to produce long-term emotional scars.

Field surveys of children's emotional reactions to real-world disasters and highly publicized media events, such as the space shuttle *Challenger* disaster and the broadcast of *The Day After* have reported predominantly short-lived, mild to moderate responses on the part of children (see Cantor, 1992). It has been argued, however, that the research process of questioning children about their responses to a traumatic event shortly after it has occurred may have a therapeutic effect and reduce the likelihood of long-term impact. There are many anecdotal reports of quasi-phobic reactions and long-term avoidance dispositions such as the one described at the beginning of this chapter, that have been precipitated by horror movies (Cantor & Oliver, 1996). These anecdotes often involve haphazard exposure to the films on television, rather than the intentional seeking out of horror films.

A recent experiment bears on long-term implications, although the data were collected immediately after exposure (Cantor & Omdahl, 1991). In this experiment, exposure to dramatized depictions of a deadly house fire (from *Little House on the Prairie*) or a drowning (from *Jaws II*) increased children's reports of worry about similar events in their own lives. In addition, these fictional depictions affected the children's preferences for normal, everyday activities that were related to the tragedies they had just witnessed: Children who had seen a movie depicting a drowning expressed less willingness than other children to go canoeing; those who had seen the program about a house fire were less eager than other children to build a fire in a fireplace. Although the duration of such effects was not measured, the effects were expected to be short-lived, because debriefings were employed at the end of the session to reduce the probability that children would experience long-term distress. It is difficult to estimate the long-term effects that occur in children whose viewing is unguided and unobserved and who do not have the opportunity to discuss unreasonable or disproportionate fears with a concerned adult.

In many of the classes I have taught over the past decade, I have asked students to write a report on one program, film, or event in the mass media that had scared them a great deal or to report that no media event had had such a profound effect. What is striking about these papers, initially, is that very few students have reported not having had an intense fright experience. Most reports, such as the one excerpted at the beginning of this chapter, include vivid and detailed memories of fright reactions. These reports are interesting, not only because of the intensity of the fear they usually convey. They are also striking because of the range of offerings that are cited as producing intense fright, often programs that parents would never be suspicious of at all, and the range of behaviors affected:

> The sitter and I and my younger brother watched a Walt Disney movie. The boy, Tom (Sawyer) or Huck (Finn), crept away from the mourners and slipped into another room, where the casket lay alone. I watched with horror as the boy approached the casket and I trembled as he lifted its lid. Suddenly, a hand reached out from inside the coffin and grabbed for the boy's neck. That is all I saw, because I ran screaming in terror from the room.
>
> Shortly after this, I was in the hospital to have my tonsils and adenoids removed. It was a frightening experience because I could never quite get the picture of something lurking within that coffin out of my mind. For several months after, I had an uncontrollable fear of the dark and especially of a corner in my bedroom, which was just the right size to hold a casket. It took about 6 months before I was able to face that corner of the room in the dark. (L. N., female)

I remember always having been horrified by the scene in *Willy Wonka and the Chocolate Factory* where Augustus, one of the lucky kids on the tour of the factory, is sipping from the chocolate river, falls in, and gets sucked up the tube leading to the fudge room.

As a side note, it hadn't occurred to me until just now, but there's probably a connection between having seen and been scared by this movie and my extreme fear of having to jump off the diving board at our local YWCA pool. I wasn't scared about the water but worried about coming too close to the grating at the bottom of the pool; I feared that if I got too close, I would get sucked in. (A. R., female)

Recollections of responses to frightening media are not only intense, but many of the responses are reported to last into adulthood:

One Friday evening when I was about nine years old, I sat down to watch Rod Serling's *Twilight Zone*. . . . It concerned a person who kept discovering that he could go to the 14th floor of a department store that had only 13 floors. The strange thing about this extra floor was that the real-life people that were seen in the store during the day, turned into mannequins that resided on this extra floor at night. There were several very spooky scenes involving this people-to-mannequin switch, and I know it was probably the scariest media experience I had had in my life.

To this day, I have hated mannequins in department stores and I can recall many times when a feeling of horror has set in at the sight of one of them. As a child I can remember being genuinely afraid of mannequins. (G. S., male)

At times, I have received similar anecdotal reports from parents:

When our youngest daughter was about 5 we were traveling in the northwestern United States. One night, in Seattle, we watched a James Bond movie on television, containing a scene of a shark that was released into a swimming pool from a grate in the side of the pool. For several days thereafter our daughter refused to go into swimming pools, even at the insistent urging of her older brother and sister. For several years she claimed to be nervous about going into pools where it looked like an underwater shark cage could be hidden.

Implications for Parental Guidance

The data presented here, amplified by these retrospective reports, should lead parents to question how much disturbing television, both real and fictional, it is appropriate to allow children to view. Joshua Meyrowitz (1985) expressed the general problem of children's exposure to what television has to offer in *No Sense of Place,* when he said,

The widespread use of television is equivalent to a broad social decision to allow young children to be present at wars and funerals, courtships and seductions, criminal plots and cocktail parties. . . . Young children may not fully understand the issues of sex, death, crime, and money that are presented to them on television. . . . Yet television nevertheless exposes them to many topics and behaviors that adults have spent several centuries trying to keep hidden from children. Television thrusts children into a complex adult world, and it provides the impetus for children to ask the meanings of actions and words they would not yet have heard or read about without television. (p. 242)

Problems of Communicating With Children About Threats

The last sentence of Meyrowitz's quotation highlights one of the challenges that exposure to television presents to parents, teachers, and other caregivers dealing with children's fears. Our research shows that it is extremely hard to reassure children about real threats, no matter how unlikely it is that these dangers could be directly experienced by the child. And the process is further complicated by the need in some cases to warn children about the existence of a threat that they must avoid, without inducing an overly intense emotional reaction.

In our study of responses to *Raiders of the Lost Ark* (Wilson & Cantor, 1987), for example, we found that telling young children that most snakes are not poisonous made them more, rather than less, scared. In another study (Cantor & Hoffner, 1990), we found it extremely difficult to communicate information about the likelihood of encountering a threat and especially difficult to get children to differentiate between threats that were highly likely and those that were very unlikely to occur.

Studies we have conducted on children's comprehension of common language terms may help us understand part of the problem. Our studies show that many young children have not fully grasped the differences between important relative quantifiers, such as "some" and "most" (as in "some snakes are poisonous, but most are not"), and probabilistic terms, such as "possibly," "probably," and "definitely" (as in "this will probably not happen to you," Badzinski, Cantor, & Hoffner, 1989; Hoffner, Cantor, & Badzinski, 1990).

In addition to these problems, our study in which we manipulated the appearance and behavior of the elderly female protagonist in a drama (Hoffner & Cantor, 1985) revealed how difficult it is to communicate to young children in situations in which the outward appearance of something or someone belies a contrary internal disposition. In other words, it is extremely difficult to communicate to young children that something that looks scary is, in fact, benign and something that looks attractive is really dangerous.

These practical problems bring to light the importance of learning more about how to communicate effectively with children on the subject of coping with the threatening aspects of their environment. It is important to recognize that some level of fear is appropriate and indeed may be important to survival in certain situations. For example, children need to protect themselves from drowning without developing a phobia of the water, and they must learn to engage in self-protective behaviors to avoid child abuse or kidnapping, without becoming socially withdrawn. On the other hand, overburdening children with fears of horrendous disasters that are either highly unlikely to threaten them personally or are unpredictable and unpreventable, may add undue stress to the process of growing up.

Because our research indicates that it is difficult to "reason away" the media-induced fears of a young child, prevention of exposure to highly disturbing fare, where possible, seems preferable for children who have shown themselves to be susceptible to long-term distress reactions. In giving advice to parents, however, it must be recognized that in addition to the difficulty of predicting how a child will respond to a given media offering, it is often difficult to anticipate what content a child will be exposed to in a particular program. The disturbing content of a program or film is not always predictable from its title or genre. Many programs ostensibly created for children, such as the series *Little House on the Prairie,* have confronted enormously disturbing issues, such as kidnapping, child molestation, and accidental death.

One proposed solution to the difficulty in determining what to let children see, at least where movies are concerned, has been proposed by Wilson, Linz, and Randall (1990). These researchers have advocated a change in the MPAA's movie rating system that would take into account a movie's impact on young viewers, based on developmental considerations such as those discussed in this chapter. Their scheme involves a category for "horror," which would indicate the age group that would be expected to be the most susceptible to fright reactions. Such G-rated Disney films as *Sleeping Beauty* and the classic, unrated "family" musical *The Wizard of Oz* would be suggested as problematic for 3- to 7-year-olds because of the visually grotesque aspects of some of their characters. A scheme such as this would indeed be helpful for parents, many of whom expect that all Disney films are appropriate for children and that a G-rating implies that a movie is "safe." A recent movie that was advertised in an extremely inviting way for children (*My Girl*) and that featured a favorite child actor (McCaulay Culkin) shocked both children and their parents when they discovered that in an early scene, one of the attractive child characters dies from a bee sting and her funeral is featured prominently.

Now that the leaders of the entertainment industry have agreed that all television programs will be rated, and "v-chips" will allow parents to block reception of unwanted materials, there will be the opportunity to provide parents with advance warning of the contents of television programs. It would certainly be helpful to parents if the new rating system were sensitive to developmental issues regarding children's fright.

Given the number of channel choices that are available now, however, it will be difficult for even the most alert and astute parent to keep up with all the available content if children are allowed to view large amounts of television alone and unsupervised. Because of the unpredictability of what programs have to offer and furthermore because children have been shown to have fright reactions even from televised advertising for frightening movies (the placement of which is never predictable), it would seem to be prudent for the parents of easily frightened children to limit the amount of time their children watch television and to closely monitor the television they watch.

In summary, the overarching message of this chapter can be summarized as follows: Because television is one of children's major sources of information about the world, we need to be able to make reasoned decisions about what types of content to expose our children to and when. We also need to be able to help them cope with their fears in age-appropriate ways. Because many of the findings of research in this area are not intuitively apparent, it is important that what is known about these issues be communicated effectively to parents, teachers, and mental health professionals.

References

Angelino, H., Dollins, J., & Mech, E. V. (1956). Trends in the "fears and worries" of school children as related to socioeconomic status and age. *Journal of Genetic Psychology, 89,* 263-276.

Badzinski, D. M., Cantor, J., & Hoffner, C. (1989). Children's understanding of quantifiers. *Child Study Journal, 19,* 241-258.

Bettelheim, B. (1975). *The uses of enchantment: The meaning and importance of fairy tales.* New York: Vintage Books.

Birch, H. B., & Bortner, M. (1966). Stimulus competition and category usage in normal children. *Journal of Genetic Psychology, 109,* 195-204.

Blumer, H. (1933). *Movies and conduct.* New York: Macmillan.

Bowlby, J. (1973). *Separation: Anxiety and anger.* New York: Basic Books.

Bruner, J. S. (1966). On cognitive growth I & II. In J. S. Bruner, R. R. Oliver, & P. M. Greenfield (Eds.), *Studies in cognitive growth* (pp. 1-67). New York: John Wiley.

Buzzuto, J. C. (1975). Cinematic neurosis following *The Exorcist. Journal of Nervous and Mental Disease, 161,* 43-48.

Cantor, J. (1989). Studying children's emotional reactions to mass media. In B. Dervin, L. Grossberg, B. O'Keefe, & E. Wartella (Eds.), *Rethinking communication. Vol. 2: Paradigm exemplars* (pp. 47-59). Newbury Park, CA: Sage.

Cantor, J. (1992). Children's emotional responses to technological disasters conveyed by the mass media. In J. M. Wober (Ed.), *Television and nuclear power: Making the public mind* (pp. 31-53). Norwood, NJ: Ablex.

Cantor, J. (1994). Fright responses to mass media. In J. Bryant & D. Zillmann (Eds.), *Media effects: Advances in theory and research* (pp. 213-245). Hillsdale, NJ: Lawrence Erlbaum.

Cantor, J., & Hoffner, C. (1990). Children's fear reactions to a televised film as a function of perceived immediacy of depicted threat. *Journal of Broadcasting and Electronic Media, 34,* 421-442.

Cantor, J., Mares, M. L., & Oliver, M. B. (1993). Parents' and children's emotional reactions to televised coverage of the Gulf War. In B. Greenberg & W. Gantz (Eds.), *Desert Storm and the mass media* (pp. 325-340). Cresskill, NJ: Hampton.

Cantor, J., & Oliver, M. B. (1996). Developmental differences in responses to horror. In J. B. Weaver & R. Tamborini (Eds.), *Horror films: Research on audience preference and reactions* (pp. 63-80). Hillsdale, NJ: Lawrence Erlbaum.

Cantor, J., & Omdahl, B. (1991). Effects of televised depictions of realistic threats on children's emotional responses, expectations, worries, and liking for related activities. *Communication Monographs, 58,* 384-401.

Cantor, J., & Reilly, S. (1982). Adolescents' fright reactions to television and films. *Journal of Communication, 32*(1), 87-99.

Cantor, J., & Sparks, G. G. (1984). Children's fear responses to mass media: Testing some Piagetian predictions. *Journal of Communication, 34*(2), 90-103.

Cantor, J., Sparks, G. G., & Hoffner, C. (1988). Calming children's television fears: Mr. Rogers vs. the Incredible Hulk. *Journal of Broadcasting and Electronic Media, 32,* 271-288.

Cantor, J., & Wilson, B. J. (1984). Modifying fear responses to mass media in preschool and elementary school children. *Journal of Broadcasting, 28,* 431-443.

Cantor, J., & Wilson, B. J. (1988). Helping children cope with frightening media presentations. *Current Psychology: Research & Reviews, 7,* 58-75.

Cantor, J., Wilson, B. J., & Hoffner, C. (1986). Emotional responses to a televised nuclear holocaust film. *Communication Research, 13,* 257-277.

Cantril, H. (1940). *The invasion from Mars: A study in the psychology of panic.* Princeton, NJ: Princeton University Press.

Collins, W. A. (1983). Interpretation and inference in children's television viewing. In J. Bryant & D. R. Anderson (Eds.), *Children's understanding of television* (pp. 125-150). New York: Academic Press.

Comstock, G. A., & Rubinstein, E. A. (Eds.). (1972). *Television and social behavior.* Washington, DC: Government Printing Office.

Dysinger, W. S., & Ruckmick, C. A. (1933). *The emotional responses of children to the motion picture situation.* New York: Macmillan.

Eisenberg, A. L. (1936). *Children and radio programs.* New York: Columbia University Press.

Flavell, J. (1963). *The developmental psychology of Jean Piaget.* New York: Van Nostrand Rienhold.

Greenberg, B., & Gantz, W. (1993). *Desert Storm and the mass media.* Cresskill, NJ: Hampton.

Hess, R. D., & Goldman, H. (1962). Parents' views of the effects of television on their children. *Child Development, 33,* 411-426.

Himmelweit, H. T., Oppenheim, A. N., & Vince, P. (1958). *Television and the child.* London: Oxford University Press.

Hoffner, C., & Cantor, J. (1985). Developmental differences in responses to a television character's appearance and behavior. *Developmental Psychology, 21,* 1065-1074.

Hoffner, C., & Cantor, J. (1990). Forewarning of a threat and prior knowledge of outcome: Effects on children's emotional responses to a film sequence. *Human Communication Research, 16,* 323-354.

Hoffner, C., Cantor, J., & Badzinski, D. M. (1990). Children's understanding of adverbs denoting degree of likelihood. *Journal of Child Language, 17,* 217-231.

Horowitz, M. J. (1976). *Stress response syndromes.* New York: Appleton-Century-Crofts.

Jersild, A. T., & Holmes, F. B. (1935). Methods of overcoming children's fears." *Journal of Psychology, 1, 75-104.*

Johnson, B. R. (1980). General occurrence of stressful reactions to commercial motion pictures and elements in films subjectively identified as stressors. *Psychological Reports, 47,* 775-786.

Kelly, H. (1981). Reasoning about realities: Children's evaluations of television and books. In H. Kelly & H. Gardner (Eds.), *Viewing children through television* (pp. 59-71). San Francisco: Jossey-Bass.

Lazarus, R. S. (1966). *Psychological stress and the coping process.* New York: McGraw-Hill.

Lyle, J., & Hoffman, H. R. (1972). Children's use of television and other media. In E. A. Rubinstein, G. A. Comstock, & J. P. Murray (Eds.), *Television and social behavior* (Vol. 4, pp. 129-256). Washington, DC: Government Printing Office.

Manis, F. R., Keating, D. P., & Morison, F. J. (1980). Developmental differences in the allocation of processing capacity. *Journal of Experimental Child Psychology, 29,* 156-169.

Mathai, J. (1983). An acute anxiety state in an adolescent precipitated by viewing a horror movie. *Journal of Adolescence, 6,* 197-200.

Maurer, A. (1965). What children fear. *Journal of Genetic Psychology, 106,* 265-277.

Melkman, R., Tversky, B., & Baratz, D. (1981). Developmental trends in the use of perceptual and conceptual attributes in grouping, clustering, and retrieval. *Journal of Experimental Child Psychology, 31,* 470-486.

Meyrowitz, J. (1985). *No sense of place: The impact of electronic media on social behavior.* New York: Oxford University Press.

Morison, P., & Gardner, H. (1978). Dragons and dinosaurs: The child's capacity to differentiate fantasy from reality. *Child Development, 49,* 642-648.

Palmer, E. L., Hockett, A. B., & Dean, W. W. (1983). The television family and children's fright reactions. *Journal of Family Issues, 4,* 279-292.

Pearl, D., Bouthilet, L., & Lazar, J. (Eds.). (1982). *Television and behavior: Ten years of scientific progress and implications for the eighties* (DHHS Publication No. ADM 82-1196). Washington, DC: Government Printing Office.

Preston, M. I. (1941). Children's reactions to movie horrors and radio crime. *Journal of Pediatrics, 19,* 147-168.

Sarafino, E. P. (1986). *The fears of childhood: A guide to recognizing and reducing fearful states in children.* New York: Human Sciences Press.

Schofield, J., & Pavelchak, M. (1985). *The day after:* The impact of a media event. *American Psychologist, 40,* 542-548.

Schramm, W., Lyle, J., & Parker, E. P. (1961). *Television in the lives of our children.* Stanford, CA: Stanford University Press.

Simons, D., & Silveira, W. R. (1994). Posttraumatic stress disorder in children after television programmes. *British Medical Journal, 308*(6925), 389-390.

Singer, J. L. (1975). *Daydreaming and fantasy.* London: Allen and Unwin.

Smetak, J. R. (1986). Steven Spielberg: Gore, guts, and PG-13. *Journal of Popular Film and Television, 14*(1), 4-13.

Sparks, G. G. (1986). Developmental differences in children's reports of fear induced by the mass media. *Child Study Journal, 16*, 55-66.

Sparks, G. G., & Cantor, J. (1986). Developmental differences in fright responses to a television program depicting a character transformation. *Journal of Broadcasting and Electronic Media, 30*, 309-323.

Stein, E. (1982, June 20). Have horror films gone too far? *New York Times* (Arts & Leisure), pp. 1, 21-22.

Taylor, P. (1991, February 6). War may not be news young children can use. *Washington Post*, p. A3.

von Feilitzen, C. (1975). Findings of Scandinavian research on child and television in the process of socialization. *Fernsehen und Bildung, 9*, 54-84.

Wartella, E. (1979). The developmental perspective. In E. Wartella (Ed.), *Children communicating: Media and development of thought, speech, understanding* (pp. 1-19). Beverly Hills, CA: Sage.

Weiss, A. J., Imrich, D. J., & Wilson, B. J. (1993). Prior exposure to creatures from a horror film: Live versus photographic representations. *Human Communication Research, 20*, 41-66.

Wertham, F. (1953). *Seduction of the innocent.* New York: Rinehart.

Wilson, B. J. (1987). Reducing children's emotional reactions to mass media through rehearsed explanation and exposure to a replica of a fear object. *Human Communication Research, 14*, 3-26.

Wilson, B. J. (1989a). Desensitizing children's emotional reactions to the mass media. *Communication Research, 16*, 723-745.

Wilson, B. J. (1989b). The effects of two control strategies on children's emotional reactions to a frightening movie scene. *Journal of Broadcasting and Electronic Media, 33*, 397-418.

Wilson, B. J., & Cantor, J. (1987). Reducing children's fear reactions to mass media: Effects of visual exposure and verbal explanation. In M. McLaughlin (Ed.), *Communication Yearbook 10* (pp. 553-573). Newbury Park, CA: Sage.

Wilson, B. J., Hoffner, C., & Cantor, J. (1987). Children's perceptions of the effectiveness of techniques to reduce fear from mass media. *Journal of Applied Developmental Psychology, 8*, 39-52.

Wilson, B. J., Linz, D., & Randall, B. (1990). Applying social science research to film ratings: A shift from offensiveness to harmful effects. *Journal of Broadcasting and Electronic Media, 34*, 443-468.

Wilson, B. J., & Weiss, A. J. (1991). The effects of two reality explanations on children's reactions to a frightening movie scene. *Communication Monographs, 58*, 307-326.

Zillmann, D. (1978). Attribution and misattribution of excitatory reactions. In J. H. Harvey, W. Ickes, & R. F. Kidd (Eds.), *New directions in attribution research* (Vol. 2, pp. 335-368). Hillsdale, NJ: Lawrence Erlbaum.

Zillmann, D. (1980). Anatomy of suspense. In P. H. Tannenbaum (Ed.), *The entertainment functions of television* (pp. 133-163). Hillsdale, NJ: Lawrence Erlbaum.

Zillmann, D., Hay, T. A., & Bryant, J. (1975). The effect of suspense and its resolution on the appreciation of dramatic presentations. *Journal of Research in Personality, 9*, 307-323.

Zoglin, R. (1984, June 25). Gremlins in the rating system. *Time*, p. 78.

5

Television Violence Viewing
and Aggressive Behavior

Eric F. Dubow
Laurie S. Miller

Aggressive behavior among children represents a major clinical and social problem. One third to one half of all clinical referrals are for behavior problems (Kazdin, 1987), which often include aggressive behavior. According to the diagnostic manual of the American Psychiatric Association (APA, 1994), approximately 9% of boys and 2% of girls in the United States have severe behavior disorders, and the incidence of specific behaviors that comprise these disorders (e.g., aggression) is much higher (Kazdin, 1987). Children who display disruptive patterns of behavior often continue to require attention from mental health and criminal justice systems, making disruptive behavior an extremely costly problem for society.

Aggressive patterns of interacting are observable very early in life and remain relatively stable into adulthood, especially for males (Farrington, 1982; Huesmann, Eron, Lefkowitz, & Walder, 1984; Loeber & Dishion, 1983; Magnusson, Duner, & Zetterblom, 1975; Olweus, 1979; Parke & Slaby, 1983; Robins & Ratcliff, 1980). Preschool-age children who exhibit high levels of impulsivity, irritability, and aggressive behaviors are likely to display serious conduct problems in middle childhood. These highly aggressive children are likely to become academic underachievers and to be rejected by their peers. In time, many of these children begin to affiliate with deviant peer groups and may develop substance use problems, drop out of school, and commit criminal offenses. As adults, they are likely to have marital problems, poor employment patterns, and are prone to involvement in violent and criminal activities (Caspi, Elder, & Bem, 1987; Huesmann & Eron, 1984; Rutter & Giller, 1983). In most cases, adult antisocial and violent behavior can be traced back to early childhood. In other words, it is rare to find an antisocial adult who was not an aggressive or disruptive child (Robins, 1966).

To summarize, child aggression is one of the best predictors of adolescent and adult antisocial and violent behavior. But, what causes children to behave aggressively? The early emergence and relative stability of aggressive behavior is consistent with both biological and learning models of development. Most researchers interested in the development of aggression agree that aggressive behavioral patterns result from the convergence of a number of interacting biological and psychosocial factors across individual, family, and environmental domains. Whereas biological factors may predispose a child toward aggression, it is the child's early learning experience that socializes him or her toward or away from aggressive behavior. Parents usually serve as the main socialization agents for young children. Thus, although children's temperaments may predispose them toward impulsive or aggressive behavior, their parents can teach them to regulate and control their behavior. Alternatively, children can learn aggressive patterns of interaction through parental reinforcement of their aggressive behavior, by observing family violence, or both. Beginning early in a child's development, other sources of information also influence the socialization process. For example, peers and siblings are important influences on children's social development, as are other adults (e.g., teachers, extended family members, babysitters), and the media (e.g., television, movies, video games, books). Regarding the potentially influential power of the media, recent studies have shown that even infants can internally represent and imitate information presented on television (Meltzoff, 1988).

In this chapter, we examine the role of television violence viewing in the development of aggressive behavior in children. Although most of the research that we review focuses on violence displayed on television, the conclusions reached in these studies apply to violence displayed in other media as well (e.g., films, videos). We will consider three questions in turn:

1. First, what is the research evidence of the link between violence viewing and aggressive behavior?
2. Second, what are the processes through which violence viewing influences aggressive behavior?
3. Third, how can parents, teachers, clinicians, and others intervene to mitigate the influence of television violence on aggressive behavior?

We want to emphasize at the outset that, as our three questions indicate, our focus in this chapter is on television violence and aggressive behavior. The American Psychological Association's task force report on television and society (Huston et al., 1992) concluded that there are two other likely effects of viewing TV violence that are not reviewed in this chapter. The first is the fear effect, which Joanne Cantor discusses in Chapter 4 of this book. The second effect, which is not reviewed in this chapter or elsewhere in this book, is that viewing violence may result in desensitization. "Children and adults who are exposed to television violence show reduced physiological arousal, and they are less likely than unexposed individuals to seek help for victims of violence or to act on behalf of victims" (Huston et al., 1992, p. 57; with details of the references for this statement provided).

TV Violence and Aggressive Behavior: Research Evidence

Since the advent of television nearly 40 years ago, there has been growing concern over its potentially negative socialization influences, particularly on the development of aggressive behavior. In their report of the American Psychological Association's Task Force on Television and Society, Huston et al. (1992) highlighted the major investigations in the United States of the TV violence viewing-aggression debate. In the 1950s, a congressional investigation began to explore the relation between TV violence viewing and aggression, followed by the Commission on the Causes and Prevention of Violence (Baker & Ball, 1969), the Surgeon General's Scientific Advisory Committee on Television and Social Behavior (1972), the National Institute of Mental Health (Pearl, Bouthilet, & Lazar, 1982), and the American Psychological Association (1985). In Canada, there have been investigations by the Ontario Royal Commission on Violence in the Communications Industry (1977) and, on several occasions since then, the Canadian Radio-Television and Telecommunications Commission. These investigations have had the opportunity to review a wide range of research studies and reports; over 1,000 articles on the role of TV violence viewing in the development of aggressive behavior have been published since the 1950s (Huston et al., 1992).

Although a detailed review of these findings is beyond the scope of this chapter, a few points should be made. Some researchers believe that findings from studies conducted in the laboratory should not be used as evidence that the same effects occur in the real world, and that there is weak evidence that cumulative exposure to TV violence leads to aggressive behavior outside the laboratory (Freedman, 1984, 1986; McGuire, 1986; Milavsky, Stipp, Kessler, & Rubens, 1982). These researchers, however, are in the minority. There is a [*others believe differe*] majority consensus among social scientists that TV violence viewing is one of many causes of aggressive behavior (Friedrich-Cofer & Huston, 1986; Huston et al., 1992). In 1985, the American Psychological Association's Board on Social and Ethical Responsibility for Psychology reviewed the available research and concluded that repeated observation of real and dramatized violence during childhood is one factor contributing to the development of stable patterns of aggressive and antisocial behavior (APA, 1985).

In this section, we provide a brief overview of the evidence for a link between violence viewing and aggressive behavior from studies using a variety of methodologies and samples. No single methodology is ideal for studying this link, but the findings from a considerable body of research conducted over the past several decades converge to support the hypothesis that repeated viewing of violence on television facilitates the development of aggressive behavior.

Experimental Studies

[*minimized the amount of T.V.*] In a typical laboratory study, the researcher is able to control the amount ① of violence viewed. For example, the experimenter might have one group of children come into the laboratory and view 30 minutes of a violent film (often excerpts from a television show) a few times a week, while another group of children views nonviolent films for the same period. Or, this might be done ② in a day care setting. These studies have consistently demonstrated that under such well-controlled conditions, the observation of violence causes children and adolescents to behave more aggressively (see reviews by Comstock,

1980; Friedrich-Cofer & Huston, 1986; Geen, 1990). Such experiments have shown that viewing violence causes children to display more aggression toward other children (Bjorkqvist, 1985; Josephson, 1987), as well as toward inanimate objects (e.g., inflated plastic "Bobo" dolls). These effects go beyond the simple imitation of aggressive behavior; children often display aggressive behavior that differs from the behavior they observe in the filmed displays (Geen & Thomas, 1986). Viewing violent media displays in the laboratory has also been shown to have immediate effects on violent thoughts (e.g., thoughts having aggressive connotations) and emotional responses related to aggressive behavior (e.g., increases in systolic blood pressure) (Bushman & Geen, 1990). In addition, studies with adults have revealed that exposure to media displays of sexual aggression elicits thought patterns condoning sexual violence that may contribute to sexually aggressive behavior in the viewer (Malamuth, 1989). Because other factors can be carefully controlled in experimental studies, they allow us to make causal inferences—that is, to conclude that the violence viewing caused the subsequent aggressive thoughts and behavior.

Observational Studies

Findings from the laboratory enable us to conclude that television viewing can cause viewers to behave more aggressively. But these studies do not allow us to draw conclusions about the effects of television violence viewing in natural settings. The laboratory findings are complemented by results obtained in field studies (in the "real world"), which also have shown a positive relation between the frequency with which children watch violent television and their current aggressive behavior (Comstock, 1980; Eron, 1963; Eron, Huesmann, Lefkowitz, & Walder, 1972; Huesmann & Eron, 1986; Parke, Berkowitz, Leyens, West, & Sebastian, 1977; Singer & Singer, 1981; Stein & Friedrich, 1972).

Two very interesting real-world research studies have focused on differences in people's aggression before and after TV was introduced to their communities. As Tannis MacBeth described in the introductory chapter of this book, she (Williams, 1986) and her colleagues (see Joy, Kimball, & Zabrack, 1986) had the opportunity to study the behavior of children in three Canadian towns: "Unitel" (a town that had been receiving one television channel for 7 years), "Multitel" (a town that had been receiving several TV stations for 15 years), and "Notel" (a town that was just about to receive television). The community of Notel had been without television previously because its geographic location prevented transmitter reception. In all three towns, the elementary school children's behavior was studied just prior to the arrival of television in Notel, and also 2 years later. The children's teachers and peers reported on the children's aggressive behavior, and trained observers rated the children's aggression during free play on the playground. Although the Notel children did not differ in their aggression from the Unitel or Multitel children before the Notel children received TV, the Notel children were higher in aggression than children in the other two towns after TV was introduced in Notel. (The lack of differences in aggression between Notel children and children in the other towns before Notel received TV is explained as follows: social constraints in the play group may have controlled children's aggression initially, but the introduction of TV in Notel may have broken down these constraints, allowing Notel children to express their aggression.) The pattern of increased aggression in Notel children following the introduction of TV was true of both physical and verbal aggression, for both genders, across grade levels, and regardless of the children's initial levels of aggression.

In another real-world study, Centerwall (1989) compared homicide rates in South Africa to those in the United States and Canada before and after 1975 (when TV was introduced to South Africa). After the introduction of TV to the United States, Canada, and South Africa, homicide rates doubled. Centerwall attributes the dramatic change in homicide rates to television viewing, because other variables failed to account for the change in homicide rates (e.g., changes in alcohol consumption, availability of firearms, economic conditions). There was about a 10-15 year lag between the introduction of television and the increase in homicide rates; Centerwall argues that this is because TV's effects are mainly on children, who presumably must "come of age" to commit homicide.

Overall, the majority of observational studies suggest that the relation between TV violence viewing and the development of aggressive behavior is small compared to the relation between other salient environmental variables (e.g., parenting practices) and child aggression. Nevertheless, the significant effect has been repeatedly replicated and is large enough to be considered socially significant (Rosenthal, 1986). In contrast, by adulthood, relations between violence viewing and aggressive behavior are rarely significant. This pattern of findings is expected given the belief that TV violence viewing leads cumulatively to increased aggression over time.

Longitudinal Studies

Although it is clear that aggressive children watch more violent television and that children exposed to media violence in the laboratory display increased aggression in the laboratory, the critical question of interest is whether children's violence viewing leads to increases in patterns of aggressive behavior over time. The data available from longitudinal studies conducted in several countries, in which the same children were studied on two or more occasions, support this hypothesis (see Huesmann & Miller, 1994). Although it is difficult to separate clearly cause from effect in nonexperimental studies, findings from a number of investigations using special statistical analyses (e.g., multiple regression, structural modeling) demonstrate that TV violence viewing predicts later aggressive and antisocial behavior, even after early aggressive behavior is statistically controlled (Botha & Mels, 1990; Huesmann & Eron, 1986; Lefkowitz, Eron, Walder, & Huesmann, 1977; Weigman, Kuttschreuter, & Baarda, 1986). In addition, exposure to television violence appears to have its major influence early in development, prior to adolescence. That is, adolescent or adult violence viewing does not appear to have a significant influence on their general tendency to behave aggressively. It is the violence viewed during childhood that influences the development of aggressive behavior into adolescence and adulthood. It should also be noted, however, that some adolescents and adults who developed aggressive patterns of behavior in childhood commit "copycat crimes," that is, carry out acts of violence against other people in imitation of violence that they have seen relatively recently on television or in films (see Comstock, 1983, for a review of the evidence of copycat crimes, which are sometimes also called bizarre replications).

Meta-Analytic Studies

Meta-analysis is a special technique for summarizing the results of an entire set of studies, taking into account the magnitude of the results (the "effect size") and the size of the group in each individual study. Two recently published meta-analyses summarize the findings of the past 30 years of research on media violence and aggression. Comstock and Paik (1991) calculated the obtained effect sizes for over 1,000 comparisons from 185 different studies that used a variety of methodological approaches. They found that the observed association between media (TV and film) violence viewing and aggressive behavior was extremely robust. Similarly, Wood, Wong, and Chachere (1991), in their meta-analytic study of 30 comparisons from 23 studies, found that exposure to media violence significantly enhanced viewers' aggressive behavior.

How Does TV Violence Viewing Influence Aggressive Behavior?

The literature reviewed in the preceding section has shown that TV violence viewing is one of the factors that independently contributes to the development of aggressive behavior. Such an effect has been demonstrated in both laboratory and field investigations, and in cross-cultural studies. It is clear, however, that only some individuals are vulnerable to the psychological and behavioral effects of violent media displays, prompting researchers to examine the processes underlying the TV violence viewing-aggression relation, and the roles played by situational-environmental factors (e.g., the amount of aggression displayed by family members) and individual characteristics (e.g., the person's gender, the person's attitudes about aggression).

In this section, we describe an "information processing" model that can be applied to understanding how exposure to TV violence influences aggressive behavior. This model draws from two similar cognitive perspectives, one proposed by Berkowitz (e.g., Berkowitz, 1984, 1986; Berkowitz & Heimer, 1989) and the other by Huesmann (e.g., Huesmann, 1986, 1988; Huesmann & Eron, 1984). Both investigators describe the important roles of individual characteristics and situational influences in determining whether observing violent displays will affect behavior. Knowledge of individual characteristics and situational influences is necessary if we are to develop practical methods of intervening to decrease the potentially negative effects of media violence viewing.

The TV Violence Viewing-Aggression Relation From a Cognitive Social Information-Processing Perspective

A number of learning theorists believe that aggressive behavior is a result of both "enactive learning" (being rewarded or punished for one's own behavior) and "observational learning" (observing the effects of others' behavior) (see Huesmann, 1988). Bandura's pioneering research (e.g., Bandura,

Ross, & Ross, 1961, 1963a, 1963b) illustrated the power of observational learning: The mere observation of aggressive models led children to imitate aggression even though the children did not have the opportunity to perform the behavior or to receive reinforcement (a reward) during the observation period. The imitation of aggression was also shown to be a function of having vicariously experienced the consequences (i.e., watching the models receive rewards or punishments for their behavior). Bandura (1977) hypothesized that for modeling influences to occur, the observer must (a) notice and attend to the model's behavior, (b) commit the model's behavior to memory in a symbolic form (a visual or verbal code) that allows for access to the code for later performance, (c) enact the behavior, and (d) evaluate the outcomes of performing the behavior. Bandura's work provided a foundation for the development of other contemporary information processing models that further explain the contribution of TV violence viewing to the development of aggressive behavior.

Although learning theories of the development of aggressive behavior are similar, they do differ with regard to what is learned (Huesmann, 1988). According to Huesmann (1988), as a result of the child's own behavior and observation of others' behaviors, the child encodes, or represents in memory, "scripts" for the behavior. A script reflects our knowledge of the typical sequence of events in a particular social situation (e.g., being provoked on the playground) (Fiske & Taylor, 1984). In everyday language, a script is like a stereotype reflecting a set of expectations about a sequence of events, such as those involved in going to a restaurant. Each script contains props or objects commonly encountered during the event, social roles of participants (e.g., aggressor, victim), and rules describing the steps to be expected during the social sequence. Scripts guide our information processing and facilitate our social behavior; we attempt to fit incoming information into the appropriate script, and we behave according to the script. Interestingly, our interpretation and memory of, and our response to, a given social event may be distorted in the direction of consistency with the script. Just as is the case for stereotypes, we tend to notice information that is consistent with our scripts and to ignore information that is inconsistent. Even if we initially notice inconsistent information, we are more likely to distort it or forget it. This is why stereotypes and scripts are so difficult to change.

According to Berkowitz's "cognitive neoassociationistic" perspective (e.g., Berkowitz, 1984; Berkowitz & Heimer 1989; Geen & Thomas, 1986), we commit to memory cue-feeling, cue-thought, and cue-behavior connections. Specifically, the observation of a violent display triggers a primitive experience of anger or negative emotion, and aggressive behavior tendencies that are connected to the anger-emotion "associative pathways." (One might think of the associative pathway as strands of a spider web connecting nodes that represent thoughts, feelings, and behaviors.) After triggering the initial negative emotional responses, more complex mental processing is activated. Thus, we make appraisals and attributions about the situation that may further elaborate, differentiate, and perhaps even suppress the initial negative emotion. Because aggressive feelings, thoughts, and behaviors are all connected within the same associative pathway, activation of any one component would spread along the pathway to activate the other components, giving rise to "feeling-activated ideas" and "thought-activated feelings." In laboratory studies, researchers have demonstrated the connections amongst violent cues in media displays, violent cognitions, and hostile feelings (e.g., Berkowitz & Heimer, 1989; Bushman & Geen, 1990).

Berkowitz does not specify exactly how the cue-feeling, cue-thought, and cue-behavior connections develop, although primitive cue-activated negative emotion is assumed to be built into humans by nature, and cue connections to more complex mental processes (e.g., making decisions about how to solve the problem) are likely to be learned. Huesmann believes that scripts develop early in life through repeated exposure to similar situations, resulting in the script becoming more and more abstract and complex. One approach to integrating Berkowitz's and Huesmann's models would be to recognize that an important component that children build into their scripts includes the feelings and thoughts of the actors in the scripts; thus, repeated exposure to similar situations would lead to the development and strengthening of event-feeling and event-thought associations.

What is the role of television in the development and maintenance of scripts and associative pathways? Long-term exposure to TV violence provides children with a greater opportunity to establish aggressive scripts in their memory. Short-term exposure to violent portrayals triggers already acquired aggressive scripts, and activates aggression-related thoughts and feelings. "Aggressive behaviors seen in the media activate ideas, emotions, and implicit behaviors associated with them. Thus, the sight of two people fighting may elicit thoughts of aggression learned in other contexts, associated emotions such as anger . . . , and a behavioral readiness to aggress with whatever means are available" (Geen & Thomas, 1986, p. 12). This implies that repeated exposure to violent TV programs could lead to the maintenance of aggressive scripts and strengthening of aggression-related pathways by reinforcing aggressive scripts and pathways that have already been established. In fact, heavy exposure to violent displays could lead the child to develop more general strategies for aggressive behavior than the specific ones already in memory.

Aggressive scripts may further be maintained and generalized through active rehearsal, which may include daydreaming or role-playing activities (e.g., the child fantasizing that he or she is a super hero). In a cross-national study, children who watched more violent television programs reported that they were more likely to daydream and fantasize about aggressive and heroic acts, such as "daydreaming about hitting and hurting someone" they did not like, and pretending that they were "a brave hero who saves someone or captures a bad guy." These results were found for boys in three countries (Finland, Poland, and the United States), and for girls in four countries (Australia, Israel, Poland, and the United States) (Huesmann & Eron, 1984).

Given that aggressive scripts have been placed into, and maintained in, the child's memory, the next important issue is under what conditions these scripts will be retrieved and used in the immediate situation. Both Huesmann (1986) and Berkowitz (1986) suggest that the person's attention to the cues in the immediate situation are critical to script retrieval and cue-activated thoughts and feelings. Thus, if a cue in the immediate situation is identical to a cue that was also present at the time the script was memorized, this increases the likelihood of the script being triggered, along with its associated thoughts and feelings. For example, Josephson (1987) had second- and third-grade boys view a violent film that included walkie-talkies as props. Then, before taking part in a floor hockey game, the boys were interviewed by an adult with either a walkie-talkie or a tape recorder. The most aggressive boys in the floor hockey game were those who were rated as highly aggressive by their teachers and who had been interviewed by the adult with a walkie-talkie, which presumably functioned as a retrieval cue reactivating aggressive emotions and ideas presented in the violent film.

In addition to cues in the immediate situation, several other important factors affect script establishment, maintenance, and retrieval: situational-environmental factors (e.g., family television environment, presence of other people when viewing the violent display) and individual characteristics (e.g., emotional arousal, understanding of the violent display, attributions about the other person's behavior). The next section will focus on these factors because they are believed to play an important role in determining which individuals are likely to be affected by violence viewing.

Situational-Environmental Factors Influencing the TV Violence Viewing-Aggression Relation

Not all children who are exposed to violent television content memorize, maintain, retrieve, and use aggressive scripts when faced with conflictual social situations. Various situational and environmental factors might account for why only some children are vulnerable to the potentially negative effects of violence viewing. Three factors discussed here are the salience of the violent display, aspects of the family environment, and the presence of others during viewing.

Salience of the Display. Attention to the violent display is a critical determinant of whether the child will commit the display to memory (Bandura, 1977; Huesmann, 1988). Research has shown that material is more likely to be attended to if it is salient, and children are more likely to attend to media displays that contain high amounts of action, laden with special visual and sound effects (Huston & Wright, 1989; Rule & Ferguson, 1986; Wright & Huston, 1983). This describes many violent displays, although nonviolent programs may also share these characteristics. In addition, presenting individuals with "high imagery aggressive words" can cue aggressive-related thoughts, emotions, and behaviors (Berkowitz, 1984). Readers may recall episodes of the *Batman* program in which fight scenes routinely included large and brightly colored displays of such words as "SOCK, BAM, POW!"

It should be stressed, however, that violent content is not the only means by which television programs can attract children's attention. The "formal characteristics" of television programs (e.g., action, special auditory and visual effects) may be more important in attracting children's attention than the actual content (e.g., violence) of the programs (Huston & Wright, 1989). In a study of preschool boys, animated and live programs characterized by rapid action with low levels of aggression attracted the children's attention as much as programs with rapid action and high levels of aggression (Potts, Huston, & Wright, 1986). These findings contradict the argument, often made by executives in the media industry, that a certain level of violence is necessary to hold children's attention. In the same study, although violent content led the preschoolers to be more aggressive, high-action programs with low levels of aggression did not lead to more aggression. Therefore, not only does rapid action result in increased attention, but it also does not appear to lead to increased aggression. Children's and women's voices, lively music, animation, and humorous sequences also attract and maintain children's attention to the program.

Family Environment. Children's aggression and delinquency can be predicted from their parents' aggression and criminality (e.g., Huesmann et al., 1984; West & Farrington, 1977). Authoritarian parents (those who rely on power-assertive discipline) are more likely to have children who imitate these coercive approaches to solving problems (Sears, Maccoby, & Levin, 1957). Thus, a family environment characterized by high levels of aggression provides many opportunities to develop scripts for these behaviors. In addition, the child might internalize norms (e.g., "everyone acts aggressively") and attitudes (e.g., "aggression works") that lay the groundwork for violent TV displays to be committed to memory because the displays are consistent with the child's internalized standards (Huesmann, 1988).

Another important aspect of the family environment that appears to influence the effects of violence viewing is the "family television environment," or the degree to which television is a focus of family recreation. Typically, North American preschoolers and school-age children spend 2 to 4 hours per day with television; there are about five violent acts displayed during each hour of prime-time evening programming, and 20-25 violent acts per hour in children's Saturday morning programming (Huston et al., 1992). "By the time the average child graduates from elementary school, she or he will have witnessed at least 8,000 murders and more than 100,000 other assorted acts of violence. Depending on the amount of television viewed, our youngsters could see more than 200,000 violent acts before they hit the schools and streets of our nation as teenagers" (Huston et al., 1992, pp. 53-54).

How much of this television viewing occurs together with a parent? Half to two thirds of preschool children's viewing occurs with a parent present (Wright, St. Peters, & Huston, 1990). The amount of coviewing varies with the type of program. For example, whereas general audience programs are viewed with at least one parent present about 75% of the time, children's programs are viewed with a parent only about 25% of the time. Wright et al. (1990) concluded that parents are not always aware of the content of what their children are viewing, and by not coviewing, miss out on the opportunity to possibly moderate the effects of the display (e.g., by offering comments about the plot, disapproving of the violent means used to solve problems, and so on). Aletha Huston and John Wright describe some of their more recent findings about parent-child coviewing in Chapter 2 of this book. Relatively few parents set rules for viewing television (e.g., limit the number of hours or shows), discourage the viewing of violent programs, or make comments about the program's content (Abelson, 1990; Wright et al., 1990).

Whether or not parents view and discuss television programs with their children may be part of a general child-rearing approach and family environment "style." Perhaps parents who view television programs with their children and who discuss the content of the programs are more likely to approach child rearing with reasoning, explanation of rules, and appeals to the child's pride (Abelson, 1990). In a series of studies, Singer and Singer (1986) found that the more imaginative and less aggressive children came from homes in which there was less television viewing during the preschool years, television was less likely to be valued as a source of recreation, parents established television viewing rules, mothers valued imaginativeness, and parents used less power-assertive punishment. The authors also noted that the more television was emphasized in the family, the more likely the child was to believe that the world is "scary" (e.g., the neighborhood is dangerous, there is a lack of justice outside the home). The Singers believe that television introduces and reinforces aggressive scripts. Furthermore, they suggest that children need to develop verbal skills, play skills, and fantasy skills to cope with frustration and social conflict situations. These skills are best developed through imaginative activities during the early years (e.g., play with parents and peers, reading, parents' storytelling). Time to engage in these activities may be preempted by television viewing.

Behavior of Others Present While Viewing. Reactions to media violence can either be facilitated or inhibited by the behavior of others who are present during viewing (Berkowitz, 1986). Specifically, viewing with others who approve of the displayed aggression facilitates aggressive behavior, whereas viewing with others who disapprove inhibits aggressive behavior. For example, in one study (Dunand, Berkowitz, & Leyens, 1984), undergraduate college students watched a boxing film with a coviewer who either sat quietly during the movie, or a coviewer who was active and made enthusiastic comments supportive of the aggression (e.g., "Good hit!" "Get up!" "Come on!"). Students who watched with the approving coviewer behaved more aggressively in a laboratory task after the movie. Perhaps someone who approves of aggression relaxes the viewer's inhibitions about behaving aggressively. It is also possible that the other viewer's comments communicate normative standards regarding aggression.

A coviewer can enhance the possible positive effects of television programs and reduce the possible negative effects (Huston et al., 1992). For example, an adult who views a program with a child could help the child understand the plot, express disapproval of any violent means used by the actors to solve problems, discuss nonviolent values with the child, and so forth. When adults view and discuss the television program with the child, this has been referred to as "mediation." In one study, 5- to 10-year-old children viewed a *Batman* episode with an adult who either made neutral comments or who made explanatory and judgmental comments such as, "It is bad to fight" and "It is better to get help." Children exposed to the adult who made explanatory and judgmental comments were less likely to say that people hit, steal, and hurt others, and were also less likely to say that it is all right for them to hit, steal, and hurt others (Corder-Bolz, 1980).

Individual Characteristics Influencing the
TV Violence Viewing- Aggression Relation

A major strength of the information processing perspective is the central role it assigns to individual characteristics that influence the effects of violence viewing on subsequent behavior. With respect to Huesmann's model, individual characteristics can affect the establishment, maintenance, retrieval, and use of aggressive scripts. With respect to Berkowitz's model, individual characteristics can facilitate or inhibit cue-activated thoughts, feelings, and behavior tendencies. This section reviews a number of individual characteristics that have been identified by researchers as important.

Emotional Arousal. Berkowitz (1986) believes that people who are angry just prior to watching violent media are more likely to respond aggressively. Consistent with the associative pathway model, a preexisting angry state prepares aggression-related thoughts and feelings to be readily reactivated by the violent media display. Furthermore, Huesmann (1988) believes that the child's preexisting emotional state, which consists of both a relatively stable physiological predisposition and whatever arousal has been recently induced just prior to the current situation, affects the child's attention to environmental cues and his or her evaluation of those cues. For example, an already angry (perhaps aggressive) child who views a violent media display might focus on only one or two salient cues (e.g., details of a fight scene), but ignore other cues that might have led to the inhibition of aggressive tendencies (e.g., motives, consequences). By contrast, a relatively nonaggressive child who is not angry might focus on different cues or on a broader range of cues. Dodge and his colleague (e.g., Dodge & Frame, 1982) suggest that an angry child might be more likely to attribute hostile intent to the actors when no such intent was present (e.g., the violent outcome was accidental). By comparison with the nonaggressive children in their study, aggressive children made more hostile attributions when interpreting ambiguous behaviors of others. For example, compared to a nonaggressive child, an aggressive child who was told a story about a youngster who lost a pencil and later sees another classmate holding that pencil, was more likely to say that the classmate in the story stole the pencil. Thus, aggressive children would be more likely to consider a hostile counterattack as justified.

In addition to the possible effects of the individual's preexisting level of arousal, investigators have examined how arousal is affected by viewing. Immediate reactions to violent displays include either the maintenance of a preexisting state of physiological arousal or increased arousal (see Rule & Ferguson, 1986; Zillmann, 1979). The systolic blood pressure of college students who watched violent videotapes increased significantly, and perhaps more important, they reported having more violent thoughts (Bushman & Geen, 1990). Geen and Thomas (1986) contend that the increased arousal triggers aggressive thoughts that are connected along the associative pathway. There is some evidence, however, that repeated violence viewing is associated with "emotional habituation," or decreased arousal (Rule & Ferguson, 1986); this emotional habituation is also believed to increase aggressive tendencies, perhaps by reducing the individual's concerns and inhibitions about aggression.

Understanding of the Media Display. Developmental considerations play a role in the information processing model, especially in terms of the child's ability to evaluate violent portrayals and alternative scripts that are activated by the violent displays. Perhaps the most important developmental issue concerns the child's ability to understand the violent display. In one study, children in the primary grades remembered less information about the plot of a program than did older children (Collins, 1979). In fact, varying the order of the scenes had no effect on younger children's memory. The younger children also failed to make inferences about information that was only implicitly presented. Perhaps younger children have yet to develop more sophisticated thinking skills that would allow them to evaluate and compare important information about each actor's motives and the appropriateness of each actor's behavior. This may be in part because younger children tend to have difficulty seeing a situation from a variety of perspectives, and thinking about how different people might be likely to think about it. In addition, younger children probably understand less about the future consequences of aggression than do older children (Rule & Ferguson, 1986). Huesmann (1988) believes that if a child is unable to evaluate the inappropriateness of aggressive acts, or to predict the future consequences of enacting alternative scripts, an aggressive act or series of acts that ostensibly solves the immediate problem will be a likely choice.

Thus, from the standpoint of the development of children's thinking (e.g., understanding of the violent display, memory for events, ability to focus on future consequences of behavior, ability to consider the perspectives that other people have on the same situation), younger children seem to be most vulnerable to the potentially negative effects of television violence viewing. Some researchers argue that there may be a sensitive period, during the preadolescent years, in which television violence viewing is most detrimental (Centerwall, 1989; Eron, Huesmann, Brice, Fischer, & Mermelstein, 1983).

Attributions About the Actor's Behavior. Perceptions and evaluations of the actor's intent in a given violent display affect the observer's aggressive thoughts and behavior. For example, several experimental studies demonstrated that people who viewed a film suggesting "justified" aggression were subsequently more punishing toward a provocateur than were people who viewed a film suggesting unjustified aggression (Berkowitz, 1984). Presumably, the first film triggered aggression-related ideas of justified aggression. In addition, as noted earlier, aggressive children tend to attribute hostile intent to ambiguous actions (Dodge & Frame, 1982). Thus, in a given social situation, if an individual thinks that the other's behavior was intentional and that he or she deserves to be punished, aggressive scripts will be retrieved along with congruent aggression-related thoughts, feelings, and behavior tendencies.

Attitudes and Self-Regulating Standards. Attitudes about aggression and self-regulating standards are also believed to affect the establishment, retrieval, and use of aggressive scripts. For example, if the child evaluates a violent media display as containing appropriate behavior, he or she is more likely to commit that script to memory and use it when faced with a social conflict. In one study, aggressive children evaluated aggressive solutions to hypothetical conflict situations more positively (e.g., good, strong, wise, brave, successful) by comparison with nonaggressive children (Deluty, 1983). In another study, aggressive children were more likely than nonaggressive children to expect that they would get what they wanted by acting aggressively, and that by acting this way, they would teach others not to treat them in a negative manner (Perry, Perry, & Rasmussen, 1986). For example, aggressive children were more likely to say that they were "very sure" that they could get to the front of the line at a drinking fountain by pushing another child out of the way, and that calling other kids names to get them to stop teasing them would prevent them from being teased in the future. Consistent with these findings, Huesmann (1988) suggests that TV portrayals that are consistent with the child's internalized attitudes and social norms are likely to be noticed and remembered, whereas displays that are inconsistent with preexisting attitudes are not. As an example, Rule and Ferguson (1986) suggested that different cultural values and attitudes may explain why Huesmann and Bachrach (1988) found a significant relation between TV violence viewing and aggressive behavior in Israeli city-dwelling children but not in kibbutz children.

Perceived Reality of the Display. If the viewer perceives the violent TV display as realistic, this will facilitate the establishment, maintenance, and retrieval of aggressive scripts, and will trigger aggressive thoughts and feelings (Berkowitz, 1986; Huesmann & Eron, 1984). Huesmann and his colleagues (Huesmann, 1988; Huesmann et al., 1984) also reported that children who identify with aggressive television characters (e.g., said they act like *The Incredible Hulk* or *The Six Million Dollar Man*) are more likely to behave aggressively. "The child constructs scripts for behavior that have subjective utility as potential strategies for social problem solving. Aggressive acts perceived as unreal and performed by actors with whom the child cannot identify do not fulfill this requirement" (Huesmann, 1988, p. 21). These authors found evidence supporting a cyclical process whereby aggressive children identify more with their aggressive television heroes, and in turn tend to watch more television, especially violent programs.

Academic Achievement. There is a sizable overlap between aggressive behavior and academic underachievement (see Hinshaw, 1992), although how this comes about is not yet clear. There are several possibilities. Recent studies suggest that aggressive, antisocial behavior may interfere with adequate school achievement (e.g., Huesmann, Eron, & Yarmel, 1987; Tremblay, Masse, Perron, & Leblanc, 1992). Huesmann et al. (1987) suggest that aggressive children engage in negative social interactions with their teachers and peers, and this precludes the positive interactions necessary for the development of academic skills. Television violence viewing may play a role in this relation in a variety of ways. In one study, children who were more aggressive and who had poorer academic skills also watched more violent television and believed the shows to be more realistic (Huesmann & Eron, 1986). The link between academic achievement and television viewing may be bidirectional: Heavy viewing interferes with academic achievement, and "children who cannot obtain gratification from success in school turn to heroic television shows to obtain vicariously the successes they miss in school" (Huesmann, 1988, p. 134). The child then commits to memory the aggressive behaviors because they are viewed as realistic and easy ways to solve social problems.

Gender. The literature suggests that boys and girls may be differentially affected by the violent media that they watch. In some studies (e.g., Joy et al., 1986), both boys and girls increased in their aggressive behavior following exposure to violence on television, but several other studies have demonstrated significant effects of television violence viewing only on boys', not girls', behavior (e.g., Eron et al., 1972). In their review of the development and regulation of childhood aggression, Slaby and Conklin Roedell (1982) suggested several reasons why television violence viewing might be more detrimental for boys than girls: Boys choose to watch more violent television; boys perceive the programs as more realistic; there are more violent males than females on television; and the violent acts committed by male characters are more likely to lead to positive outcomes than are the violent acts committed by female characters (who are more likely to be victims than perpetrators). It is also possible that societal attitudes are more accepting of aggression in boys (Lytton & Romney, 1991), and that boys are more impulsive and less self-regulating of their behavior than are girls. Some recent studies do, however, show socialization effects on girls' aggression (Eron, 1992).

Implications for Intervention

The critical findings reviewed so far in this chapter are the following: (a) Aggressive children grow up to be aggressive adults; (b) TV violence viewing early in development, during childhood, can have a long-term influence on adult behavior; and (c) Scripts for behavior are also constructed early in development, and it is likely that continued exposure to media violence influences the development of aggressive scripts. Attempts to diminish the link between televised violence and aggressive behavior need to occur early in development, therefore, during childhood, before aggression becomes an ingrained, characteristic, and intractable method of solving interpersonal problems. The information processing model presented in this chapter suggests that there are several environmental and individual characteristics that influence whether violent media displays viewed by children will be committed to memory, maintained, retrieved, and used. This in turn points to a number of specific ways to reduce the potentially negative effects of TV violence viewing.

Targeting Environmental Factors

What aspects of the environment can be altered to reduce the negative effects of violence viewing? Before answering this question, we should again stress that television is only one source for the development of aggressive scripts. If aggression is prevalent in the child's family, simply reducing the child's violent TV diet would likely have little effect; in this case, intervention must be directed toward the family.

Television Networks and the Government. One obvious way to reduce children's exposure to televised violence is for the industry to limit the production of violent programs. Eron (1986) argued that this is unlikely because the networks dismiss the findings that violence viewing is one cause of aggressive behavior, and such programs often attract high ratings. In the past few years, however, public outcry against televised violence in both the

United States and Canada has placed significant pressure on television executives to reduce the level of violent content on television. In the United States, in October 1993, during a Senate Commerce Committee hearing on TV violence, Attorney General Janet Reno sent the following warning to media executives:

> Television violence and the development of our youth are not just another set of public policy problems. They go to the heart of our society's values. The best solutions lie with industry officials, parents, and educators, and I don't relish the prospect of government action. But if immediate steps are not taken (to reduce violent content) and deadlines established, government should respond, and respond immediately. (Wines, 1993, p. B16)

Three bills are currently under consideration in the U.S. Congress. The proposed legislation would ban violence in programs targeted toward children; require that network and cable television programs be rated for violent content; and demand that broadcasters provide warnings prior to the airing of all violent programs, regardless of the age of the intended viewer. In June 1993, network executives volunteered to post warnings to alert viewers to programs that contained high levels of violence. Children's action-oriented cartoons, programs that typically contain a great deal of violent content, however, would not be included (Wines, 1993). There appears to be overwhelming public support for a violence rating system for televised programs. In a recent national poll, 71% of adult Americans indicated that they would support such a rating system ("Los Angeles Times poll," 1989).

In Canada, a striking and influential example of public outrage over TV violence was the 1992 petition, signed by over 1 million people, that called for government legislation to reduce televised violence. The petition was organized by a Quebec teenager who believed that TV violence contributed to her sister's rape and murder. Government officials warned broadcasters to develop self-regulatory codes or they would face government restrictions. In October 1993, the Canadian Radio-Television and Telecommunications Commission (CRTC) announced that it had approved the "toughest" self-regulatory codes in North America aimed at reducing TV violence. The code was developed by the Canadian Association of Broadcasters, an organization representing private TV and radio companies. Although the code applies only to private broadcasters, the CRTC has requested that Canadian public television, cable, pay-TV, and specialty services also develop self-regulatory standards. The CRTC rules include the following: (a) a ban on "gratuitous" violence, or violence that is not necessary to the plot. One study found that 69% of the televised violence on U.S. and Canadian networks in prime time was gratuitous (Williams, Zabrack, & Joy, 1982); (b) a ban on programming that promotes violence against women, minorities, and animals; (c) later broadcast times (after 9 p.m.) of adult-oriented programs that contain violence; (d) viewer advisories warning about violent content; (e) guidelines for broadcasting violent scenes on news programs; and (f) detailed codes for children's programs (e.g., violence should not be portrayed as a problem-solving method, consequences of violence must be included). Compliance with the code is to be monitored by a committee established by the Canadian Association of Broadcasters; applications for license renewals by noncompliant companies could be denied (Harris, 1993).

Not surprisingly, the television and motion-picture industries are opposed to government regulation, insisting that such attempts violate their right to free speech. And, despite their claims of self-regulation, some industry representatives downplay the degree to which the media influence the level of violence in society, citing the roles of other sources such as the family.

Parents. If some type of violence rating system is developed, either voluntarily by the media industry or through mandated government regulation, the burden still falls on parents to use these ratings to make decisions about which programs their children may watch. Parents can intervene by developing rules for TV viewing, especially for young children who may be most vulnerable. For example, the American Psychological Association Task Force on Television and Society (Huston et al., 1992) suggested that parents might set weekly viewing times, rule out television viewing during certain times of the day or week, and keep a list of alternative activities on hand for their children when they complain of being "bored." In addition, instead of using television as a major source of family recreation, parents could read stories with their children and encourage their children to play imaginative games with their siblings, friends, or both (Singer & Singer, 1986). Not only would these activities limit the opportunities to develop aggressive scripts from heavy TV viewing, but children would develop the fantasy and play skills necessary to cope with frustration and interpersonal conflict.

Parents can view programs with their children and play a mediating role by voicing disapproval of the violence, pointing out how the plots may be unrealistic, and suggesting alternative ways to solve problems. Unfortunately, it may be difficult to encourage parents to play such a role. Corder-Bolz (1980) found that only 55% of the parents in a sample of 3,321 Texas families reported talking to their children about the TV program content. It is also important to note the practical problem involved—if parents do try to discuss the program content during viewing, this prevents continuous viewing. And children who have a TV set in their own room, as is increasingly the case, are less likely to watch with their parent(s).

Singer and Singer (1981) carried out an intervention for the parents of 141 nursery school children. One group of parents attended three TV training sessions designed to educate them about the positive and negative aspects of TV viewing, the research evidence of the relation between violence viewing and aggressive behavior, factors to consider in choosing which programs to watch, and the need to become active rather than passive viewers (i.e., play the role of mediator). Another group of parents received training on how to develop their children's imagination and play skills. A third group of parents received training on how to develop their children's language skills. A fourth (control) group of parents received no training. Contrary to the Singers' expectations, the TV intervention had no effect on the first group of children's TV viewing habits or their aggression. Their parents reported that their efforts to monitor and limit their children's viewing were met with resistance. The children whose parents received the imagination (second group) and language interventions (third group), however, did show slight improvement in TV viewing habits compared to the children of control group parents (fourth group). Perhaps instructing parents to restrict their children's TV viewing without providing alternative positive activities is an ill-fated strategy.

The American Psychological Association's task force (Huston et al., 1992) suggested the following sources for parents and teachers seeking more detailed recommendations for enhancing the positive benefits of television and reducing the possible negative effects of violence viewing: (a) *Taking Advantage of Media: A Manual for Parents and Teachers* (Brown, 1986); (b) *Getting the Most Out of TV* (Singer, Singer, & Zuckerman, 1981a); and (c) *Teaching Television: How to Use TV to Your Child's Advantage* (Singer, Singer, & Zuckerman, 1981b).

Targeting Individual Characteristics

The information processing model identifies several individual characteristics that seem to influence the TV violence viewing-aggression relation.

Children are more vulnerable to the potentially negative effects of TV violence viewing if they have a preexisting higher level of arousal (or are aggressive to begin with); are younger; do not understand key aspects of the plot (including the inappropriateness of the aggressive act and its consequences); attribute hostile intent to actors' behaviors and believe retaliation is morally justified; hold values and norms consistent with the performance of aggressive behavior; perceive the TV-portrayed violence as realistic; and identify with the aggressive actor. Thus, modifying children's thoughts so that they are inconsistent with the acquisition and retrieval of aggressive scripts would seem to be a reasonable intervention strategy.

One such approach has been to teach young children "critical viewing skills" (Corder-Bolz, 1980; Singer, Zuckerman, & Singer, 1980), ways of thinking that are more typical of older children, in the hope that enhancing the children's understanding of television would prevent them from developing aggressive scripts. Singer et al. (1980) developed an eight-lesson curriculum to enhance third and fourth graders' awareness of the different types of programs, the degree of reality of TV portrayals, how TV affects viewers' feelings and behaviors (especially how violence viewing might affect aggression), and the purposes and types of commercials. Three months later, children exposed to the curriculum had more knowledge about TV than a group of children who did not receive the curriculum, but there was no assessment of the children's aggressive behavior or attitudes. Thus, it is unclear whether or not the development of critical viewing skills decreased the relation between TV violence viewing and aggressive behavior. Williams (1986) believes that curricula such as these should incorporate discussions of how some tasks (e.g., reading, studying) require enough mental effort that they should not be shared with television viewing; she also believes that children should learn to consider the pros and cons of choosing alternative activities to television viewing. Abelson (1990) applauds "critical viewing skills" curricula because they might serve to stimulate parents' interest in their children's viewing, and encourage parents' to reassess the role of television in the family.

Huesmann, Eron, Klein, Brice, and Fischer (1983) developed an intervention program based on Huesmann's information processing model. The general goal of the program, designed for first and third graders who were in the upper 25% of violence viewers in a larger sample of children, was to modify beliefs about TV violence. The specific goals were to change children's attitudes about (a) the desirability of imitating the aggressive behavior of TV characters, (b) the degree to which television programs reflect real life, and (c) the consequences of imitating TV violence. Children were asked to help produce a film to change the attitudes of other school children who have been fooled by television and have gotten into trouble because they imitated violent acts seen on TV. The participants were told that they "knew better" than to believe that TV programs were like real life. These manipulations were geared toward facilitating attitude change by creating in the children a feeling of personal choice in their participation (i.e., they were asked to participate), encouraging them to commit to an important cause (i.e., to help children who have been fooled by TV), producing a sense of responsibility for the consequences of their behaviors (i.e., the children were to try to change the attitudes of other children), and generating attitudes the experimenters wanted them to adopt (i.e., you "know better" than to believe that TV is realistic).

The intervention consisted of two sessions in which the children prepared arguments about the negative aspects of television violence, how it does not portray real life, and what the consequences could be if one were to imitate TV violence. The children wrote their arguments and read them during a videotaped "talk-show," which was later replayed to them. This procedure was intended to create in the group a norm of anti-TV violence, and more generally, anti-aggression. Children in a comparison group followed similar procedures but produced a film about their favorite hobbies; that is, there was no attempt to change their attitudes toward TV violence. Four months later, children who had received the TV attitude change intervention were less likely to be nominated by their peers as aggressive than were children in the comparison group. Those who had decreased the most in aggression were children who had identified less with TV characters prior to the intervention, and whose attitudes had changed toward the view that TV violence could be harmful. Of further interest, the improvement of children in the experimental group occurred even though they still watched as much TV violence as before the intervention. Thus, there was no longer a significant relation between TV violence viewing and being nominated by peers for aggression in the experimental group, but there was still a significant relation in the comparison group. It appears that the attitude change procedure buffered the children from the negative effects of violence viewing. The authors attributed the success of the program to attitude changes that may have reduced the likelihood that participants would adopt and later retrieve the aggressive scenarios observed on television.

Summary and Conclusions

Aggressive behavioral patterns develop early in life and remain relatively stable over time. The etiology, or development of aggressive behavior, is believed to include a convergence of a number of interacting biological and psychosocial factors across individual, family, and environmental domains. This chapter has focused on one source of socialization contributing to aggressive behavior—the influence of violent media portrayals. Most of the evidence from laboratory, observational, and cross-cultural longitudinal studies indicates that violence in television and other media plays a causal role in the development of aggression. Most researchers acknowledge that television violence viewing is only one of many causes of aggression (other causes include family environment characteristics), but conclude that it is nevertheless of social significance.

It is more difficult to study and determine how televised violence influences viewers' aggressive behavior. In an attempt to understand this, we have presented a cognitive social information processing model based on the work of both Huesmann and Berkowitz. Children are believed to commit to memory scripts for behavior as a result of both their own behavior and observing the behavior of others (observational learning). TV and other media provide one important source for observational learning, although this framework is clearly relevant to understanding how aggression is learned in other contexts as well. Scripts contain rules describing the sequence of events during a social interaction, as well as the feelings and thoughts of the actors portrayed in the situation. Thus, when the child is exposed to later situations similar to an already established script, he or she might use the relevant script for coping with the situation. If many aggressive scripts have been placed into and maintained in memory, and one way this might happen would be through heavy exposure to television violence, the likelihood of retrieving an aggressive script would be increased, especially if the child has few other scripts.

The information processing model provides a good basis for developing interventions to mitigate the effect of TV violence viewing on aggressive behavior because the model posits several environmental and individual characteristics that affect whether children will develop and use aggressive scripts. For example, a violent family environment might lead to the development of aggression-related norms and attitudes that would increase the likelihood that the child would place into memory violent scenes portrayed in televised media. In terms of individual characteristics, children are more vulnerable to the potentially negative effects of TV violence viewing if they have a preexisting higher level of emotional arousal; fail to understand the content of the violent display, perhaps because they have yet to develop the ability to consider the motives of each actor in the situation and the future consequences of the aggressive behavior; and perceive the TV violence as presenting realistic strategies to solve interpersonal problems.

Interventions have targeted these environmental and individual factors, and have demonstrated varying degrees of success in decreasing the TV violence viewing-aggression relation. As we have stressed several times throughout this chapter, however, television violence is only one cause of habitual aggressive behavior. Interventions to decrease aggression must be more broadly focused than simply attempting to change parents' and children's attitudes about television violence viewing, or encouraging children to be more knowledgeable consumers of television. Such media-oriented interventions could be one component of a comprehensive intervention that targets other socializers of aggressive behavior—families, peer groups, and schools.

References

Abelson, R. (1990). Determinants of parental mediation of children's television viewing. In J. Bryant (Ed.), *Television and the American family* (pp. 311-326). Hillsdale, NJ: Lawrence Erlbaum.

American Psychological Association. (1985). *Violence on television.* Washington, DC: APA Board of Social and Ethical Responsibility for Psychology.

American Psychiatric Association. (1994). *Diagnostic and statistical manual of mental disorders* (4th ed.). Washington, DC: Author.

Baker, R. K., & Ball, S. J. (1969). *Violence and the media: A report to the national Commission on the Causes and Prevention of Violence.* Washington, DC: Government Printing Office.

Bandura, A. (1977). *Social learning theory.* Englewood Cliffs, NJ: Prentice Hall.

Bandura, A., Ross, D., & Ross, S. A. (1961). Transmission of aggression through imitation of aggressive models. *Journal of Abnormal and Social Psychology, 63,* 575-582.

Bandura, A., Ross, D., & Ross, S. A. (1963a). Imitation of film-mediated aggressive models. *Journal of Abnormal and Social Psychology, 66,* 3-11.

Bandura, A., Ross, D., & Ross, S. A. (1963b). Vicarious reinforcement and imitative learning. *Journal of Abnormal and Social Psychology, 67,* 601-607.

Berkowitz, L. (1984). Some effects of thoughts on anti- and prosocial influences of media events: A cognitive neoassociationistic analysis. *Psychological Bulletin, 95,* 410-427.

Berkowitz, L. (1986). Situational influences on reactions to observed violence. *Journal of Social Issues, 42,* 93-106.

Berkowitz, L., & Heimer, K. (1989). On the construction of the anger experience: Aversive events and negative priming in the formation of feelings. *Advances in Experimental Social Psychology, 22,* 1-37.

Bjorkqvist, K. (1985). *Violent films, anxiety, and aggression.* Helsinki: Finnish Society of Sciences and Letters.

Botha, M. P., & Mels, G. (1990). Stability of aggression among adolescents over time: A South African study. *Aggressive Behavior, 16,* 361-380.

Brown, L. K. (1986). *Taking advantage of media: A manual for parents and teachers.* Boston: Routledge and Kegan Paul.

Bushman, B. J., & Geen, R. G. (1990). Role of cognitive-emotional mediators and individual differences in the effects of media violence on aggression. *Journal of Personality and Social Psychology, 58,* 156-163.

Caspi, A., Elder, G. H., & Bem, D. J. (1987). Moving against the world: Life course patterns of explosive children. *Developmental Psychology, 23,* 308-313.

Centerwall, B. S. (1989). Exposure to television as a cause of violence. In G. Comstock (Ed.), *Public communication and behavior* (Vol. 2, pp. 1- 58). San Diego, CA: Academic Press.

Collins, W. A. (1979). Children's comprehension of television content. In E. Wartella (Ed.), *Children communicating: Media and development of thought, speech, understanding.* Beverly Hills, CA: Sage.

Comstock, G. A. (1980). New emphases in research on the effects of television and film violence. In E. L. Palmer & A. Dorr (Eds.), *Children and the faces of television: Teaching, violence, selling* (pp. 129-148). New York: Academic Press.

Comstock, G. A. (1983). Media influences on aggression. In A. Goldstein (Ed.), *Prevention and control of aggression: Principles, practices, and research.* New York: Pergamon.

Comstock, G. A., & Paik, H. (1991). The effects of television violence on aggressive behavior: A meta-analysis. In *A preliminary report to the National Research Council on the understanding and control of violent behavior.* Washington, DC: National Research Council.

Corder-Bolz, C. R. (1980). Mediation: The role of significant others. *Journal of Communication, 30*(3), 106-118.

Deluty, R. H. (1983). Children's evaluations of aggressive, assertive, and submissive responses. *Journal of Clinical Child Psychology, 12*(2), 124-129.

Dodge, K. A., & Frame, C. L. (1982). Social cognitive biases and deficits in aggressive boys. *Child Development, 53,* 620-635.

Dunand, M., Berkowitz, L., & Leyens, J. (1984). Audience effects when viewing aggressive movies. *British Journal of Social Psychology, 23,* 69- 76.

Eron, L. D. (1963). The relationship of TV viewing habits and aggressive behavior in children. *Journal of Abnormal and Social Psychology, 67,* 193-196.

Eron, L. D. (1986). Interventions to mitigate the psychological effects of media violence on aggressive behavior. *Journal of Social Issues, 42,* 155-169.

Eron, L. D. (1992). Gender differences in violence: Biology and/or socialization? In K. Bjorkqvist & N. Pirkko (Eds.), *Of mice and women: Aspects of female aggression* (pp. 85-97). San Diego, CA: Academic Press.

Eron, L. D., Huesmann, L. R., Brice, P., Fischer, P., & Mermelstein, R. (1983). Age trends in the development of aggression, sex-typing, and related television habits. *Developmental Psychology, 19*(1), 71-77.

Eron, L. D., Huesmann, L. R., Lefkowitz, M. M., & Walder, L. O. (1972). Does television violence cause aggression? *American Psychologist, 27,* 253-263.

Farrington, D. P. (1982). Longitudinal analyses of criminal violence. In M. E. Wolfgang & N. A. Weiner (Eds.), *Criminal violence* (pp. 171-200). Beverley Hills, CA: Sage.

Fiske, S. T., & Taylor, S. E. (1984). *Social cognition.* Reading, MA: Addison-Wesley.

Freedman, J. L. (1984). Effect of television violence on aggressiveness. *Psychological Bulletin, 96,* 227-246.

Freedman, J. L. (1986). Television violence and aggression: A rejoinder. *Psychological Bulletin, 100,* 372-378.

Friedrich-Cofer, L., & Huston, A. C. (1986). Television violence and aggression: The debate continues. *Psychological Bulletin, 100,* 364-371.

Geen, R. G. (1990). *Human aggression.* Pacific Grove, CA: Brooks/Cole.

Geen, R. G., & Thomas, S. L. (1986). The immediate effects of media violence on behavior. *Journal of Social Issues, 42*(3), 7-27.

Harris, C. (1993, October 29). CRTC ratifies stricter rules to crack down on TV violence. *The Globe and Mail,* pp. A1, A2.

Hinshaw, S. (1992). Externalizing behavior problems and academic underachievement in childhood and adolescence: Causal relationships and underlying mechanisms. *Psychological Bulletin, 111,* 127-155.

Huesmann, L. R. (1986). Psychological processes promoting the relation between exposure to media violence and aggressive behavior by the viewer. *Journal of Social Issues, 42*(3), 125-139.

Huesmann, L. R. (1988). An information processing model for the development of aggression. *Aggressive Behavior, 14*(1), 13-24.

Huesmann, L. R., & Bachrach, R. S. (1988). Differential effects of television violence in kibbutz and city children. In R. Patterson, & P. Drummond (Eds.), *Television and its audience: International research perspectives* (pp. 154-176). London: BFI Publishing.

Huesmann, L. R., & Eron, L. D. (1984). Cognitive processes and the persistence of aggressive behavior. *Aggressive Behavior, 10,* 243-251.

Huesmann, L. R., & Eron, L. D. (Eds.). (1986). *Television and the aggressive child: A cross-national comparison.* Hillsdale, NJ: Lawrence Erlbaum.

Huesmann, L. R., Eron, L. D., Klein, R., Brice, P., & Fischer, P. (1983). Mitigating the imitation of aggressive behavior by changing children's attitudes about media violence. *Journal of Personality and Social Psychology: Attitudes and Social Cognition, 44,* 899-910.

Huesmann, L. R., Eron, L. D., Lefkowitz, M. M., & Walder, L. O. (1984). The stability of aggression over time and generations. *Developmental Psychology, 20,* 1120-1134.

Huesmann, L. R., Eron, L. D., & Yarmel, P. W. (1987). Intellectual functioning and aggression. *Journal of Personality and Social Psychology: Personality Processes and Individual Differences, 52,* 232-240.

Huesmann, L. R., & Miller, L. S. (1994). Long-term effects of repeated exposure to media violence in childhood. In L. R. Huesmann (Ed.), *Aggressive behavior: Current perspectives* (pp. 153-180). New York: Plenum.

Huston, A. C., Donnerstein, E., Fairchild, H., Feshbach, N. D., Katz, P., Murray, J., Rubinstein, E. A., Wilcox, B. L., & Zuckerman, D. (1992). *Big world, small screen: The role of television in American society.* Lincoln, NE: University of Nebraska Press.

Huston, A. C., & Wright, J. C. (1989). The forms of television and the child viewer. In G. Comstock (Ed.), *Public communication and behavior* (Vol. 2, pp. 103-158). San Diego, CA: Academic Press.

Josephson, W. L. (1987). Television violence and children's aggression: Testing the priming, social script, and disinhibition predictions. *Journal of Personality and Social Psychology, 53,* 882-890.

Joy, L. A., Kimball, M. M., & Zabrack, M. L. (1986). Television and children's aggressive behavior. In T. M. Williams (Ed.), *The impact of television: A natural experiment in three communities* (pp. 303-360). Orlando, FL: Academic Press.

Kazdin, A. E. (1987). Treatment of antisocial behavior in children: Current status and future directions. *Psychological Bulletin, 102,* 187- 201.

Lefkowitz, M. M., Eron, L. D., Walder, L. O., & Huesmann, L. R. (1977). *Growing up to be violent.* New York: Pergamon.

Loeber, R., & Dishion, T. J. (1983). Early predictors of male delinquency: A review. *Psychological Bulletin, 94*(1), 68-94.

Los Angeles Times poll. (September 19, 1989). Television, sex, and violence (Poll 196). *American Public Opinion Data.* Louisville, KY: Opinion Research Service.

Lytton, H., & Romney, D. M. (1991). Parents' differential socialization of boys and girls. A meta-analysis. *Psychological Bulletin, 109*(2), 267-296.

Magnusson, D., Duner, A., & Zetterblom, G. (1975). *Adjustment: A longitudinal study.* Stockholm: Almqvist & Wiksell.

Malamuth, N. M. (1989). Sexually violent media, thought patterns, and antisocial behavior. In G. Comstock (Ed.), *Public communication and behavior* (Vol. 2, pp. 159-204). San Diego, CA: Academic Press.

McGuire, W. J. (1986). The myth of massive media impact: Savagings and salvagings. In G. Comstock (Ed), *Public communication and behavior* (Vol. 1, pp. 173-257). San Diego, CA: Academic Press.

Meltzoff, A. N. (1988). Imitation of televised models by infants. *Child Development, 59,* 1221-1229.

Milavsky, J. R., Stipp, H. H., Kessler, R. C., & Rubens, W. S. (1982). *Television and aggression: A panel study.* New York: Academic Press.

Olweus, D. (1979). The stability of aggressive reaction patterns in human males: A review. *Psychological Bulletin, 85,* 852-875.

Ontario Royal Commission on Violence in the Communications Industry. (1977). *Report of the Ontario Royal Commission on Violence in the Communications Industry.* Toronto: Government of Ontario.

Parke, R. D., Berkowitz, L., Leyens, S. P., West, S., & Sebastian, R. S. (1977). Some effects of violent and nonviolent movies on the behavior of juvenile delinquents. In L. Berkowitz (Ed.), *Advances in experimental social psychology* (Vol. 10, pp. 136-172). New York: Academic Press.

Parke, R. D., & Slaby, R. G. (1983). The development of aggression. In P. Mussen (Ed.), *Handbook of child psychology* (3rd ed., pp. 547-642). New York: John Wiley.

Pearl, D., Bouthilet, L., & Lazar, J. (Eds.). (1982). *Television and behavior: Ten years of scientific progress and implications for the eighties, technical reviews* (Vol. 2). Washington, DC: Government Printing Office.

Perry, D. G., Perry, L. C., & Rasmussen, P. (1986). Cognitive social learning mediation of aggression. *Child Development, 57,* 700-711.

Potts, R., Huston, A. C., & Wright, J. C. (1986). The effects of television form and violent content on boys' attention and social behavior. *Journal of Experimental Child Psychology, 41*(1), 1-17.

Robins, L. N. (1966). *Deviant children grown up: A sociological and psychiatric study of sociopathic personality.* Baltimore: Williams and Wilkins.

Robins, L. N., & Ratcliff, K. S. (1980). Childhood conduct disorders and later arrest. In L. N. Robins, P. J. Clayton, & J. W. Wing (Eds.), *The social consequences of psychiatric illness* (pp. 248-263). New York: Brunner/Mazel.

Rosenthal, R. (1986). Media violence, antisocial behavior, and the social consequences of small effects. *Journal of Social Issues, 42,* 141-154.

Rule, G. R., & Ferguson, T. J. (1986). The effects of media violence on attitudes, emotions, and cognitions. *Journal of Social Issues, 42*(3), 29-50.

Rutter, M., & Giller, H. (1983). *Juvenile delinquency: Trends and perspectives.* New York: Guilford.

Sears, R. R., Maccoby, E. E., & Levin, H. (1957). *Patterns of child-rearing.* Evanston, IL: Row, Peterson.

Singer, J. L., & Singer, D. G. (1981). *Television, imagination, and aggression: A study of preschoolers.* Hillsdale, NJ: Lawrence Erlbaum.

Singer, J. L., & Singer, D. G. (1986). Family experiences and television viewing as predictors of children's imagination, restlessness, and aggression. *Journal of Social Issues, 42*(3), 107-124.

Singer, D. G., Singer, J. L., & Zuckerman, D. M. (1981a). *Getting the most out of TV.* Santa Monica, CA: Goodyear.

Singer, D. G., Singer, J. L., & Zuckerman, D. M. (1981b). *Teaching television: How to use TV to your child's advantage.* New York: Dial Press.

Singer, D. G., Zuckerman, D. M., & Singer, J. L. (1980). Helping elementary school children learn about TV. *Journal of Communication, 30*(3), 84-93.

Slaby, R. G., & Conklin Roedell, W. (1982). The development and regulation of aggression in young children. In J. Worell (Ed.), *Psychological development in the elementary school years* (pp. 97-147). New York: Academic Press.

Stein, A. H., & Friedrich, L. K. (1972). Television content and young children's behavior. In J. P. Murray, E. A. Rubenstein, & G. A. Comstock (Eds.), *Television and social behavior: Television and social learning* (Vol. 2, pp. 202-317). Washington, DC: Government Printing Office.

Surgeon General's Scientific Advisory Committee on Television and Social Behavior. (1972). *Television and growing up: The impact of televised violence.* Washington, DC: Government Printing Office.

Tremblay, R., Masse, D., Perron, D., & Leblanc, M. (1992). Early disruptive behavior, poor school achievement, delinquent behavior, and delinquent personality: Longitudinal analyses. *Journal of Consulting and Clinical Psychology, 60*(1), 64-72.

Weigman, O., Kuttschreuter, M., & Baarda, B. (1986). *Television viewing related to aggressive and prosocial behavior.* The Hague: Stitching voor Onderzoek van het Onderwijs.

West, D. J., & Farrington, D. P. (1977). *The delinquent way of life.* London: Heineman.

Williams, T. M. (Ed.). (1986). *The impact of television: A natural experiment in three communities.* Orlando, FL: Academic Press.

Williams, T. M., Zabrack, M. L., & Joy, L. A. (1982). The portrayal of aggression on North American television. *Journal of Applied Social Psychology, 12,* 360-380.

Wines, M. (1993, October 21). Reno chastises TV executives over violence. *New York Times,* pp. A1, B16.

Wood, W., Wong, F. Y., & Chachere, G. (1991). Effects of media violence on viewers' aggression in unconstrained social interaction. *Psychological Bulletin, 109,* 371-383.

Wright, J., & Huston, A. (1983). A matter of form: Potentials of television for young viewers. *American Psychologist, 38,* 835-843.

Wright, J. C., St. Peters, M., & Huston, A. C. (1990). Family television use and its relation to children's cognitive skills and social behavior. In J. Bryant (Ed.), *Television and the American family* (pp. 227-252). Hillsdale, NJ: Lawrence Erlbaum.

Zillmann, D. (1979). *Hostility and aggression.* Hillsdale, NJ: Lawrence Erlbaum.

The *Bizarro* cartoon by Dan Piraro is reprinted courtesy of
Chronicle Features, San Francisco, California. All rights reserved.

6

Indirect Effects of Television
Creativity, Persistence, School Achievement, and Participation in Other Activities

Tannis M. MacBeth

M any questions raised about television and other media focus on potentially positive or negative effects of its programming or content. Several of these important questions are addressed in the other chapters of this
book. In this chapter I want to focus on some other questions that have been
asked by researchers and the public, questions for which any possible effects
of television would be more indirect. As a context for addressing these
questions I will use some of the findings from our study in Notel, Unitel, and
Multitel. In the introductory chapter, I provided an overview of the design of
that study to highlight some of the methodological issues involved in trying
to use natural experiments to answer the questions of whether television can
and does have effects in real-life settings. In this chapter, I will describe some
of the results from that natural experiment as well as congruent and contradictory evidence from previous and subsequent studies. Let me begin by
providing some information on the background and nature of our own
study.

Notel, Unitel, and Multitel as Context

One of the most important landmarks for research on the effects of television in North America is referred to as *The Surgeon General's Report*. Concern in the United States about the possible effects of television on social behavior, and in particular on aggression, led to the establishment in 1969 of the Surgeon General's Scientific Advisory Commission on Television and Social Behavior. This commission, which funded new research in addition to evaluating previous research, produced their much-heralded five-volume report in 1972 (Comstock & Rubinstein, 1972a, 1972b; Comstock, Rubinstein, & Murray, 1972; Murray, Rubinstein, & Comstock, 1972; Rubinstein, Comstock, & Murray, 1972).[1] In evaluating the evidence, the commissioners noted the problem of being unable to make causal inferences regarding some findings for which the only evidence was correlational, because it had been obtained after almost everyone in North America was a regular TV viewer. They lamented not having the opportunity to get around the chicken-and-egg problem I discussed in this book's introductory chapter by studying people both before and after they became regular viewers.

In the summer of 1973, just after the U.S. Surgeon General's report was published, I learned[2] that a town in my province of British Columbia was going to get television reception for the first time. This was an especially good opportunity to study the effects of television because this town, to which we gave the pseudonym "Notel," was not isolated. It had road, train, and bus service and should have had television reception, but the transmitter intended by the Canadian Broadcasting Corporation (CBC)[3] to bring it their English channel did not succeed in doing so because of the way in which Notel was located in a valley. That transmitter did succeed in bringing CBC to a similar town about an hour's drive away, so we also studied that town, which we dubbed "Unitel." In addition, we studied another comparison or control town, called "Multitel," because we thought the effects of one CBC channel might differ from the effects of four channels. Multitel received CBC and the three major private U.S. networks then available, ABC, CBS, and NBC. In Phase 1 of this natural experiment we conducted a number of studies in Notel, Unitel, and Multitel just before Notel obtained one channel—CBC. We then went back to all three towns to collect Phase 2 data 2 years later—that is, after Notel residents had had 2 years of CBC television reception. If you have read the introductory chapter (this volume), you are familiar with the methodology of this natural experiment. If you have not yet read it, you may want to turn to it now for more details of our study before proceeding with this chapter.

Since the publication of the book describing our findings[4] (Williams, 1986b), the central or main results have been fairly widely reported and discussed by other researchers and by some media outlets. I find, myself, that I tend to mention only those main findings when talking about our study, whether with other researchers or interested professionals, students, parents, etc. This is especially true when an interviewer from the media wants a 30-second summary (of a 450-page book!). In this chapter I will highlight some of our less well-known and perhaps more provocative results, in addition to summarizing those that are better known.

Creativity and Imagination

The questions of whether television has an impact on its viewers' creativity or imagination, either positively or negatively, and whether viewers who differ in creativity or imagination use television differently have been addressed by a number of researchers. I will first describe our findings for children and adults in Notel, Unitel, and Multitel, and then review other relevant findings.

Results From Notel, Unitel, and Multitel

School-Age Children. We assessed the creative thinking of students in Notel, Unitel, and Multitel in two ways (Harrison & Williams, 1986). Both measure ideational fluency—the generation of many ideas—and ideational originality—the generation of unique ideas. Our primary measure was the Alternate Uses task, in which the child is asked to think of all the different ways a common item (magazine, knife, shoe, button, key) could be used. This task, which was developed by Guilford and his colleagues (e.g., Guilford, 1975), is considered one of the best measures of ideational fluency and has been widely used as a measure of creativity and divergent thinking (Barron & Harrington, 1981). Our second measure was the Pattern Meanings task (developed by Wallach & Kogan, 1965). Each item is a drawing on a card, and the child is asked to think of all the things each complete drawing could be. In Phase 1, before Notel had television reception, we gave both tasks individually to 160 students in Grades 4 and 7 in the three towns. Two years later, we retested 137 (86%) of the same students,[5] now in Grades 6 and 9, who were still available, and 147 new students in Grades 4 and 7.[6] An interviewer wrote down the child's answers and tried to create a relaxed, playful atmosphere, with no time limits, which facilitates creative performance (Wallach & Kogan, 1965).

In Phase 1, before Notel had television, Notel students obtained higher Alternate Uses creativity scores than did students in both Unitel and Multitel, who did not differ. This was true for both total-idea and original-idea scores. In Phase 2, after 2 years of regular television viewing, the Alternate Uses scores of Notel students did not differ from those of Unitel or Multitel students.[7] From Phase 1 to Phase 2 Notel students' total-idea scores decreased significantly, whereas the scores of Unitel and Multitel students did not change. This pattern of results, which is illustrated in Figure 6.1 for the total-idea scores, indicates that children who did not have the opportunity to watch television on a regular basis obtained higher creativity scores than those who were regular viewers. But not growing up with television did not provide an "inoculation"; after 2 years of regular viewing, Notel students' scores had fallen significantly. Whereas they previously had had higher Alternate Uses scores than their age mates in Unitel and Multitel, they no longer differed from them, implying that whatever had facilitated their before-TV performance no longer was doing so. The kinds of responses given by Notel children in Phase 1 suggested that they had had a wider variety of experiences than did Unitel and Multitel children. They more often mentioned activities such as camping, hiking, crafts, and doing various projects, which points to an indirect effect of television.

Our hypothesis that any effect of television on creativity is indirect—that is, that other activities may foster mental elaboration and reflection or may provide a wider range of experience on which children may draw when generating ideas—is supported by some of our other findings. First, there was no relationship between Alternate Uses scores and hours of TV viewing per week in Phase 1 for Unitel and Multitel students. This also was true in Phase 2 for all three towns combined, for Notel alone, and for Unitel and Multitel. Second, Alternate Uses scores were significantly and positively related to some other activities. The pattern varied depending on whether the correlation was for Phase 1, for Phase 2, or across both phases; and whether gender or gender and IQ or neither was taken into consideration (i.e., controlled) in the analyses. In general, students with higher Alternate Uses scores participated

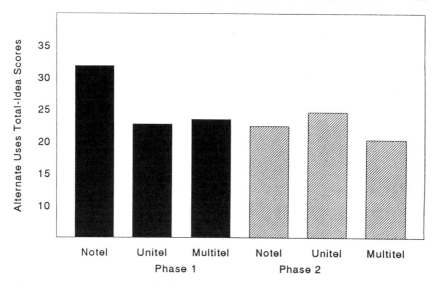

Figure 6.1. Alternate Uses Total-Idea Creativity Scores of Notel, Unitel, and Multitel Grade 4 and 7 Students Before (Phase 1) and 2 Years After (Phase 2) Notel Obtained Television Reception

in community activities more than did students with lower scores both in total and in sports in particular. They also participated more in other private leisure activities, both in total and for book reading and radio listening in particular (the latter findings were for Phase 2 so were not due to the absence of TV in Notel). Thus, hours of TV viewing did not vary systematically with Alternate Uses scores, but students who scored higher on this measure of ability to generate ideas did tend to participate more in community activities and in certain other private leisure activities than did students with lower Alternate Uses scores.

Whereas the findings for the Alternate Uses task formed a pattern clearly suggesting a negative, indirect effect of the availability of television, those for the Pattern Meanings task were much less clear. There were no differences among the scores of Notel, Unitel, and Multitel students in Phase 1 or Phase 2. For the three towns combined in Phase 2, students with higher Pattern Meanings scores watched less TV than did students with lower Pattern Meanings scores. Although this negative relationship was statistically significant, it was small, and the relationship was not significant for Unitel and Multitel in Phase 1. As was true for Alternate Uses scores, students with higher

Pattern Meanings scores participated more in some other leisure activities, including both community activities (total, sports) and private activities (total, book reading, radio listening). This provides additional evidence that such activities facilitate performance on creativity tasks, that students who are more creative use their leisure time differently than do those who are less creative, or both.

For several reasons, we are inclined to place more weight on the Alternate Uses results than on the Pattern Meanings results as indicative of the role of television and other leisure activities in creativity. First, the pattern of results for comparisons among the towns for the Alternate Uses task was clear and consistent for four different sets of findings: the cross-sectional comparisons among Notel, Unitel, and Multitel; the longitudinal town comparisons from Phase 1 to Phase 2; the correlations with television use; and the correlations with other leisure activities. Second, the Alternate Uses task has a much more eminent history. It is considered to be an excellent measure of both ideational fluency and ideational originality, which in turn are considered to be among the best means of assessing creative thinking. Third, it seems possible that television viewing facilitates performance on the figural interpretation aspect of the Pattern Meanings task, whereas experiences in other activities facilitate performance on the production of ideas aspect of the task, hence the inconsistent pattern of results. The finding that in Phase 2, students with lower Pattern Meanings scores watched more TV than did those with higher scores does, however, weaken the likelihood of the first part of this possibility, namely that TV experience facilitates the interpretation of figural patterns.

When our findings have been reviewed, along with those of other researchers, the conclusions have varied. The American Psychological Association (APA) Task Force Report noted that, "Children showed reduced performance on one of two measures of creativity after television was introduced" (Huston et al., 1992, p. 90). Anderson and Collins (1988) concluded that there is little evidence that television has any effects on creativity (or on other cognitive processes, including attention and impulsivity). Others have included our findings among those that, taken together, they say indicate that television has a detrimental effect on creativity or imagination (e.g., Greenfield et al., 1993; Singer, 1993). In the next sections of this chapter, I will review findings obtained by other researchers so that you can evaluate the entire body of evidence yourself and draw your own conclusions.

Was there any evidence that the Notel students who were more creative in Phase 1, before television was available, used it differently 2 years later than did their initially less creative peers? I do not have an answer in terms of the type of programming they watched (although given that they had only one channel, the choices were limited), but in terms of amount of TV viewing, the answer is no. We divided the Notel students into those who were above and below the median[8] in Phase 1 Alternate Uses total-idea scores, and they did not differ in hours of TV viewing per week in Phase 2. The same was true for Pattern Meanings scores.

Adults. We assessed the creative problem-solving skills of adults in Notel, Unitel, and Multitel individually in their homes with problems designed to measure flexibility in thinking (Suedfeld, Little, Rank, Rank, & Ballard, 1986). In Phase 1, we used the Duncker (1945) Candle Problem. We provided a vertical cardboard surface, a box of thumbtacks, a candle, and a book of matches and asked each person to "affix the candle to the cardboard wall, using any of the objects on the table, so it stays there and burns freely without being held." The trick is to "break set" or think of the objects differently, by emptying the box of tacks, tacking the box to the cardboard, and putting the candle in or on the box. This relatively difficult problem was solved by 40.4% of the 57 Notel adults, 25.5% of the 51 in Unitel, and 30% of the 55 in Multitel.[9] Among those who solved the problem, Notel residents did so more quickly (151 seconds) than did Unitel (251 seconds) and Multitel (263 seconds) residents. Furthermore, Unitel and Multitel residents who solved the problem reported watching less TV ($M = 18.1$ hours per week than did those who failed to solve it ($M = 33.4$ hours).

We used a different problem in Phase 2, the Nine Dot Problem (Dworetzky, 1982), and it proved to be exceptionally difficult. Each adult was given a sheet of paper on which nine dots formed a three-by-three square and was asked to connect all the dots using no more than four straight pencil lines without retracing any portion of a line or lifting the pencil off the paper (but the lines could cross). The trick in this case is to go outside the square twice, but the tendency is to think of the outer dots as a boundary. Only 7 of the 188 adults solved this problem so we could not compare either the proportions of solvers across the towns or their speed. We therefore looked to see if each person had "broken set" at least partially by attempting to link the dots by going outside the square. In Notel, 25% of the 64 adults did so, compared with 15% (of 60) in Unitel and 9.4% (of 64) in Multitel, a marginally significant pattern. Averaging across the three towns, the adults who succeeded on this problem reported watching significantly less TV ($M = 12.75$ hours per week) than those who did not (*M* = 23.4 hours), and a similar significant pattern occurred for those who broke set (17.2 hours) versus those who did not (24.7 hours).

This set of results for creative problem-solving by adults is consistent with the results for children on the Alternate Uses task in indicating that creative thinking is better in the absence of television than when it is available. Again, this seems likely to be an indirect effect resulting because some other activities (including, perhaps, doing puzzles of one form or another) may facilitate performance. The finding of a marginal difference favoring Notel adults in the proportion who partially broke set after 2 years of regular viewing provides a small hint that, once acquired, flexible thinking skills may be lost more slowly in adulthood than in childhood as television replaces other activities (recall that on the Alternate Uses task there were no differences among the towns in Phase 2).

Other Research and Reviews

In her recent review of research on the effects of television on creativity, D. Singer (1993) concluded that "the evidence for negative effects of television on the creativity of children appears to be stronger than for the positive effects" (p. 85). She went on to raise a note of caution, however, citing the correlational nature of some studies, the different age levels assessed, and the small numbers in each study.

 In early studies, some researchers contended that more creative adolescents are interested in a wider variety of activities and therefore watch less television than do less creative adolescents. In Japan, Furu (1971) reported that heavy TV viewers, by comparison with print-oriented students, were inferior in "intelligence, creativity, positivity, and adaptability, and had less interest in 'thinking' and 'science' " (p. 266). In the United States, Wade (1971) found that adolescents with higher scores on creativity tasks reported watching significantly fewer hours of TV per week than did those with lower creativity scores. In both of these studies the correlational nature of the data cannot rule out the possibility that television use may influence performance on creativity tasks, although, as I have argued earlier, such an influence would at most be indirect and, in my opinion, would likely begin earlier in development when children begin to develop habits regarding how they spend their leisure time.

More recently, several researchers have investigated the potential impact of television viewing on various behaviors related to creative thinking. For example, Gadberry (1980) conducted an experiment in which 6-year-olds were blindly assigned to restricted or unrestricted viewing groups. Parents in the restricted group cut their children's viewing time by half and interacted with their child daily for 20 minutes over a 6-week period. Parents in the unrestricted group interacted similarly but set no limits on TV viewing. For leisure, reading was chosen most often by both groups. Nevertheless, 6-year-olds in the restricted TV group scored higher on a measure of reflective thinking (the Matching Familiar Figures test, MFF) that involves searching for visual details to match figures. Gadberry also found that increased leisure reading in the restricted group was associated with higher scores on a test of Picture Completion, which involved searching for missing details on common objects. She contended that the rapid changes and television motion in most programming may limit the time viewers can take to process information, whereas children's programming that is intended to be informative may encourage more reflection. She did, indeed, find that children who watched more programs such as *Sesame Street* and *Electric Company* were more reflective in terms of their MFF scores. The experimental nature of this study makes a causal interpretation of the relationship between amount of viewing and reflectivity scores more plausible than if the study were correlational. The choice of what to watch (e.g., *Sesame Street* vs. general programming), however, was presumably made by children and their parents. Thus, the relationship of particular types of programming to reflectivity scores may be due to some other relevant variable(s), for example, IQ. This finding is nevertheless interesting, because it complements very well the evidence from other studies discussed later in this chapter (Jönsson, 1986; Rosengren & Windahl, 1989; Wright, 1995) and by Huston and Wright in Chapter 2 (this volume) that watching informative children's programming and parental concern regarding children's use of TV in the early years sets in motion an upward spiral with regard to school entry skills and later academic achievements.

The complexity of stories written by children in Grades 3, 5, and 8 when asked to write from a real-life perspective versus a television perspective was studied by Watkins (1988). On one occasion, the child was instructed in this way: "(A television program shows) or (we know) a person who arrived from another country. Write a story about what happens with this person." On another occasion the instructions were as follows: "Two people (we know) or (in a television show) are angry with each other. Write a story about what they do." Complexity was defined as the amount of elaboration and inferential information, compared with the amount of visual, descriptive material, weighted for story length. Students who were low or moderate television viewers wrote more complex real-life (RL) than television (TV) stories, but the opposite was true for high viewers. The greater complexity of television stories written by heavy viewers in Grade 8 was particularly noticeable (TV mean 265, RL mean 86). For both third and fifth graders, the difference between the RL and TV complexity scores was greatest for low viewers and smallest for high viewers. "Especially for older children, televised events and characters appear to take on lives of their own, often represented in more interesting and elaborate ways than parallel people and events supposedly from real life" (Watkins, 1988, p. 181). This suggested to Watkins that because of TV's more superficial representational system, heavy viewers may lag behind light viewers in understanding the subtleties involved in human interactions. Whereas there were differences in story complexity related to age and usual amount of TV viewed, children who watched more TV did not differ substantially from those who watched less in the content they depicted. Overall, three times as many TV as RL stories included the violent use of weapons. This was expected to be especially significant for the angry stories, but it was not. No character in the TV stories traveled to escape, whereas almost half the real-life foreigners did so, and whereas the real-life story foreigners were most likely to have a positive experience, over 60% of the TV foreigners experienced rejection and failure.

Another study (Peirce, 1983) focused on both the creative (fantasy, elaboration of creative ideas, use of dialogue and point of view) and structural (grammar and so forth) aspects of the writing abilities of fifth, seventh, eighth, and ninth graders in Florida. The author reported details of the results (which I describe later in this chapter under the heading *School Achievement*) only for the structural writing abilities but said the results for creative writing were similar and correlated. In brief, hours of TV viewing was the most important, and negative, predictor of writing abilities. Both book reading and parental interest in the child's use of books and TV contributed positively to creative writing scores, although not as strongly as TV viewing. This pattern of results held up even after parent's educational level was controlled.

Comparative Studies of Media as a Stimulus to Creativity

Whereas the work I've reviewed so far asked whether television has an impact on creative thinking and problem solving and whether use of TV differs according to creativity, other researchers have asked whether some media are better than others at stimulating children's imagination or fantasy on a short-term basis. For example, Greenfield, Geber, Beagles-Roos, Farrar, and Gat (1981) asked 6- to 11-year-olds who had listened to an incomplete story on radio or television to "tell a story about what you think will happen next" (p. 7). The radio presentation stimulated more ideas the researchers judged to be novel, whereas the children who had seen the televised version based their conclusions more directly on the story. In another study, students in Grades 6 and 7 had to invent solutions to a series of problems (Meline, 1976). They were given sample solutions for each problem through either solely verbal media (audiotape or printed text) or through audiovisual media. The solutions invented by students given the solely verbal media were rated as more creative (more stimulus-free and transformational ideas) than the solutions of students in the videotape group, who stuck more closely to the facts and concepts provided.

In a third study (Runco & Pezdek, 1984), children in Grades 3 and 6 listened to or saw one of two stories (*A Story, A Story,* which is an African folktale, or *Strega Nona,* about a magical old woman). A female narrator created a new soundtrack for the color animated videotapes, and that same soundtrack was used for the radio version. After listening to and watching the story individually, the child was given an adaptation of the creativity task, "Just Suppose" (Torrance, 1974), with 5 minutes to answer a specific set of "Just Suppose" questions about the story. Each child's responses were scored for ideational fluency (number of ideas), flexibility (number of distinct, different conceptual categories of ideas), and originality (number of unique or statistically infrequent ideas relative to the complete sample). Creativity scores were not related to verbal ability scores, and there were no differences for any of the three creativity scores between children who received the radio versus television story versions at either the third or sixth grade levels. Thus, whereas Greenfield et al. (1981) found that a story presented on radio stimulated more novel ideas than did a story on television, and Meline (1976) found solely verbal media to be superior to audiovisual media, Runco and Pezdek (1984) found no difference. They suggested that the three studies, which used different measures of imagination and creativity, may have been assessing different cognitive processes. They also emphasized that their three measures of divergent thinking reflect a "trait" theory of creativity, in which performance would be expected to be relatively stable rather than susceptible to short-term influence. They pointed out, in addition, that none of the three studies tested the possibility that creativity may be influenced significantly by longer term media exposure. These points may be important for understanding the results of these three studies in relation to our findings for Notel, Unitel, and Multitel (Harrison & Williams, 1986). Like Runco and Pezdek (1984), we used ideational fluency and originality measures of creativity, albeit different ones, but whereas theirs was a study of short-term exposure, ours was a study of long-term exposure.

In a follow-up study to her 1981 work, Greenfield and her colleagues (Greenfield, Farrar, & Beagles-Roos, 1986) responded to the points made by Runco and Pezdek (1984), which I described earlier, about their different findings. In the 1986 follow-up, children at two different age levels (Grades 1-2 vs. 3-4) were given one incomplete story in a radio format and another in a television format, rather than only one or the other (as in Greenfield et al., 1981, and in Runco & Pezdek, 1984). To make the study more readily comparable to the Runco and Pezdek (1984) study, the same stories (*A Story, A Story* and *Strega Nona*) were used. To be rated as imaginative, story completions had to introduce new elements that were not part of the incomplete versions. The radio versions stimulated imagination more than did the television versions. Moreover, students who heard the radio story first showed enhanced imagination in responding to their subsequent television story, whereas seeing the TV story first seemed to depress imagination for the subsequent radio story.

The enhancing versus diminishing effect of presenting the radio versus television story first also occurred in a subsequent study (Greenfield & Beagles-Roos, 1988) with African American and white children in Grades 1 and 2 and 3 and 4 from middle- and working-class families. There were two radio and two TV versions of two incomplete stories, with each child exposed to one radio and one TV story. Again, radio stimulated more imaginative story completions on average (especially for children who heard the radio story first and for white children). Greenfield and her colleagues (1986) suggested that Runco and Pezdek (1984) may have obtained a different pattern of results—that is, no difference in the extent to which radio and TV stimulated imagination—because their procedure elicited so little creative imagination (a mean of less than one response per child vs. eight in the Greenfield et al., 1986 study) that media differences could not manifest themselves. To solve this potential problem, Greenfield and her colleagues used incomplete stories, because they had found in pilot work that children who were given a complete story, as in Runco and Pezdek's study, did not elaborate further. They also noted that Runco and Pezdek's instructions may have oriented the children toward problem solving (one right answer) rather than creative thinking (in which an unlimited number of equally "right" responses would be sought) and that they may have created a serious rather than a playful tone. A relaxed, playful atmosphere has the effect of stimulating creative thinking (as Wallach & Kogan, 1965, demonstrated). Greenfield and her colleagues (1986) concluded that their results support McLuhan's (1964) contention that "the medium is the message" (p. 23)—that is, that there are some specific effects related to the content of the stories, as the Singers have found (e.g., Tower, Singer, Singer, & Biggs, 1979), but the more general effects are due to the medium in which the content is presented—that is, radio versus television.

A final consideration when comparing the effectiveness of different media for stimulating children's creativity or imagination is the evidence of developmental differences in children's ability to understand the story or narrative and to remember the temporal order of its events, depending on the medium of presentation. In one study, for example, children aged 5 to 6, 8 to 9, and 10 to 12 heard or saw an audio-only, video-only, or audiovisual presentation of a story (Hoffner, Cantor, & Thorson, 1988). The 5- to 6-year-olds in the video-only group did more poorly on comprehension questions and did not remember the temporal order of events (as tested by a picture-ordering task) as well as did their age-mates in the audio-only and audio-visual groups or as well as did the older students in all three groups. Thus, perhaps contrary to intuitive wisdom, young children found it more difficult to understand and integrate the temporal aspects of a narrative when the story was presented visually than when there was a verbal component to the presentation. As these researchers pointed out, the visual-only condition of this study displayed rapidly changing still drawings, and young children may better understand characters and events shown in motion. Nevertheless, to the extent that children's ability to understand the order of events in a story is limited by any medium, their ability to respond creatively or imaginatively to the story would also likely be limited. In this study, comprehension of the audio-only and audiovisually presented stories was equally good, but some other researchers (e.g., Gibbons, Anderson, Smith, Field, & Fischer, 1986) have found audiovisual presentations to be superior.

Mindfulness and Mindlessness

The work of Langer and Piper (1988) on mindfulness and mindlessness in how viewers watch television seems relevant to this discussion of creativity.

Mindfulness involves the process of "drawing distinctions, creating categories, making the unknown known, or making the novel familiar" (p. 250), whereas in *mindlessness,* individuals rely on rigid distinctions or on "familiarity without an awareness of other ways the object (person, event, idea) might exist" (p. 250). Langer and Piper asked 20- to 60-year-olds to watch one television program of their choice each day for a week. Half were told that television is often relaxing, because it is familiar, which may make people feel secure and enable them to relax. They were asked to watch television in a familiar way. The other half, the mindful group, were told to watch TV from a different perspective each night, their own and then one the researchers suggested (e.g., a lawyer, a child). The two groups differed on a posttest. In particular, "several converging measures in this study suggested that watching television in a mindful way apparently results in greater flexibility in one's thinking" (p. 255). This could be interpreted as additional evidence, under certain conditions, that television has the potential to stimulate some aspects of creative thinking.

Imaginative or Fantasy Play

As the APA Task Force's report (Huston et al., 1992) points out, "any casual observer of children is well aware that television characters and content serve as the basis for a great deal of imaginative play" (p. 90). On one hand, Anderson and Collins (1988) have argued that it is arbitrary to decide that one type of imagining is of higher quality than another. On the other hand, there is some evidence that the kind of imaginative play in which children engage can be influenced by television content. In my opinion, researchers who reach this conclusion do not necessarily argue, as Anderson and Collins (1988) implied they did, that certain types of imagining are better than others.

Several studies of the potential impact of television on young children's imagination have been conducted at Yale University by the Singers (e.g., Singer & Singer, 1981, 1983, 1986, 1990; Tower et al., 1979; Zuckerman, Singer, & Singer, 1980). In one study, 4-year-olds were randomly assigned to watch *Mister Rogers' Neighborhood* (MR), *Sesame Street* (SS), or neutral films about animals, health, and nature (N) half an hour per day for 10 days. Their imaginative play, defined as the extent to which they transcended reality (e.g., by using one object to represent another, adding symbolic vocalizations, or introducing a story line) was observed before and after the viewing period. "Both television programs helped the initially low-imagination children improve, whereas the films did not; MR helped them particularly in developing their imaginative play" (Tower et al., 1979, p. 278). In another, longitudinal study of preschoolers who were followed up into the early elementary school years, the Singers found that children who were more imaginative at age 8, either in their block play or in their responses to inkblots, had a history of watching less television and had parents who described themselves as imaginative and creative (Singer & Singer, 1983). In another study, third, fourth, and fifth graders who were rated by their teachers as more imaginative had higher IQ scores and watched fewer fantasy-violent TV programs (e.g., *The Incredible Hulk*) than did their peers who were rated as less imaginative in their play, suggesting that "fantasy violent programs may inhibit or take the place of imaginative play or imaginative behavior" (Zuckerman et al., 1980 p. 173).

Patricia Greenfield and her colleagues have used the following definition of imagination in several studies of media effects: Imagination is any form of representational activity that creates entities or events not found in the current or immediately preceding situation (Greenfield & Beagles-Roos, 1988; Greenfield et al., 1987; Greenfield et al., 1986; Greenfield et al., 1993). In their most recent study, they assessed variations in the play of first and second graders according to whether the toys were cartoon related (Smurfs) or not (Trolls) and whether the child had watched a toy-related cartoon (Smurfs) or played a neutral game (connect-the-dots). In a pretest, the children, who were in same-sex pairs, were given a set of four toys (Trolls or Smurfs) and asked to tell a story together using the toys (no time limit). Then, for 10 minutes, they either played the game of connect-the-dots or watched the Smurfs cartoon. Then, in a posttest, they were asked to tell another story using the same toys as in the pretest. Thus, the sequence of events for the experimental group was Smurf toys, Smurf cartoon, Smurf toys; for one control group it was Smurf toys, dot game, Smurf toys; and for the other control group, Troll toys, Smurf cartoon, Troll toys.

Each pair of children received a score for both the pretest and posttest on "transcendent imagination," defined as the extent to which the children's ideas transcended or went beyond the immediate situation—that is, the toys. Playing with a Smurf toy and calling it a "bunny rabbit" would receive a transcendent score, whereas calling it a "baby Smurf" would not. Symbolically creating actions, feelings, mental states, or character dialogue also received credit for transcendent imagination. On the posttest, but not the pretest, transcendent scores were divided into creative and imitative imagination.

Creative imagination transcended both the immediate toy situation and the preceding experimental one (the cartoon or dot game, which is why it could be discerned only on the posttest). If a representation in the story was found in the earlier cartoon or game it was called imitative imagination.

There were no differences among the three groups in transcendent imagination on the pretest. That is, scores for children who told a story about Smurfs (cartoon-related toys) were similar to those for children who told a story about Trolls (neutral toys) on the pretest. On the posttest, the combination of product-based television (Smurf cartoon) and thematically related toys (Smurfs) resulted in the lowest proportion of creative imagination and highest proportion of imitative imagination. The combination of cartoon (Smurfs) plus neutral toys (Trolls) yielded intermediate proportions of creative imagination, and the combination of game (connect-the-dots) plus cartoon-related toys (Smurfs) yielded the highest proportion of creative imagination. This pattern was stronger for the second graders than for the first graders. Some children's stories that were coded as creative came from other media sources (e.g., one pair of children used the Smurfs to reenact *Charlie and the Chocolate Factory*), so as the authors stated, "it is probably more accurate to say that television and program-related toys change the source of imagination, rather than its creativity or quantity" (Greenfield et al., 1993, p. 69).

In their recently published review of research on television's impact on children's fantasy play, van der Voort and Valkenburg (1994) included all research conducted in both North America and Europe up to mid-1992. They noted that earlier reviews (e.g., Anderson & Collins, 1988; Singer, 1982; Singer & Singer, 1981) had dealt in addition with creativity and inner fantasy, whereas they focused just on fantasy play (also interchangeably called "imaginative," "pretend," "dramatic," and "make-believe" play). They also pointed out that Anderson and Collins's (1988) review discussed only a selection of the research. Fantasy play was defined by van der Voort and Valkenburg (1994) as "play in which the child transcends the constraints of reality by acting 'as if.' " Children pretend "that they are someone else, that an object represents something else and/or that the participants are in a different place and time" (p. 27).

As van der Voort and Valkenburg (1994) point out, almost all the research on the relation between television and fantasy play has been done with preschoolers, who, developmentally speaking, most often engage in it (Singer & Singer, 1990). They reviewed the research in four categories:

(1) quasi experimental studies of the influence of television on the amount of time spent in play, (2) qualitative studies of the influence of television on the content of play, (3) correlational studies of the relation between television viewing and fantasy play, and (4) experimental studies of the influence of program characteristics on fantasy play. (p. 29)

They noted that only short-term effects have been studied, so there is a need for research into long-term effects and longitudinal studies. Furthermore, they reviewed a few studies indicating that television's influence on fantasy play may vary with background variables such as gender, socioeconomic status (SES), and predisposition to engage in imaginative play, so further research should explore the potentially moderating role of such variables.

One of van der Voort and Valkenburg's (1994) conclusions, namely that there is evidence that television watching displaces play time in general, seems to me to be only weakly supported by the evidence they reviewed. Two studies of the introduction of television (Maccoby, 1951; Schramm, Lyle, & Parker, 1961) provided some evidence for this conclusion. Another did not (Murray & Kippax, 1978), but van der Voort and Valkenburg (1994) questioned the validity of the time estimates given by children in that study, especially the younger children (van der Voort & Vooijs, 1990). Unfortunately, in Notel, Unitel, and Multitel we did not obtain any information about preschool children or about older children's play, either in general or fantasy play in particular. As van der Voort and Valkenburg (1994) acknowledged, only a portion of total playtime is spent in fantasy play. They did conclude, however, that "when total playtime decreases, the time spent in fantasy play is likely to decrease as well, although this was not investigated" (p. 32) in the studies of the introduction of TV that they reviewed.

The other conclusions drawn by van der Voort and Valkenburg (1994) seem to me to be more strongly supported. In particular, the type of program watched on TV is central to its effects on the content of fantasy play. The results of experimental studies indicate that fantasy play is decreased by programs with a high level of violence and action. It is not clear whether this effect occurs through an arousal mechanism, an anxiety mechanism, or both. In addition, the correlational studies indicate that high exposure to or amount of time spent viewing adventure programs, violent programs, and realistic action programs is associated with lower levels of imaginative play. By contrast, benign, nonviolent children's programs—such as puppet films, *Sesame Street*, and programs with low levels of action and violence—were found neither to increase nor to decrease fantasy play. Although there is no evidence that watching television in general stimulates imaginative play, there is evidence that children's programs specifically designed to stimulate constructive imaginative play (e.g., *Mister Rogers' Neighborhood*) are successful in doing so, particularly for preschoolers who are initially less imaginative (Tower et al., 1979).

Finally, van der Voort and Valkenburg (1994) concluded that although it is clear that television content is used by children in fantasy play both during and after viewing, it has not been established (a) how often children use television elements in their fantasy play; (b) whether television-related play is more or less imaginative than play that is not derived from television; and (c) whether television influences the frequency with which children engage in fantasy play.

Summary

In the natural experiment we studied in Notel, Unitel, and Multitel, we found that the availability of television and normal patterns of viewing, had, on average, a negative effect on creative thinking for both children (Harrison & Williams, 1986) and adults (Suedfeld et al., 1986). We also found that students who performed better on creativity measures tended to participate more in other (non-TV) activities, but in this case, we cannot assess the direction of influence. In other studies, TV viewing has been negatively related to a variety of behaviors related to creative thinking (e.g., Furu, 1971; Gadberry, 1980; Peirce, 1983; Wade, 1971; Watkins, 1988). Researchers who have compared the ability of audiovisual versus other forms of media to stimulate creativity on a short-term basis have obtained mixed results. In several studies radio or other solely verbal media were superior to audiovisual media in stimulating creativity, in others there were no differences, and in a couple of studies, radio had an enhancing effect whereas TV had a diminishing effect on imaginative responses. Research on how adults view TV indicates that it has the potential to stimulate some aspects of creative thinking if watched mindfully rather than mindlessly. Studies of the short-term impact of TV on preschoolers' imaginative or fantasy play indicate that high levels of violence and action have a negative impact, but programs specifically designed to stimulate constructive, imaginative play can have a positive impact. In sum, my review of the literature reveals more evidence of a negative influence of television on creativity and imagination than evidence of no relationship or a positive impact.

Persistence

As a result of growing up with television, are children these days less attentive in school and less able to be focused and task oriented? This widely heard criticism (e.g., Healy, 1990; Postman, 1979; Swerdlow, 1981; Winn, 1985) is sometimes tied to the emphasis on the entertainment rather than informative functions of most of North American television programming. Some teachers say, for example, that they find it hard to gain and keep children's attention in the classroom and that they cannot compete with the slick production values to which children are accustomed by the time they start school at age 5 or 6. Are these concerns and criticisms supported by any research evidence? The answer is, "not much," but that is primarily because of lack of evidence rather than because of evidence that supports or contradicts popular claims regarding persistence and task-orientation.

Other Research and Reviews

If there is any effect of television on persistence, it seems to me most likely to be a relatively indirect, longer-term effect. After watching a particularly action-filled program with lots of boisterous music and sound effects a young child may be wound up and less able to concentrate or focus on a task, but any such effect seems likely to be relatively short-lived. In one of the few studies of short-term exposure, preschoolers watched an hour of relatively fast-paced or slow-paced programming (Anderson, Levin, & Lorch, 1977). There were no differences between the two groups in attention or perseverance on a task completed after viewing. If short-term effects were at the root of teachers' concern, however, they probably would say that children's persistence is affected when first at school in the morning or when first back at school after going home for lunch, but their concern seems to be broader and to cover most, if not all, of the school day. It seems more likely to me that if television has any effect on persistence, the effect occurs because of the nature of television viewing as the primary leisure activity of children and adults in our society. Turning regularly to television as a relatively easy way to be entertained (easier, for example, than playing some board or other games), to avoid boredom, or both may have the side effect of seeking easy solutions in other situations or giving up more readily when a solution is not found. Or, any possible effect of television on persistence may be even more indirect. Perhaps persistence and task orientation develop as a result of experiencing the rewards that come with persistence, including finding a solution and feeling the pleasure and satisfaction of doing so. If so, the focus and emphasis should be on providing children with such experiences rather than on use of television per se. The type of programming watched and motivation for doing so (e.g., to learn from a program with a "curriculum" intended to inform and educate, perhaps even about task persistence, vs. to relax and be entertained) also strike me as important for any effects that TV may have in this area. The findings of a study by Friedrich and Stein (1973) are consistent with these speculations.

In their field experiment, which was conducted in preschools, Friedrich and Stein (1973) observed self-regulation in free play over a 9-week period. They compared the children's behavior during an initial baseline period (3 weeks); a viewing period (4 weeks) in which the children watched either prosocial programs (*Mister Rogers' Neighborhood*), aggressive cartoons (*Batman, Superman*), or neutral children's films that had little or no aggressive or prosocial content; and a postviewing period (2 weeks). Some of the most clear-cut differences among the three different viewing groups occurred for self-regulation. In general, children who saw aggressive cartoons declined and those who saw the prosocial programs increased. With regard to task persistence in particular, there was an increase in persistence over the study period for high-IQ children who saw *Mister Rogers,* a drop for children who saw neutral films, and a larger drop for those who saw aggressive cartoons, but for lower-IQ children there was few differences among the three groups. Friedrich and Stein (1973) noted that,

> It is possible that these themes are subtle or complex and are more easily grasped by brighter children. It is also likely that bright children have more successes when they do persist at a task, so there may be more environmental reinforcement for them. (p. 57)

The anecdotal belief that heavy TV viewing is associated with poor self-control was one of the topics of interest to the Singers when they studied a group of children longitudinally from the preschool to early elementary years (Singer, Singer, & Rapaczynski, 1984). Observers assessed each child's motoric restlessness during an apparently natural waiting period before an interview. The children who were more restless while waiting had in the previous 3 years been watching more violent television (both realistic and fantasy), had parents who were more tolerant of TV, were brighter or more verbal, and had a mother who described herself as less creative and imaginative. In another aspect of this study, observers assessed self-restraint when the child was asked to be like an "astronaut" and sit quietly for as long as possible. Children who in the preceding years watched more TV, particularly realistic action TV, were less likely to sit quietly for several minutes. This study did not focus on task persistence but did find that restlessness and lack of self-restraint, which would presumably make persistence more difficult, were related to the child's previous television viewing experiences.

The claim that television viewing reduces preschoolers' perseverance, increases their impulsivity, and induces restlessness was assessed in a study of 328 five-year-olds conducted by Collins (1991). Observers noted how long the child worked on a difficult wooden puzzle before looking away, the number of times she or he looked away, and the total time spent on the task. The child also was assessed with the Kansas Reflection-Impulsivity Scale for Preschoolers (KRISP). Prior to these assessments, the child's parent completed a 14-day television viewing diary for the child. The parent also completed the Thomas and Chess (1977) Parent Temperament Questionnaire (PTQ). Given the large number of correlations computed, the pattern of results across 17 program categories indicated no significant relationship between TV exposure and puzzle scores, PTQ distractibility, and PTQ persistence for girls or for boys, and no significant relationship between KRISP errors (impulsivity) for girls. For boys, however, although no single relationship was strong, the more KRISP errors they made, the more they watched live action, commercial, entertainment, and moderate-length content unit programs and the less they watched general informative, child informative, public broadcasting, Sesame Street, and short content unit programs. It is quite possible, of course, that more reflective (less impulsive) boys choose to watch more programs in the latter than in the former categories. Children whose parents reported that they watched more total hours of television per week were reported by their parents on the PTQ as more physically active in terms of level, frequency, and tempo. Within the group of boys who spent the same total time with TV, those who spent more time with Mister Rogers' Neighborhood had lower activity level scores than did those who spent less time with *Mister Rogers,* but this was not true for girls. As Collins (1991) pointed out,

> *if* television induces restlessness, specific program choices may have an impact on the size of the effect. Since these correlations cannot establish that television played a causal role, it is also possible that less active boys prefer to spend more time with *Mister Rogers' Neighborhood.* (p. 8)

Taken together, these findings provide some hints of a link between exposure to certain kinds of programming and activity level/impulsivity/restlessness for preschool boys, but the direction of influence cannot be determined. This particular sample of 5-year-olds was relatively high in IQ, with a mean higher than 73% of the normative sample for the Peabody Picture Vocabulary Test (PPVT), which is a verbal measure of IQ. They also were reported to watch considerably less TV per week (15.1 hours) than children in many other studies.[10] These characteristics of the sample may have reduced the likelihood of finding relationships between TV exposure and the other measures.

Some additional evidence that TV viewing and impulsivity may be linked, in this case for middle-school-aged children, was found in a Canadian study (Anderson & Maguire, 1978). Teachers rated their students on seven traits associated with hyperactivity (e.g., impulsiveness, irritability). These scores were significantly correlated with a measure assessing regular viewing of violent TV programs by students in both Grades 3 and 4 and 5 and 6. For the older group the behavioral impulsivity measure was also significantly related to viewing serious programs, situation comedies, and total viewing. Again, however, no causal inference can be made, and the correlations may very well reflect only program preferences.

Results From Notel, Unitel, and Multitel

Unfortunately, we did not have the foresight to assess task persistence by children in Notel, Unitel, and Multitel. Our finding, described earlier, that children in Notel obtained higher creativity scores on the Alternate Uses task before television was available than they did after 2 years of regular viewing and than did Unitel and Multitel children in both phases of the study, could potentially be taken as indirect evidence of greater persistence, because giving more alternate uses to a common household item requires sticking with the task and thinking up more ideas. But we did not find that Notel children in Phase 1 obtained higher scores for the Pattern Meanings task, and although it differs from the Alternate Uses task in other ways, it seems similar from the point of view of persistence.

We did measure persistence in the creative problem-solving task given to adults in Notel, Unitel, and Multitel in their homes (Suedfeld et al., 1986). As I noted earlier, some residents of each town did solve the Duncker Candle Problem in Phase 1, before Notel had television reception, but most did not solve it (59.6% in Notel, 74.5% in Unitel, and 70% in Multitel). Two years later, almost no one (only 4% across the three towns) solved the Nine Dot Problem.

In both phases, we took note of the length of time each person who was eventually unsuccessful continued to try to solve the problem before giving up. In Phase 1, Notel residents persisted statistically significantly longer (401 seconds) than did Unitel residents (280 seconds) and marginally significantly longer than did Multitel residents (332 seconds). Unitel and Multitel did not differ. Two years later, on the Nine Dot Problem, the pattern was similar; Notel residents persisted significantly longer (293 seconds) than did Unitel residents (264 seconds) and marginally longer than did Multitel residents (277 seconds). Again, Unitel and Multitel did not differ. Because the tasks used in Phases 1 and 2 were different, any comparisons across the phases must be made with great caution. It is interesting to note, nevertheless, that the most discrepant figure among the six does seem to be the Notel adults' mean persistence for 401 seconds before television reception was available.

If the finding in Phase 1 that Notel residents persisted longest in trying to solve the Duncker Candle Problem is attributable in part to their lack of television, then the finding that this also was true after 2 years of regular viewing indicates that once the tendency to persist when trying to solve problems is established, it is not quickly lost (or it persists). Helping children to persist with tasks and projects when they are frustrated and want to give up quickly will probably increase the likelihood that they will eventually be successful, and it may also help them learn to persist more generally in the face of difficulty. Again, as with other potential indirect effects of television, the focus must be on the other activities with potentially positive effects rather than on the use of television per se.

Summary

In sum, there has been relatively little research on the role of television in children's persistence at problem solving or impulsivity. The findings from the natural experiment in Notel, Unitel, and Multitel suggest that in the absence of television, adults may develop a tendency to persist longer before giving up on a difficult problem, and once that tendency is established, it is not readily lost. The results of a field experiment in preschools suggest that some types of television programming (*Mister Rogers*) can facilitate persistence for some children (in this case, high-IQ children), but typical programming for children also can reduce perseverance or increase impulsiveness (Friedrich & Stein, 1973). Some of the results obtained for preschoolers by Collins (1991) and for middle-school-aged children by Anderson and Maguire (1978) are consistent with these statements, although the correlational nature of the data does not permit the same kinds of causal inferences. Others have found no link between television viewing and preschoolers' persistence following short-term (Anderson et al., 1977) exposure. More evidence is needed before we can conclude that television viewing affects persistence, and in any event, it makes more sense to focus on determining what can be done to help children and adults develop the habit of persistence in the face of adversity.

Television Viewing and IQ

Other Research and Reviews

As others reviewing the literature on the relationship between IQ and television viewing have noted (e.g., Ball, Palmer, & Millward, 1986), it is complex and difficult to interpret causally. In their research in 10 communities in Canada and the United States assessing the uses and effects of television following its introduction in the 1950s, Schramm, Lyle, and Parker (1961) found that children who scored one standard deviation or more (115 or more) above the norm of 100 on IQ tests tended to be heavier viewers of television up to about age 11, but for older students the opposite was true. They suggested that bright young children may simply do more of everything, including reading, listening to records and radio, as well as TV viewing. Similar results were found in the U.S. Surgeon General's report for Lorge-Thorndike IQ scores (Lyle & Hoffman, 1972); higher-IQ Grade 6 students were among the heaviest viewers whereas higher-IQ Grade 10 students were more likely to be among the lighter viewers. One interesting hypothesis to explain these results was offered by Ball et al. (1986): Most television programs may be

> matched to the interests and abilities of bright younger children, who outgrow this level over time. Meanwhile, less bright children grow into this level. In any case, chronological age seems to be a complicating factor in analyzing the relationship between amount of viewing and intelligence. (p. 130)

In their review of the literature, Wartella, Alexander, and Lemish (1979) pointed out that whereas 15 years earlier mental ability tended to be related to TV use, surveys in the late 1970s (e.g., Comstock, Chaffee, Katzman, McCombs, & Roberts, 1978) indicated this was no longer the case. Wartella et al. (1979) suggested that one result of the increasing ubiquity of television may have been to reduce such differences (as well as those for socioeconomic status) found in earlier studies. What does more recent research indicate?

One of the more recent findings is that parental mediation of TV viewing varies with the child's IQ. A study by Abelman (1987) of 364 gifted (Stanford-Binet IQ score of 126 or more) and 386 average fourth graders focused on this issue. He was particularly interested in the role of child characteristics for parent perceptions of the impact of TV on their children and the type of mediation strategies they use. He had previously reported (Abelman, 1984) that

> in comparison with intellectually average or "traditional" children, gifted children: (a) spend nearly as many hours in front of the television set; (b) display a similar tendency to consume more adult-oriented fare than children's programming; (c) are more likely to watch television alone; and (d) have an equivalently high level of perceived reality of prime-time television's character portrayals. (p. 217)

In the 1987 study Abelman found that, by and large, parents of both gifted and traditional children did not consider television to be an important influence in their children's lives worthy of much consideration or intervention. They did differ, however, in the nature of their interventions. Parents of traditional children were more likely to perceive television as primarily influencing their child's behavior and to react by restricting it, whereas parents of gifted 9-year-olds were more likely to see television as influencing how their children think and what they think about. They also were more likely to say they speak with their children about the impact of television and to explain the mechanisms behind television programming than to restrict its use. In her review of this study, Singer (1993) noted that she and her colleagues had evidence that when parents take an active stance toward the use of television, children can glean more information from it (Desmond, Singer, Singer, Calam, & Colimore, 1985). Elsewhere, they have reported that parents of school-age children who are heavy TV viewers interact relatively little with their children when the TV is on, let alone engage in mediation of the child's viewing (Desmond, Singer, & Singer, 1990).

Results From Notel, Unitel, and Multitel

In our natural experiment we used several measures of IQ. First, we obtained general test IQ scores from the permanent school records of all students in Grades 1 through 12 for whom they were available. If the child had more than one score, the mean was used. These scores were based on group tests administered in the schools, which we and others readily acknowledge to be inferior to individually administered measures because the group tests depend considerably on reading ability. In addition, other relevant factors, such as fatigue, attention, and so forth, are not part of the assessment. Across the three towns, group IQ scores were available for 631 students (Harrison & Williams, 1986, p. 103). Their mean (101.7) and standard deviation (13.9) are close to those (100, 15) for the standardization samples of most tests, indicating that our sample was representative of North American students with regard to IQ.

We used the group scores primarily as a control when assessing the role of television for other variables potentially related to IQ, such as reading and creativity, but we also asked whether amount of television watched varied according to group IQ test scores (Harrison & Williams, 1986). We divided the students (combining across the three towns) into four IQ groups: those with scores one or more standard deviation below the test mean of 100 (i.e., those with scores below 85), those with scores from 85 to 99, from 100 to 115, and above 115. In Phase 2, 2 years after Notel obtained television reception, the mean hours of TV viewed per week for these four groups were 29.4, 28.0, 25.8, and 23.7, respectively, forming a statistically significant linear trend.

As I described earlier, some other researchers have found that children who vary in IQ watch different amounts of television, and the amounts vary with their age levels. We therefore asked whether the IQ-related difference in Phase 2 TV viewing varied according to town and grade level (grouping Grades 3-5,

6-8, and 9-12 to provide sufficiently large groups for the analyses) (Williams & Boyes, 1986). For this analysis two levels of IQ were used, 101 or higher and 100 or below. In the higher-IQ group, students in Grades 6 through 12 in the three towns watched approximately equal amounts of television, but in Grades 3 through 5, Notel students watched fewer hours per week (22.6) than both Unitel (28.3) and Multitel (31.6) students, who did not differ. The opposite was true for the lower-IQ students, with no town differences for Grades 3 through 5 or 6 through 9. In Grades 9 through 12, lower-IQ Multitel students watched more TV (30.0 hours) than both Notel (19.5) and Unitel (23.6) lower-IQ students. There is evidence from other studies that television viewing tends to decrease in adolescence as students spend more time with peers and popular music (Rosengren & Windahl, 1989). Our findings indicate that this characteristic dip in viewing occurred for the higher-IQ students in Grades 9 through 12 in all three towns, as well as for the lower-IQ students in Notel and Unitel, where only one channel was available. The lower-IQ Grade 9 through 12 Multitel students, however, maintained a high level of viewing relative to their peers.

When we conducted correlational analyses to ask whether individual students with higher IQ scores tended to use television and other media differently in Phase 2 than did their peers with lower scores, a very interesting pattern emerged (Williams & Boyes, 1986, p. 252). For students who grew up with television in Unitel and Multitel, students with higher IQ scores reported more radio listening; more book, magazine, and newspaper reading; and less comic reading[11] than did lower-IQ students. They did not differ in amount of TV viewing (perhaps because the pattern of relationships between IQ and TV viewing varied with age level, as just discussed, so that overall, when the data were combined, these patterns canceled each other). By contrast, in Notel, the opposite was true. IQ scores were not as consistently related to use of print media (but they were positively related to one measure of book reading and to newspaper reading) and not related to radio listening. They were, however, significantly negatively related to TV viewing. That is, Notel students with higher IQ scores tended to watch less TV in Phase 2 than did Notel students with lower IQ scores. Thus, in our study, the relationship between IQ and use of television as well as other media varied according to whether TV was unavailable (Notel, Phase 1), recently had become available (Notel, Phase 2), or was available throughout childhood (Unitel and Multitel, in both phases).

In my opinion, one of our most intriguing sets of findings concerns the relationships among IQ scores, reading ability, print use, and the availability of TV. First, before television was available in Notel—that is, in Phase 1—IQ scores were not related to print use (Williams & Boyes, 1986, p. 25) as they were in Unitel and Multitel (and as they are in most studies). Second, before TV, Notel IQ scores also were not related to performance on an individual measure of fluent reading skill (Corteen & Williams, 1986), as they were in Unitel and Multitel in both phases, in Notel 2 years later, and in most studies. And third, although Notel students' IQ scores were significantly related to their Phase 1 group reading test scores, they were significantly less strongly related to those scores than was true for Unitel and Multitel students (Corteen & Williams, 1986). This relative independence of IQ from reading skill and print use in the absence of television stands in strong contrast to the usual finding of substantial interrelations among IQ, reading skill, and amount and type of reading, and it underscores the complexity of trying to ferret out the role of television for reading and other aspects of school achievement (Comstock, 1989; Neuman, 1991). Our findings for Notel in Phase 1 have prompted me to wonder whether one of the indirect effects of television is to produce more reading dropouts than when it is not available (Williams, 1986c).

> It is tempting to speculate that when television is available, the less intelligent students, who have the most difficulty learning to read, most readily abandon reading practice in favor of TV viewing. As they grow older they continue to watch more television and read less print because they are poor readers. They do, however, read more comics by comparison with their brighter peers, since these are less demanding of reading skill and mental effort. In the absence of television, less intelligent children do practice reading enough that, on average, their competence does not differ from that of their brighter peers. They also use print media similarly. When television arrives, however, they watch more than their brighter classmates. Two years after the arrival of TV, they also read books and newspapers less frequently. These speculations, derived from our findings, are offered as hypotheses to be pursued in further research. (Williams & Boyes, 1986, p. 244)

In our natural experiment we used three other measures related to IQ, in addition to the standardized group tests already discussed. We gave the vocabulary subtest of the Wechsler Intelligence Scale for Children (WISC) to students in Grades 4 and 7 in Phase 1 and to those in Grades 4, 6, 7, and 9 in Phase 2 (Harrison & Williams, 1986). This is a productive test of vocabulary that requires the child to provide definitions for a series of words. In addition to being a measure of vocabulary, however, this test can also be considered to be a measure of IQ, because it is the subtest of the WISC most strongly related not only to the overall verbal IQ score but also to the full scale or total IQ score. The same students also were given the WISC Block Design test as a measure of spatial ability (Harrison & Williams, 1986). Again, however, this can be considered to be a measure of IQ because it is the WISC perform-ance measure most highly correlated with both the overall performance IQ score and the full scale (total) IQ score. Within our sample, averaging across the three towns, scores on these two WISC measures were not only signifi-cantly related, but both were also significantly and fairly strongly correlated with the group test IQ scores from the students' permanent school records, providing further evidence of their role as a measure of IQ.

The pattern of findings across the towns and phases for the WISC Vocabulary and Block Design scores was not consistent with the hypothesis that television influences performance on verbal or spatial measures of intel-ligence, either positively or negatively. Given that children's performance on these measures tends to be relatively stable over the school years,[12] and given that they were developed to measure intelligence, which is conceptualized as a relatively stable trait, it seems much more likely that any relationship observed between television viewing and performance on these measures occurs because students who vary in intelligence or, to be more specific, in IQ as measured by these tests, use television differently.

For scores from individual IQ measures, did use of television vary with IQ?[13] We divided the Notel students in Grades 4 and 7 in Phase 1 into those who were above and below the median for the WISC vocabulary score and found that 2 years later those who had been below the median watched significantly more TV (26.3 hours per week) than those above it (19.0 hours). We did the same analysis for the Block Design scores but found no significant difference in Phase 2 TV viewing for those below (24.2) and above (22.0) the Phase 1 median. When we combined the data from all three towns and formed three groups, those who scored one standard deviation or more above the mean in Phase 1 on the WISC vocabulary subtest watched less TV in Phase 2 (19.0 hours per week) than both those in the middle range (27.0 hours) and those who had scored one standard deviation or more below the vocabulary mean (29.2 hours); the latter two groups did not differ, but there was a significant linear trend for the three means.

Our final measures of IQ were, again, measures of vocabulary as well. They were given[14] only in Phase 1, and only in Notel and Unitel, to students in kindergarten and Grade 1. They were the Peabody Picture Vocabulary Test (PPVT, a receptive measure of vocabulary in which the child points to one of four pictures that best illustrates the word said by the interviewer) and the vocabulary test from the Stanford-Binet (S-B) test of intelligence (which, like that from the WISC, requires definitions of words). As was the case for the WISC Vocabulary and Block Design scores, the set of findings for the PPVT and S-B vocabulary measures did not support the hypothesis that the availability of television influences performance on these tests. Unfortunately, we were unable to ask whether children who varied on these measures used television differently, as we did not have adequate TV viewing information on these young children.

Summary

The natural experiment in Notel, Unitel, and Multitel provides some reasonably strong evidence that children's use of television and other media varies with IQ, as measured both individually and by group tests. Other research on this issue has yielded mixed results, and there is some evidence that the IQ-TV viewing relationship may depend on the age of the child. There is no evidence that availability or use of television affects performance on IQ measures.

School Achievement

There is disagreement among those who have reviewed the research evidence concerning the relationship between television viewing and literacy, broadly speaking, and more narrowly, the impact of television on school achievement. I will now review that complicated set of evidence, pointing out areas of disagreement. I want to note at the outset that although they disagree about the extent to which charges against the medium are well- or ill-founded—that is, the amount and consistency of evidence that television affects school achievement—there is some agreement among researchers in this area. They all say, in one way or another, that television is neither inherently good nor bad, neither "a threat" nor "a complement to school" (Jönsson, 1986), "neither villain nor redeemer" (Neuman, 1991, p. xiii; Williams, Haertel, Haertel, & Walberg, 1982, p. 35); its impact depends on how it is used.

Whether television helps children raise or lower their academic achievement depends on a lot more than simply how much they watch: It depends on what they view, what they bring to the TV set, and what is happening in the rest of their lives. (Mielke, 1994, p. 361)

For example, the longitudinal research conducted with preschoolers by Aletha Huston, John Wright, and their students at the Center for Research on the Influences of Television on Children (CRITC) at the University of Kansas clearly indicates that informative and educational programming intended for children, and *Sesame Street* in particular, effectively teaches vocabulary and other skills that are important for school readiness and entry (see Chapter 2 of this volume; see also Rice, Huston, Truglio, & Wright, 1990; Wright, 1995). Much of the debate on the relation of TV viewing to school achievement, however, focuses on general viewing and on older children.

Other Research and Reviews

In reviewing the evidence on the relationship between television viewing and school achievement, Gerbner, Gross, Morgan, and Signorielli (1984) stated the following:

It is tempting to connect the apparent decline in school performance with the rise of television and let that be the end of the discussion. The problem with such "self-evident," "commonsense" conclusions is that many other things have happened in the last 30 years that might account for the decline. (p. 10)

They went on to offer their criticisms of some of the evidence presented by the Television Information Office (TIO) of the National Association of Broadcasters in the United States (Briller & Miller, 1984) and then stated that

the central flaw in the TIO presentation is the way in which it frames the issues. It asks, in essence, whether television is *the* cause of declines in academic performance: If there is a decline in . . . [children's] ability to read and in their academic achievement, is it the fault of television? The answer is, "of course not." The question that should be asked—one that leads to a sharply different answer—is this: Does television viewing exert an independent influence on academic achievement, and if so, for whom, under what conditions, and in which direction? (p. 10)

I am inclined to modify this last question slightly from "exert an independent influence on" to "play any role, however indirect, for" academic achievement. Let's consider the evidence.

In the United States, the National Assessment of Educational Progress (NAEP) obtained information in 1979-1980 about the TV viewing habits, reading skills, leisure time reading, and homework of more than 20,000 nine-year-olds, 30,000 thirteen-year-olds, and 25,000 seventeen-year-olds. Some of the results were summarized by Searls, Mead, and Ward (1985). They reported that, "students at each age who watch over 4 hours of TV daily display the poorest reading skills. Beyond that, the relationship of TV watching and academic achievement depends heavily on the age of the students" (p. 160).

> Moderate amounts of spare time reading do appear to have a favorable impact on reading skills. Highest reading levels occur among groups that combine 1 to 2 hours of reading with what appears to be the optimal amount of TV for their age group—3 to 4 hours for 9-year-olds, 1 to 2 hours for 13-year-olds, and under 1 hour for 17-year-olds. (p. 162)

It is important to note that the association they reported between spare time reading and reading skills indicates only that better readers read more. It does make sense that reading practice through spare time reading would, over time, result in improved reading skill, but a longitudinal study in which children were assessed on more than one occasion would be required to sort out that type of causal association. The Swedish study I describe later in this chapter does provide that kind of evidence (Jönsson, 1986; Rosengren & Windahl, 1989). The finding in this U.S. study (Searls et al., 1985) that the heaviest TV viewers (over 4 hours per day) had the poorest reading skills will be echoed in most of the other studies I review in this chapter.

In a national study conducted in the United States in Grades 4, 8, and 11 in 1984, the relationship between television viewing habits and reading achievement was assessed (National Assessment of Educational Progress, 1986). At all three grade levels, students who reported watching 6 or more hours of television a day were poorer readers than those who watched less. For Grade 11, students who reported watching TV 2 hours or less were better readers than those who reported 3 to 5 hours of viewing. This pattern also held for Grades 4 and 8 but the differences were smaller. The negative relationship between excessive viewing (6 or more hours) and reading performance was worst for white students and those with well-educated parents.

A study of a nationally representative longitudinal sample of Grade 8 students in public and private schools in the United States, the National Education Study, began in 1988, with follow-ups planned for 1990 and subsequent 2-year intervals (Office of Educational Research and Improvement, 1990). Overall, 19% of the students (but 30% of Hispanic, African American, and American Indian students) were not proficient in basic mathematics skills for everyday tasks. Basic reading tasks could not be performed by 14% of all eighth graders, but for those who usually speak a language other than English, the proportion was 30%. Typical students reported spending four times as many hours each week watching television as doing homework.

In part because of these 1988 results, the United States began a campaign in 1990 to increase educational performance. Data from the 1991 National Assessment of Educational Progress report, which focused on 9- and 17-year-olds, were compared with six previous assessments in science (done between 1969-1970 and 1990), five in mathematics (1973 to 1990), and six in reading (1971 to 1990) (Office of Educational Research and Improvement, 1992; U.S. Department of Education, 1991). In math and science, 9-year-olds in 1990 did somewhat better than in the past. In mathematics, 28% in 1990 could add, subtract, multiply, and divide using whole numbers and could solve one-step problems, compared with 20% in 1978. In science, 31% could understand and apply general information from the life and physical sciences, compared with 26% in 1977. With regard to reading, however, the percentage (18%) who could search for specific information, interrelate ideas, and make generalizations was no better than in 1971. Three activities that could potentially be related to achievement were homework, reading, and television viewing.

The percentage of 9-year-olds who reported that they did not receive daily homework assignments was about the same in 1990 (31%) as in 1984 (36%). The percentage who said that they "read for fun" on their own time every day was about the same in 1990 (54%) as in 1984. Fewer, however, reported reading books, magazines, or newspapers weekly in 1990 (34%) than in 1984 (42%), and fewer reported in 1990 (29%) than in 1971 (39%) that they had four or more types of reading materials (newspapers, magazines, books, and encyclopedias) at home.

The proportion of 9-year-olds who reported watching 3 or more hours of television per day increased from 55% in 1982 to 62% in 1990, and in 1990, 23% reported watching 6 or more hours every day. The report noted that given

1 hour to go to and from school, 6.5 hours in school, and 10 hours sleeping, a child who watches television 6 hours has only $^1/_2$ hour remaining for everything else—breakfast, dinner, sports, play, homework, or reading (Office of Educational Research and Improvement, 1992).

In 1990, mathematics scores tended to be higher for children who reported watching less television than for those who reported watching 6 or more hours per day. At age 9, the mean mathematics scores for those reporting 0 to 2 hours, 3 to 5 hours, and 6+ hours of TV per day were 312, 300, and 289, respectively. At age 13, the analogous figures were 278, 272, and 259, and at age 17, 230, 234, and 220. The report acknowledges that these are not large differences, in absolute terms, but states that they do suggest a trend (Office of Educational Research and Improvement, 1992). I want to emphasize that when evaluating such findings we cannot make causal inferences. Students who do better on mathematics tests may use television differently from those who do more poorly, or they may use different bases (which may be more or less accurate) for reporting their TV use. Students who spend a lot of time with television may do less mathematics homework or other activities, such as number-based games, which might facilitate mathematics performance. Or some other factor, such as intelligence or family background and attitudes, may influence both performance on mathematics tests and time spent with television versus other activities.

In California, 99% of the 6th and 12th graders were assessed in 1980 on television exposure and mathematical, reading, and writing ability (California Assessment Program, 1981). Amount of television viewing and all three scores were negatively correlated at both grade levels, but Comstock (1989) noted some important qualifications. First, as other researchers have noted (e.g., Rosengren & Windahl, 1989, for the Swedish study discussed later in this chapter), SES was also negatively and more strongly related to achievement than was TV viewing. Second, the strongest negative relationship between amount of TV viewed and achievement occurred in the highest SES category. This may reflect greater heterogeneity of use of leisure time because more resources are available to do other things. Third, the negative TV viewing-achievement relationship was stronger in Grade 12 than in Grade 6. Fourth, at the lowest SES level, the inverse relationship between TV exposure and achievement was barely observable, and there was some evidence of a rise in achievement before a decline in relation to TV viewing appeared. As I suggest at the end of this chapter, when other resources are very limited, television may be an especially important source of stimulation and information. Fifth, for students with limited fluency in English, TV viewing was positively related to achievement. Television undoubtedly facilitates second language acquisition for viewers who need or want to communicate in that second language, as I note later in this chapter, and that in turn would facilitate school achievement in that language. Television also may be an important source of information for such students, although this seems less likely for math, reading, and writing skills than for other kinds of information. The sixth and final point regarding the California Assessment Program's (1981) findings that Comstock (1989) found noteworthy was that a substantial number of students watched a great deal of television. In Grade 6, 20% watched 4 or more hours per day and an additional 11% watched 3 to 4 hours per day. In Grade 12, the analogous proportions were 16% and 13%. Thus, almost one third of the students could be described as heavy TV viewers. At both grade levels, students who reported watching more TV also reported spending less time on homework and on reading (other than for class assignments).

Comstock (1989) described the pattern of results from the California Assessment Program (1981) as reminiscent of the findings reported by Schramm, Lyle, and Parker (1961) and said that the

> pattern invites a proposition: Television viewing is inversely related to achievement when it displaces an intellectually and experientially richer environment, and it is positively related to achievement when it supplies such an environment. The stronger inverse relationships at the 12th-grade level suggest that this pattern becomes increasingly discernible as the academic demands of schooling increase. (Comstock, 1989, p. 214)

In a follow-up conducted one year later, the California Assessment Program (1982) assessed a representative sample of 15,000 sixth graders. The results supported those obtained a year earlier for achievement, SES, and television viewing. In addition, they indicated that some households were "television-centered," in that there was a TV set in the living room or child's bedroom and that the sixth grader was likely to watch TV with his or her parents and was likely to discuss the programs with them. Such children were more likely to be heavy viewers and to watch a higher proportion of light entertainment. Grade 6 students who were light viewers "were more likely to watch news, documentary, or informational programs, or more serious or sophisticated entertainment" (Comstock, 1989, p. 215). Students who watched no TV had lower achievement scores than those who watched a minimal amount. In Comstock's (1989) opinion, TV viewing is normative for children and teens in the United States, and thus some minimum use "is an index of alert participation in and coping with the environment" (p. 214).

Evidence that the negative relationship between television viewing and educational achievement extends beyond North America to other educational systems is reported by Wober (1991), who cited a report by Keys and Foxman (1989). It focused on 13-year-olds in 12 educational systems in 6 countries. "Heavy viewing of television was negatively related with performance in each of the 12 systems examined" (Wober, 1991, p. 102), and this included the United Kingdom. "The only system in which the distinct associations found elsewhere were less marked was in South Korea, where a substantial portion of children's viewing was, perforce, to educational programming" (p. 102).

In one of the very few investigations of the relationship between television viewing and writing skills, Peirce (1983) studied 102 students in Grades 5, 7, 8, and 9 in Florida. They provided information about their television viewing (including hours per day, hours per week, favorite program and type of program, whether they watched alone, whether their viewing hours or programs were restricted, and whether their parents watched and discussed programs with them) and their reading habits and after-school activities. Parents' answers to the same questions tended to corroborate the children's answers. Parents also provided information about their own viewing habits and their education. To assess writing skills, each child wrote a story about an imagined situation. The story was judged for both writing abilities (grammar, spelling, sentence construction, idea development, punctuation) and creative writing (fantasy, elaboration of creative ideas, use of dialogue, and point of view). The results for writing ability are presented in the article (Peirce, 1983); the creative writing results are not, but are said to be similar (and scores for the two measures were significantly correlated). In an analysis to determine whether writing ability scores could be predicted from some of the other variables, hours of television viewing was the most important predictor; students who watched more TV had lower writing ability scores, and amount of TV viewing accounted for 14% of the variance in writing scores. The other significant predictors of writing ability were number of books read per month (an additional 7% of the variance) and parental interest (6%; a scale composed of the items concerning restriction of viewing hours and programs, whether the parent read to the child when she or he was small, and whether the parent watched and discussed programs with the child). Parental level of education did not add significantly to prediction from the other three variables, although it was significantly positively related to the child's writing ability. In another set of analyses the relationship between television viewing and writing remained significant even after parent education was controlled. As Peirce (1983) noted, these results do not provide any hints about the process that results in the significant relationships among children's TV viewing, number of books read, parent interest, parent education, and children's writing ability, and no causal inferences can be made.

There is evidence that children's academic achievement is related to the control strategies their parents' use (Dornbusch, Ritter, Leiderman, Roberts, & Freleigh, 1987), their parents' involvement in their school-related activities (Stevenson & Baker, 1987), and the affection their parents show toward them (Hess & Holloway, 1984). This led one team of researchers (Henggeler, Cohen, Edwards, Summerville, & Ray, 1991) to hypothesize that the nature of the family context, particularly with regard to stress, might play an important role in the association between children's TV viewing and their academic achievement. They studied 25 Grade 3 middle-class children (44% girls) and their parents; 28% were African American, 8% were Asian, and the remainder were white. There was high agreement (75%) between parent and child reports of the hours of weeknight (Sunday through Thursday) television viewing (mean 1.5 hours, range 0 to 3). Third graders who watched more weeknight TV did more poorly on the Wide-Range Achievement Test-Revised (WRAT-R; Jastak & Wilkinson, 1984), even after the influence of verbal ability (WISC-R Verbal Vocabulary subtest) was controlled (the correlation dropped from −.69 to −.66). It is noteworthy that this is a much stronger relationship than is usually found between TV viewing and school achievement, particularly after any influence of verbal IQ is controlled. I also think the weeknight measure of TV is interesting. In most studies, total viewing per week is the measure of TV use, but it was not reported by Henggeler et al. (1991). Perhaps their measure—that is, hours of viewing on evenings before school days—is more closely tied to school performance, either directly or through other relevant variables. This finding caught my eye in part because it reminds me of a family I know in which the children are not allowed to watch any television on school days or evenings before school days, but they may videotape programs for viewing on weekends. The parents want them to take school work seriously and so try to provide an environment encouraging them to do homework, take extra time for school-related projects, and so on. Because the Henggeler et al. (1991) findings were for a small middle-class sample of third graders, they may merely be unusual, although greater homogeneity—that is, less variability—in the sample would normally be expected to yield smaller rather than larger correlations.

Some researchers have suggested that the relationship between television viewing and academic achievement may not be linear, which may explain inconsistencies in some of the results obtained with strictly linear analyses. For example, Hornik (1981) and I (Williams, 1981) have both independently argued that a threshold model for the relationship between TV viewing and many behaviors may be more appropriate than one that is linear across the entire range of viewing. That is, up to some point (number of hours) there may be no effect or a positive one, then there may be a range in which there is a potentially negative effect, and beyond some point, there may be no additional effect. Just such a pattern was found by P. Williams and her colleagues (Williams et al., 1982) in their meta-analysis[15] of the literature on school achievement and TV viewing. Watching up to 10 hours per week was related to slightly enhanced achievement. Between 10 and 35 hours, achievement diminished with amount viewed. Beyond 35 hours there was relatively little additional effect, summarizing across the large number of studies reviewed in their meta-analysis.

A curvilinear relationship between amount of TV viewing and reading achievement also was found by Neuman (1986) in her synthesis of data from a number of large state and national assessments in the United States. There was a modest positive association for moderate viewers (2 to 3 hours per day) and a negative association for heavy viewers (4 or more hours per day), with a small negative overall association. She concluded that there are no deleterious effects of television on learning achievement. In a more recent study of fifth graders in Illinois, some other researchers found that the curvilinear pattern reported by P. Williams et al. (1982) did map onto their findings relating hours of TV viewing to reading comprehension scores, but only the linear component of the curve was statistically significant (Anderson, Wilson, & Fielding, 1988). In other words, they found that the students at the lowest reading comprehension percentile scores were indeed the heaviest TV viewers, and the curve did not flatten out after about 35 hours per week. In their study, however, only about 10% of the students watched 25 or more hours of TV a week so there were relatively few heavy viewers.

In a later volume that provides an extensive review of the literature on the relationship between television viewing and school achievement, particularly reading and literacy, Neuman (1991) examined several hypotheses put forth by others to explain television's potential effects. She rejected the displacement theory that television has replaced time that children either used to (before TV) or otherwise would (now) spend in more educational pursuits, in large part on the basis that most children read very little now and never did read much. She also considered information processing theory (that television affects the processes through which we think and learn), the short-term gratifications theory (that TV reduces perseverance, attention span, and concentration, while increasing impulsivity), and the interest stimulation theory (TV is a "window on the world" that informally exposes children to a wide range of information and motivation) in relation to the evidence. In her opinion, none of these theories, all of which deal with potential indirect effects of television, could explain differences in school achievement.

The results of three surveys conducted in the United Kingdom by the British Broadcasters Audience Research Board (BARB) with their Television Opinion Panels have been reported by Wober (1990, 1991, 1992). The Panels are samples of about 3,000 people who complete weekly diaries in which they report the television programs they have watched and answer some additional questions that vary week by week.

The first survey (Wober, 1990) focused on the extent to which 12- to 24-year-olds perform intellectual homework and, in particular, do so with television as an accompaniment. Among the 208 twelve- to fifteen-year-olds, 74% overall reported that they did school homework. Among these students, 50% reported doing homework with the TV on and 23% reported doing homework without the TV on. Overall, 20% did not answer the homework questions. The analogous proportions regarding "writing, on which you have to concentrate" were 58%, 39%, 21%, and 20%. Among the 50% who said they did homework with the TV on, 24% said they liked to have it on, 20% said it was usually on but it made no difference for doing homework, and 6% said it was usually on and made it difficult to do homework. Among the 39% who said the TV was usually on when they were doing writing that required concentration, the comparable proportions were 13%, 21%, and 5%. With regard to reasons for finding television a help or hindrance to work, proportions were not reported but there was evidence of support for both sides of two paired possibilities—"having a TV on helps to keep someone else in the room interested and stops them interrupting me," versus, "the TV on brings someone else into the room and I get interrupted," which Wober calls a social role; "having a TV on reassures me and I can get on with my work," versus "the activity on TV makes me feel on edge and uneasy about getting on with my work," an emotional role. There also was evidence of support for "the activity on TV distracts my attention quite a bit" but little support for "having the TV on keeps other people from distracting me."

The second survey (Wober, 1991), which focused on adults, indicated that they held a distinct character stereotype of young heavy television viewers (aged 12 to 20). By comparison with young, light viewers, young heavy viewers were rated lower on six positive attributes (keen on good manners and behavior; have a good imagination—lots of new ideas; read a great deal every day; know a lot about science and the natural world; have a good memory; know a lot about British politics) and rated higher on six negative items (be afraid to go out in the dark; have bad eating habits—eat too much or too little and at the wrong times; be a selfish person; have a quick temper and be likely to hit out; believe it is a fine thing for a woman to be a housewife; and be the kind of person who grows old early). Adults of higher SES were the most negative about young, heavy viewers.

> To put it in more colloquial terms, couch potatoes are thought to be (slightly) ignorant and unpleasant—to themselves as well as to others, but only if they are young. These images do not attach to old people who are heavy viewers. (Wober, 1991, p. 104)

Wober (1991) pointed out that the group from which teachers are most heavily drawn (older, higher SES) think most unfavorably of young heavy viewers, and even young viewers themselves do not have positive perceptions of the cognitive attributes of young heavy viewers. This may lead to negative expectations regarding their school performance, and such "stereotypes may reinforce a downward spiral in performance" (p. 107). With regard to the research evidence relating TV viewing to academic achievement, he noted that "even if some have failed to demonstrate links between heavy viewing and reduced performance, none have shown that heavy viewing enhances it, while some do report harm" (p. 107).

The third BARB survey (Wober, 1992) was answered by 842 children aged 7 to 15 years. The proportions saying they often, sometimes, and never did "school homework" were 42%, 34%, and 24%, and for "read a serious book," 22%, 40%, and 35%. These items were combined into a "textwork" item. More than 40% of the children aged 10 and over reported doing homework with a TV set on and either simply accepted it (about 25% of those 10 and over) or actually welcomed it (about 17%). Children who reported heavy viewing (defined as more than 2 hours per day) were likely to be of lower SES. Heavy viewing was not related to age, gender, or the likelihood of doing textwork at home, but if and when children did textwork, heavy viewers were more likely than lighter viewers to do it with the set on, to say that having TV on with homework is of help, to agree that home viewing helps children do well in school, to have a positive stereotype of a heavy viewer, and to reject a picture of the heavy reader as positive. In contrast, heavy readers (by comparison with lighter readers) tended to be younger, to be female, to say they do textwork at home, to deny that the set switched on helps their work, and to have a positive view of heavy readers. Some heavy readers evidently also did textwork with the TV set on, but the relationship was stronger for heavy viewers. The set of results from this third survey is interpreted as reflecting a "process of rationalization . . . in which those who reported heavy viewing themselves, were more likely to do homework with the television on, to say it helped them and that it was linked to good achievement at school" (Wober, 1992, p. 23). Overall, however, the children recognized "that working or reading with a television switched on makes work more difficult and less effective" (p. 34).

These studies by Wober provide some hints about the processes whereby heavy viewing is linked to poorer school achievement, a point on which those who otherwise take different positions seem to agree (e.g., Comstock, 1989; Neuman, 1991; Wober, 1991). Better students may do better in school in part because of their greater knowledge of their own thinking processes and abilities about activities that can be time-shared with television without loss of accuracy or poorer performance (e.g., polishing shoes, ironing) and those for which performance may suffer if time-shared (e.g., homework involving material that is difficult or has not yet been mastered). That is, perhaps the same homework could be time-shared with television by students who have mastered the skills involved without affecting performance significantly, whereas there would be greater loss for students who had not yet mastered those skills. As I have previously noted, any links between use of television and school achievement may follow a pattern reflecting an upward or downward spiral, a case of "the rich get richer" (Williams, 1986c).[16] But the causal path has yet to be charted and is undoubtedly complicated.

The metaphor of an upward or downward spiral linking television use to school achievement is strongly supported by an important longitudinal Swedish research program, Media Panel, in which 194 children were studied from the age of 6 to 12 (Jönsson, 1986; Rosengren & Windahl, 1989). This study is impressive not only because the students and their parents were studied repeatedly, in preschool, Grade 1, Grade 3, Grade 5, and Grade 6, when many academic skills are being acquired, but also because the researchers have proposed a theoretical model to account for complexities in the way TV use relates to school achievement. Their metaphor sees the "mass media use of children and adolescents as a series of positive and vicious circles" (Rosengren & Windahl, 1989, p. 224), and it spells out precisely the sort of model I had more vaguely envisioned as involving upward or downward spirals. I can provide only a brief description here so I urge those of you interested in better understanding how TV use and school achievement evolve over children's lives to read the original sources.

The theoretical model proposed for the Media Panel findings merges two traditions in media research that have historically been conceptualized in an either-or manner: "effects" and "uses and gratifications" (see Rosengren, Roe, & Sonesson, 1983, for details). Rather than asking simply whether TV use, reading habits, parental attitudes, and so on have any effect on school achievement, this model also acknowledges that low and high achievers use television differently. "High achievers used television more as a complement to school while low achievers used television more as an entertainer and pastime" (Jönsson, 1986, p. 32). Two important features of this model are its proposal (confirmed by the results) that "school influences TV as much as TV influences school, and this holds true not only for TV but for other mass media as well," and that "TV has both positive and negative effects" (Rosengren & Windahl, 1989, p. 224), depending on how it is used.

A succinct and eloquent summary of the way TV use and school achievement developed in interaction from the preschool years onward in this Swedish study is provided by the authors:

> Those parents who feel that children's use of TV should be controlled and that their TV experiences should be discussed make their children watch children's programs when they should be watched (in the preschool period) and make them watch fewer fiction programs. All this positively affects test results in Grade 1, thereby starting a positive circle which ends up with a positive influence on marks in Grade 6.
>
> Parents who, at the time of their children's preschool days, have less belief in the need for control and more confidence in TV, influence the consumption of children's programs in preschool negatively, the consumption of fiction programs positively. This starts a vicious circle; few preschool children's programs, more preschool and school fiction—worse marks—more routine motivated TV, fewer informative programs in Grade 5, more fiction and children's programs—worse marks in Grade 6. (Rosengren & Windahl, 1989, p. 225)

As Rosengren and Windahl (1989) point out, it is important to remember that although television use was significantly related to school achievement in a transactional or circular pattern in their study, this measurable influence was nevertheless modest, especially compared with the more powerful factors of class and gender. The strongest predictor of success in Grade 6 was success in Grade 1, and social background was also strongly related to marks obtained in Grade 6. Unfortunately, class and gender are not easily altered, but, as they point out, "What is hopeful in the results just presented is that they show the importance of the early TV setting offered by parents. This setting may be influenced and charged by parents themselves—and by children" (p. 227). These results for the Swedish Media Panel study (Jönsson, 1986; Rosengren & Windahl, 1989) and those reported by Aletha Huston and John Wright in Chapter 2 (this volume) for their longitudinal studies in the United States provide strong evidence for the importance of ensuring that all children have access to age-appropriate TV programming with an informative curriculum.

Further evidence that informative children's television can effectively teach school-related skills, in this case mathematical problem solving, has been demonstrated by Children's Television Workshop (CTW, the producers of *Sesame Street* and *Ghostwriter*) for their series about mathematics, *Square One TV* (Hall, Esty, & Fisch, 1990). This program has three goals: to promote enthusiasm for mathematics, to encourage the use and application of problem-solving processes, and to present sound math content in an interesting, accessible, meaningful way. Its effectiveness was evaluated in a field experiment with fifth graders in four Texas schools that had not shown the program in classrooms. In the two experimental schools, students watched one program each weekday for 6 weeks, but the teacher did not incorporate or relate *Square One TV* to the school curriculum. The two control schools maintained their usual schedules and teaching. In a pretest and posttest, children were individually given three levels of problem-solving activities (PSAs) that involved a range of mathematically rich, nonroutine, problem situations. From the pretest to posttest children in the viewing group improved significantly more than did the nonviewers, and at the posttest they scored higher than the nonviewers. The positive effects of viewing occurred for both girls and boys, who did not differ on the pre- or posttest. The effects also were similar for low- and middle-SES children. Whereas 42% of the problem-solving actions and heuristics the viewers used in the posttest were new, this was true for only 25% of nonviewers, and whereas viewers increased in their use of 11.7 of the 17 actions and heuristics, nonviewers increased in only 4.0. Preexisting differences between the groups did not account for these results. They indicate that sustained, unaided viewing of *Square One TV* can increase problem-solving performance in its target audience of 8- to 12-year-olds. Whether casual home viewing would produce similar results is not clear, because the sustained nature of exposure (5 days a week for 6 weeks), watching in the "serious" school setting, or both may have been crucial factors in the program's effectiveness. Nevertheless, at a minimum, the results indicate clearly that under those conditions, the program is an effective teacher of academically important skills, and they underscore the importance of expanding the availability of such programming.

Results From Notel, Unitel, and Multitel

The main aspect of school achievement that we studied in the natural experiment in Notel, Unitel, and Multitel was reading (Corteen & Williams, 1986). We also gave students several measures of vocabulary and a measure of spatial ability, which I discussed earlier in this chapter as measures of IQ (Harrison & Williams, 1986). Here I will discuss those findings from the vocabulary and spatial ability perspectives.

Reading. Our primary measure of reading proficiency was designed to assess the acquisition of fluent reading. At the fluent stage in reading development, children have mastered the alphabet and how to match letters with spoken words (decoding), and they are becoming "unglued from print" (Chall, 1983). They can glance at a word or phrase and read it automatically, without conscious effort. We assessed fluent reading by presenting the items of a standardized test (Gates & McKillop, 1962) under very controlled conditions rather than the usual flash card presentation (Corteen & Williams, 1986). We used a device called a tachistoscope, which is like a "box" into which the child looks, to control precisely the amount of time each card was available for the child to read. Three kinds of items were used: 20 single words, 26 phrases, and 23 nonsense words (which look like English words but have no meaning—e.g., *sked*). The results for words, phrases and nonsense words were similar so we combined them into total scores.

In Phase 1, before Notel had television, we tested 217 students in Grades 2, 3, and 8 in the three towns, and in Phase 2, we tested 206 in the same grades (cross-sectional comparison). We also retested 153 students now in Grades 4, 5, and 10 who had been in the Phase 1 sample (longitudinal comparison).

Then, an additional 2 years later (4 years after Phase 1), we tested 82 students in Grade 2 in the three towns.[17]

A practice word was given first to familiarize each child with the (tachistoscopic) "box," and if the child could not read it in the test time, the time was lengthened and the item presented again and again for longer periods until the child could read it. The actual test items were then all shown at the same time length, which was 100 milliseconds for Grades 2 through 5 and 30 milliseconds for Grades 8 and 10.

As many reviewers of the research evidence on television use and reading performance have pointed out (e.g., Hornik, 1981; Neuman, 1991), both variables tend also to be related to I.Q. When IQ is controlled the question becomes, "After IQ is controlled or partialled out, is amount of TV viewing still negatively correlated with reading skill?" and the answer becomes, "sometimes yes and sometimes no." In our study the pattern of findings was clearer and more easily interpretable when IQ was used as a covariate or control in the analyses. The results were still complicated, however, in part because there was a gender difference in Grade 2 favoring girls, although it became only marginally significant after IQ was controlled.

When we controlled for IQ in the Phase 1 (before TV) Grade 2 scores, Notel second graders (girls and boys combined) had significantly better fluent reading scores than second graders in both Unitel and Multitel, who did not differ. Four years later there were no differences between the towns for either girls or boys.[18] In Grade 3, after IQ was controlled, there were no town differences in Phase 1. Unitel and Multitel third graders in Phases 1 and 2 obtained comparable scores, but in Notel, the third graders in Phase 2 had significantly lower scores than the third graders tested in Phase 1. Indeed, in Phase 2 the Notel scores were significantly lower than the Unitel and Multitel scores, which did not differ. It is noteworthy that these Notel Phase 2 third graders had been just beginning to learn to read 2 years earlier when television arrived in November.

The combined evidence for Grades 2 and 3 suggests that the availability of television may slow down the acquisition of fluent reading, but most children do acquire such skills. The results for older students and the longitudinal analyses support this interpretation. Taken together, the results point to Grades 1 and 2 as especially important for television's potential influence on the acquisition of fluent reading skills. Some of our findings (not detailed here) suggest that, in some instances, superior fluent reading skills acquired in the absence of TV may be maintained despite the later acquisition of TV and that children who have grown up with television do not "catch up" to these students.

Our secondary measure of reading performance consisted of vocabulary, comprehension, and total scores for a standardized test, the Gates McGinitie Reading Achievement tests. We gave these group tests to the Grades 1 through 7 classes in all three towns (total 813 students) about 6 months after the arrival of TV in Notel, at the request of the schools and as a way of repaying them for their cooperation. The results tended to corroborate the findings from our primary, individually administered measure of fluent or automatic reading. IQ was an important control for both vocabulary and comprehension. Notel students in Grades 2 and 3 obtained higher comprehension scores than both Unitel and Multitel students, who did not differ. The same pattern was true for vocabulary scores for the specific comparisons among the towns. There were no town or gender differences for students in Grades 4 through 7.

Whereas our findings for the natural experiment we studied in Canada point to the greater importance of the role of television for reading skills in the early rather than later school years, results from the natural experiment Hornik (1978) studied in El Salvador indicate that it can also slow down reading improvement later on. He compared students from families who obtained a TV set when they were in Grades 7, 8, or 9 with students whose families had had a set throughout those grades (and were of higher SES) and with students who had no set during the same period (and were of lower SES). Students in the first group—that is, those who recently obtained TV—did about 10% worse on a reading test relative to the other two groups, and this was true for three different samples or cohorts.

As I have already noted, some researchers, myself included, have hypothesized (Hornik, 1981; Williams, 1981) and others have found in meta-analyses (Neuman, 1986; P. Williams et al., 1982) that a curvilinear, threshold, or other nonlinear model may better account for the relationship between television viewing and academic achievement. We therefore analyzed our data from Notel, Unitel, and Multitel to see how reported TV viewing related to reading. Both our fluent reading and group measures were negatively correlated with hours of TV viewing even after controlling for IQ. That is, students who obtained higher individual and group reading test scores tended to report watching less TV than did students with lower reading scores, whatever their IQ level. In addition, students who obtained higher group reading test scores tended to report watching less TV 18 months later than did students with lower group reading scores. The relationships were not strong, but they were more linear than not and did not vary with IQ.

As I mentioned earlier, one of the most intriguing findings from our study that is often overlooked is that in the absence of television in Notel (that is, in Phase 1), the relationship between IQ and our fluent reading scores was not statistically significant.[19] Moreover, the correlations between IQ and the group reading scores were significant for all three towns, but the correlations for Notel were significantly lower than those for Unitel and Multitel. In other words, the typical finding that IQ and reading achievement are related was true when television was available, but when it was not, they were more independent. Why? These results could be due to chance, but they also may indicate that when television is available, there is an increase in the proportion of lower IQ children who do not acquire reading skills to the point of automaticity in the early elementary grades.

In addition to assessing the possible impact of television on reading performance and achievement in the ways I have already described, we also obtained some information in Phase 2 about Notel, Unitel, and Multitel children's reading habits. The proportion of Notel students aged 6 to 18 who reported using the town's library (76.3%) was significantly greater than that for Multitel (68.0%). The Unitel proportion (70.4%) did not differ significantly from that for Notel or Multitel. When these overall proportions were broken down by age level, an interesting pattern emerged. Averaging across the towns, 80% or more of the students in the 6 and 7, 8 through 10, and 11 and 12 age groups reported using the town library, and variations among the towns were small. Among 13- to 15-year-olds, however, the proportion of Notel students (70.4%) who reported doing so was still relatively high and significantly higher than the proportions for both Unitel (51.5%) and Multitel (53.4%), which did not differ significantly. This apparent drop-off in library use with age in Unitel and Multitel for 13- to 15-year-olds was even more evident for 16- to 18-year-olds; only 43.6% reported using the library and there were no town differences. This suggests that students who grew up to age 11 to 13 without TV in Notel maintained their earlier library use habits pattern at age 13 to 15, whereas there was a fall-off for students who grew up with TV. By 16 to 18, however, the greater appeal of other adolescent activities, such as music, doing things with peers, and so on that typically are associated with a decrease in TV viewing (Comstock & Paik, 1991; Huston et al., 1992) and, in Unitel and Multitel, in library use, was also true for library use in Notel.

With regard to the number of books read per month and reading comics, 2 years after the arrival of TV, Notel students were similar to Unitel and Multitel students (unfortunately, we did not obtain this information in Phase 1). Across the towns, children who watched more TV reported reading fewer books and less radio listening, but more comic reading.

Taken as a set, our findings and those obtained by others are consistent with the following hypothetical scenario (Williams, 1986c):

> In the absence of television most children practice reading enough to become fluent to the point that decoding letters, words, and phrases is automatic. Practice is hard work, and children cannot read during this stage for entertainment or information (Chall, 1983). Television provides a more attractive alternative for most children, but especially for those who have most difficulty learning to read and who need the practice most, namely, those who are less intelligent (or have a learning disability). The brighter children either need less practice and get enough in school or practice more. Differences related to socioeconomic status (SES) emerge (Roberts, Bachen, Hornby, & Hernandez-Ramos, 1984) because more children in higher SES families are given encouragement and assistance, raised in a print-oriented environment, and so on. In subsequent elementary and high school years, children who have not acquired good reading skills enjoy reading less than the better readers, so they spend less time reading and more time with television. This provides even less opportunity to hone their skills. This hypothesized chain of events results in the typical finding for high school students that poor readers are less intelligent, are of lower SES, read less, and watch more television than students who are better readers (Morgan & Gross, 1982). The chain begins because television displaces reading practice, and this leads to more reading "dropouts" in the long run. There always have been and will be people who do not become fluent readers, but the numbers may be greater when television is available. Parents and educators who want children to read well should ensure that they practice enough in the early grades to become fluent and should foster positive attitudes toward print throughout childhood and adolescence. Television's influence is indirect; reducing the child's involvement with television may be necessary, but it is not likely to be sufficient. (p. 397)

In his review of research relating TV use to scholastic achievement, Comstock (1989) described this explanation as "certainly plausible" and added that it "also could readily apply to mathematical and writing skills" (p. 216).

A study of 155 Grade 5 students in Illinois provides support for the contention that television's role in relation to reading achievement is at best indirect and that other activities are more important (Anderson et al., 1988). The students kept daily diaries (mean 57 days) of the time they spent in 14 activities. The researchers took several steps to ensure that the forms were completed and that students were trained in how to fill them out, how to estimate time, and so on. With regard to book reading, their time estimates were used in the analyses only if they also answered one or both additional questions: "The book was called _____. It was written by _____." Reading books in Grade 5 was the best predictor of several measures of reading achievement, including gains the students previously made between Grades 2 and 5. The typical child did very little book reading ($M = 10.1$, $Mdn = 4.6$ minutes per day) in comparison, for example, with TV viewing (the comparable figures were 131.1 and 111.0), listening to music (30.8, 18.0) or going out (98.6, 93.7). This was not because he or she did a lot of other reading; the figures for comics were 2.1, 0.2; for mail, 1.4, 0.4; and newspapers and magazines, 4.8, 2.0. But there was enormous variation in book reading. At the 90th percentile, students reported 65.0 minutes of book reading per day (that is, only 10% of the students spent more than 65 minutes a day reading books, and 90% spent less time doing so), but the 50th percentile was *not* roughly half an hour—that is, half that figure. It was only 4.6 minutes per day, and the 10th percentile was only 0.1 minutes per day. Teachers seemed to have a significant influence on their students' book reading; the class that read the most averaged 16.5 minutes per day, whereas the class that read the least averaged only 4.1 minutes. Watching television had only a small, negative relationship to reading proficiency that did not quite reach statistical significance. There was no strong evidence that watching TV or any other out-of-school activity interfered with book reading. In this particular sample, however, very few students reported the sort of heavy viewing patterns found in some other studies, with only 10% watching TV 25 hours a week or more.

Vocabulary and Spatial Ability. As I described earlier in the section on IQ, we gave several vocabulary tests (WISC vocabulary subtest, Stanford-Binet or S-B vocabulary test, and PPVT) and a measure of spatial ability (WISC Block Design) to students in Notel, Unitel, and Multitel (Harrison & Williams, 1986). We did so because we thought that television would have a positive influence on vocabulary, particularly for children in the early elementary grades who could not yet read for pleasure on their own (as Schramm et al., 1961 found). We also thought that the visual aspect of television viewing might facilitate spatial ability or that children high in spatial ability might spend more time watching TV. These hypotheses about possible positive effects of television were not supported by our findings. In the case of spatial ability, they were actually contradicted by significant negative correlations in Phase 2 between hours of TV viewing and Block Design scores. In addition, students who obtained high vocabulary scores in Phase 1 tended to watch less TV 2 years later than did those who obtained low scores, and participation in other leisure activities, particularly book reading, was positively related to performance on the WISC vocabulary subtest. When we chose measures for the natural experiment I thought of the WISC, S-B, and PPVT tests primarily as measures of vocabulary and spatial ability, but on looking back at the pattern of results over the entire study, I now believe that they are better conceptualized as measures of IQ, as I discussed earlier in this chapter.

In his recent review of studies of the effects of visual media (film, television) on spatial intelligence, Messaris's (1994) conclusions were consistent with our findings.

> Neither the empirical evidence we have reviewed nor the theoretical arguments we have considered build a particularly strong case in favor of the idea that experience as a spectator of still pictures or film and television is a significant contributor to general spatial intelligence. (p. 445)

For example, in one field experiment 4-year-olds were randomly assigned to watch a 24-minute TV program dealing with shape recognition (circles, triangles, squares, and so on) or to follow their regular preschool program (Hofmann & Flook, 1980). There was no evidence that the TV program facilitated shape recognition, which was tested haptically (i.e., using touch). Visual recognition, which would have been a more direct test, was not assessed, as the researchers were interested in assessing the effectiveness of children's TV programs on general cognitive development, from the perspective of Piagetian theory.

Children undoubtedly do learn some vocabulary from television, but our findings and those obtained by others (e.g., Schramm et al., 1961) indicate that for most school-age children, television may not significantly boost vocabulary over what it otherwise would have been. In the absence of television, some children may acquire more of their vocabulary from being read to, reading themselves, or conversationally. This is not to argue that television plays no role in language acquisition, which it clearly does, particularly in the preschool years (Hoff-Ginsberg & Shatz, 1982; Lemish & Rice, 1986; Rice et al., 1990; Wright, 1995; see also Chapter 2, this volume). In our multicultural society it may play a particularly important role in second-language acquisition for children and adults who speak another language in their home. Where I live, in the third largest Canadian city, that is true of more than 50% of the school children. Unfortunately, there has been little research in this area, although anecdotal evidence indicates that motivated adults can improve their proficiency in a second or subsequent language through TV viewing. For example, while skiing in British Columbia, I had a conversation in English with a man from a small town in Quebec, whose first language was French, who said he had learned all of his English by watching TV.

Conclusions Regarding Television and School Achievement

In sum, there is a body of evidence that amount of television viewing is negatively related to academic achievement, and another body of evidence indicating no relationship. There does not seem to be any evidence that viewing more television in general relates positively to academic achievement (recall the quotation from Wober, 1991, p. 107, which I cited earlier). There is considerable evidence (including that discussed by Huston & Wright, Chapter 2, this volume) that viewing children's programming intended to be informative is positively related to young children's vocabulary, letter, and number skills, as well as their later school achievement (Jönsson, 1986; Rosengren & Windahl, 1989; see also Comstock & Paik, 1991; Dorr, 1986; Huston et al., 1992; Murray, 1993, for reviews). With regard to developmental level, there is some evidence (Beentjes, 1989; Salomon, 1984) that 12-year-olds are more mentally active or "invest more mental effort" (Salomon, 1983) in reading than in television viewing. Younger children may habitually invest more effort in television viewing than do older children because they have more difficulty comprehending programming aimed beyond their developmental level. Age-appropriate programming intended to be informative may, therefore, be especially effective for younger children.

After carefully sifting and weighing all of the evidence, most reviewers, myself included, have concluded that the relationship between use of television and school achievement is very complex. We all acknowledge its potential to have a positive impact through programming intended to inform and educate. Some reviewers tend to downplay the evidence of a negative relationship for general viewing (e.g., Neuman, 1991), whereas others consider it to be more important (e.g., Comstock, 1989; Gerbner et al., 1984). I am inclined to agree with Comstock (1989) that "television can hardly be said to be without implications for scholastic achievement. . . . It is certain that children and teenagers doing poorly in school and watching vast amounts of television somehow should be persuaded to spend their time otherwise" (p. 217). Despite her generally less critical opinion of television's potential for negative effects, Neuman (1991) apparently agrees; "Excessive viewing of generally over 3 hours per day is clearly related to lower proficiency scores in reading" (p. 199), as shown in her analysis of results for over 2 million children. The more recent research (e.g., Anderson et al., 1988) I've reviewed in this chapter adds further support to the following conclusion:

> Those students who say they spend relatively more time watching television are more likely to get lower scores on achievement tests. There can be no doubt or disagreement about the consistency of this finding across numerous studies all over the country.[20] Even the TIO[21] acknowledges the basic finding that heavy viewing tends to be associated with lower test scores. (Gerbner et al., 1984, p. 10)

It has long been established that one of the best predictors of school achievement is class or socioeconomic status (SES); children from privileged families tend to do better in school than children from less privileged families. One might, therefore, ask whether any relationship between use of television and school achievement simply reflects the role of SES, because, as Wober (1992) found in the United Kingdom, heavy viewing may be more character-istic of students from lower SES families. Based on my review of the literature, the answer is no. I am struck by the converging evidence from several studies conducted in several different countries that use of television seems to interact with SES in relation to school achievement. For example, Comstock's (1989) review of the California Assessment Program's (1981) findings indicated that the negative relationship between television exposure and mathematical, reading, and writing ability that generally held true was strongest for students in the highest SES category and barely observable in the lowest SES category. Moreover, for students with limited fluency in English, TV viewing was positively rather than negatively related to achieve-ment. Similarly, in the U.S. National Assessment of Educational progress (1986), the negative relationship between excessive viewing (6 or more hours per day) and reading performance was worst for white students and those with well-educated parents. Evidence that TV use contributes to achievement in interaction with SES, but not just as a marker of SES, can be seen in Peirce's (1983) finding in Florida that the relationship between TV viewing and students' writing skills remained significant even after parental education was controlled. And in the longitudinal Swedish Media Panel study (Jönsson, 1986; Rosengren & Windahl, 1989) television use was significantly related to school achievement in a transactional set of upward or downward spirals, over and above the more powerful effects of class and gender.

As we have seen, in much of the research relating school achievement to television use, it is tempting to make causal inferences, but they are not warranted. Comstock (1989) proposed two possible models to account for the negative relationship found in some studies. In the first model, television could either contribute directly and independently to lower achievement, or TV could independently influence some other variable, which would, in turn, independently contribute to lower achievement. In the second model, greater television viewing (especially of programs not intended to be informative) "is simply the sign of some other factor such as lower intellectual ability, poorer prior grades in school, conflict with the family, estrangement from peers, and the like" (p. 215). He went on to point out, however, that even if, in the second model, television cannot be said to *cause* lower achievement, it remains part of the problem *requiring* treatment, particularly for heavy viewers.

The problem that has not yet been solved is how "to capture the subtleties of television's influence on literacy and school achievement" (Neuman, 1991, p. 46). In her opinion, "the causal path may be just too difficult to chart" (p. 46), but I disagree. Researchers are making excellent progress, particularly through longitudinal studies. They are coming up with increasingly sophisticated models of the paths of influence that include not only amount but type of TV viewing and how that varies with the child's stage of development.

Participation in Other Activities

Watching television is the most popular discretionary activity of North Americans. How does TV viewing relate to participation in other leisure activities? Several models have been proposed to account for television's role in relation to other activities, and there is some evidence to support each model.

Television may displace other activities that might otherwise have had some positive or negative effects. "When more time is spent viewing, less time must be spent doing something else" (Robinson, 1981, p. 128). But although there is evidence that television does displace some other activities that are incompatible with or "compete with" TV viewing (Robinson, 1981), in other studies little or no relationship between viewing time and participation in other activities was found (e.g., Lyle & Hoffman, 1972). Perhaps in part because of such findings and a growing awareness that if some form of displacement does occur, it is not a simple, straightforward process, Wright (1995) and his colleagues have used the phrase "concurrent trade-offs in time use" when discussing some of their results in which young children's school readiness and achievement were related positively (+) and negatively (–) to their previous exposure to informative children's television programming (+), other programming (–), print media (+), other educational activities (+), and video games (–).

Evidence that some individuals who watch a lot of TV also have high participation rates for other leisure activities led Meyersohn (1968) to propose "the more, the more" hypothesis—namely, that what motivates someone to watch a lot of television also motivates her or him to pursue other leisure activities; in this model, they reinforce rather than compete with one another. In one study (Selnow & Reynolds, 1984), students in Grades 6, 7, and 8 were interviewed about their use of various media, memberships in groups and clubs, and miscellaneous pastimes (hobbies, sleeping, and so on). Some findings were consistent with "the more, the more" hypothesis; as TV viewing increased, so did time spent listening to music and, to a lesser degree, radio listening and hobby activities. There also, however, were at-home activities that competed with or seemed to trade off with TV viewing. As viewing increased, playing home video games, sleeping, and playing musical instruments declined. TV also competed, as Robinson (1981) found for adults, with group memberships away from home.

The default hypothesis sees TV viewing as something that's done when the individual is near a TV set and not doing something that conflicts with viewing (Kubey & Csikszentmihalyi, 1990). For example, Robinson (1981) found that for adults, some home activities complement television viewing in the sense of being positively correlated with it (e.g., resting), many away from the home compete with television (e.g., paid work, bars, and parties), and some activities in the home (e.g., child care, housework) and away from it (e.g., entertainment) fall in between. In general, people who spend more time at home have more time available to spend with television, and some are less able for reasons of age, health, domestic responsibilities, finances, and so on to participate in activities outside the home or to participate in incompatible ones in the home (e.g., because they cannot afford a musical instrument).

The fourth hypothesis, functional equivalence, refers to use of television in relation to use of other media, although it is sometimes extended to other activities as well. It states that media will replace other media as well as other activities to the extent that they satisfy the same needs (e.g., Comstock et al., 1978; von Feilitzen, 1976) and because television is one of the least specialized media, it therefore may satisfy many needs or satisfy more of them best.

Do our results from the natural experiment in Notel, Unitel, and Multitel and those obtained by other researchers support or contradict these four hypotheses? Is there any evidence that use of television does relate to participation in other activities?

Results From Notel, Unitel, and Multitel

One of the clearest kinds of evidence that television does relatively directly displace some activities can be seen in attendance at films shown in movie theaters. In the United States, annual attendance at movies declined from 82 million in 1946 to 41 million in 1960 and 19 million in 1970 (Comstock, 1980). Multitel first obtained TV reception in 1958, and Unitel in 1966 (Williams, 1986a). Both had had indoor movie theaters, but they had gone out of business prior to Phase 1 of our study (1973-1974). Unitel had a drive-in movie theater that was still in business in Phase 2 (1975-1976). It operated only in summer and was not the sole income of the owners, who told us that attendance had dropped dramatically following the introduction of television to Unitel in 1966. Notel still had an indoor movie theater when TV reception arrived in late 1973, but by Phase 2, only 2 years later, it had gone out of business. In the Australian natural experiment studied by Murray and Kippax (1978), all three towns still had an indoor movie theater, but children in the No-TV town reported spending significantly more of their leisure time at the cinema than did children in the Low-TV (1 year's experience with TV) and High-TV (2 year's experience) towns. Thus, the results of both the Canadian and Australian natural experiments indicate that the availability of television led to a decrease in attendance at films shown in theaters, and in Notel, Unitel, and Multitel, in the opportunity to do so.

What did we learn from the residents of Notel, Unitel, and Multitel about the role of television for their participation in other leisure activities (Williams & Handford, 1986)? We were primarily interested in community activities, both organized (e.g., league sports, public dances) and unorganized (e.g., parks, local natural swimming places), but we also surveyed both indoor (e.g., knitting) and outdoor (e.g., hiking) private leisure activities. The pattern of results for these private activities was not clearly linked to the availability of television,[22] although there were a few hints in that direction, so I'll focus here on the community activities.

To study participation in public activities we needed a relatively objective method of quantifying each town's characteristics into equivalent, meaningful units, and we found it in a system called "psychological ecology" or "behavior settings analysis" developed by Barker and his associates (Barker, 1968; Barker & Gump, 1964; Barker & Wright, 1955/1971). It is based on the idea that each environmental unit, or behavior setting, constrains or places limits on the type of behavior likely to occur there, for both physical reasons (you can't swim if there's not enough water) and social reasons (people behave differently at weddings and funerals). They used this system to study a town slightly larger than Notel, Unitel, and Multitel, which they called Midwest. A team of participant observers spent a year in Midwest, noting the number and characteristics of people who went to various activities and places, and so forth. The imminent arrival of TV in Notel and insufficient funds meant we could not use this method. Instead, we used the method Barker and Gump (1964) developed for their survey of the behavior settings used by high school students.

We began by exploring each town and its vicinity, chatting with residents and asking about sights to see, places to meet, parks, and so on. After interviewing 6 to 8 key informants (which included school teachers, police, clergy, children, retailers, officers of organizations, elected officials, and so on), new settings emerged less and less frequently. We then went through all the weekly community newspapers for the preceding year to identify additional activities, organizations, special events, and so on. For each town in each phase we ended up with about 275 items, which we grouped on the questionnaires into the 12 categories used to describe Midwest (Barker & Wright, 1955/1971): Sports; Open Areas, such as playgrounds, hangouts; Businesses; Civic Activities, such as the post office and town hall; out-of-school Educational Activities, such as music lessons, adult classes; Medical Activities, such as the health unit, doctors' offices; Dances, Parties, and Suppers; Special Days, such as weddings, elections, funerals; Religious Activities of the churches and bible camps; Entertainment, such as bingo and parades; and Other Activities, such as cleanup campaigns, fund-raising events.

All students in Grades 7 through 12 completed the questionnaires in school, and we mailed questionnaires to a random sample of adults on the electoral lists, for a total of 1,023 in Phase 1 and 1,369 in Phase 2. Each person indicated whether and how they had been involved in each activity during the preceding year. Thus, Notel residents were indicating what they had done in the year prior to the arrival of television reception and then again during the period from 1 to 2 years after obtaining reception.

Summing across the 12 categories, total participation before TV was available in Notel ($M = 66$ community activities) was significantly higher than in Unitel ($M = 54$, thus Notel was 22% higher), which in turn was higher than in Multitel ($M = 47$, with Unitel 15% and Notel 40% higher). These figures are based on the entire Phase 1 sample and are shown in Figure 6.2. In Phase 2 when total participation by the complete sample in each town was considered (see Figure 6.2), Notel residents still participated significantly more ($M = 45$) than did Unitel residents ($M = 41$), who in turn participated more than Multitel residents ($M = 36$), but the differences were much smaller than in Phase 1 (Notel was 10% rather than 22% higher than Unitel and 25% rather than 40% higher than Multitel). For the subset of those who completed questionnaires in both phases—that is, the longitudinal sample—the participation of Notel youths (18 and under) fell significantly (from 72 to 50, by 31%), but there was no significant change in Unitel ($M = 52$) or Multitel ($M = 47$). Among adults, there was a significant decrease in all three towns, but it was greater in Notel (from 62 to 49, a 21% decrease) than in Unitel (53 to 45, 15%) and Multitel (48 to 45, 6%). These results for comparisons among the towns and across the phases, which indicate that television does affect participation in community activities, were corroborated by other analyses. For example, individuals in Unitel and Multitel who participated in more of their community's activities tended to report watching less television than did those who participated in fewer community activities.

The effects of the availability of TV were particularly strong for active involvement in Sports. Attendance at Dances, Parties, and Suppers, particularly by youths, and at Meetings of organizations, particularly by adults, also was affected. The results for Special Days and Entertainment were not as clear, but there was some evidence that the availability of TV may have had an impact on these events. There were some town differences for Open Areas, Businesses, Civic, Educational (nonschool), and Other activities, but the pattern of findings indicated that the town differences were not related to television. There were no systematic differences among the towns in attendance at Medical and Religious activities.

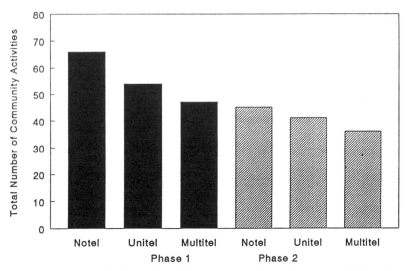

Figure 6.2. Mean Number of Total Community Activities Participated in During the Previous Year, by Town and Phase
NOTE: All participants in each phase.

Was there any evidence that participating in other activities was related to any of the topics reviewed earlier in this chapter? For creativity, the answer is yes. As I mentioned earlier, students with higher Alternate Uses and Pattern Meanings total-idea scores participated more than did students with lower scores in both total community activities and sports in particular. In addition, they participated more in other private leisure activities, both in total and in book reading and radio listening in particular. Unfortunately, we do not have all the relevant data we would need to try to answer this question for persistence and academic achievement.[23]

For most of the other behaviors we studied in Notel, Unitel, and Multitel for which we found differences related to television (e.g., creativity, reading), they seemed to be due mainly to the availability of TV (that is, Notel vs. the other towns in Phase 1 and changes in Notel from before to after obtaining TV) rather than to the number or type of channels available. But in the case of participation in community activities we found both kinds of differences. For example, participation in total community activities was greater in Unitel than in Multitel in both Phase 1 and Phase 2. One explanation for this Unitel-Multitel difference may be the large number of people surveyed, so a smaller difference would be required to be statistically significant than if fewer people had been surveyed. It also is true, however, that Multitel residents reported watching more TV than did Unitel residents (about 7 hours more per week for youths and 6 for adults), which may account for some of the difference in participation in community activities. In addition, whereas Unitel had had television reception for 7 years in Phase 1, Multitel had had it for 15 years. Participation in community activities may fall off gradually rather than abruptly, in part because of social pressure to keep them going. The finding that although participation in Notel dropped following the introduction of TV, it did not fall to the level of Unitel and Multitel by Phase 2, despite the novelty of TV when its effects would be likely to be greatest, is consistent with this hypothesis of a gradual rather than abrupt change.

One of our findings has implications for successful aging and for integration versus segregation of age groups. Before television was available, the older residents (aged 56 and over) in Notel participated as much in their community's activities as did the younger adults and much more than adults 56 and over in Unitel and Multitel. In Unitel and Multitel, there was a substantial drop-off in participation by adults 56 and over by comparison with younger adults. Two years later, this drop-off also was apparent for the 56 and over group in Notel. This pattern held true for active participation in sports as well as for total community activities. Unfortunately, we did not assess the fitness levels of either students or adults, but it seems likely that fitness, and perhaps other aspects of health as well, would vary in relation to patterns of participation in sports and some other activities. The "use-it-or-lose-it" theme of successful aging would suggest that while being able to stay home to watch TV may be more appealing than going out and being more active, particularly in winter (as some older Notel residents told us after the advent of TV), it may have its costs. In addition, if fewer older people are out attending community activities, younger people may have less interaction with them, and there may be more age segregation.

Other Research

In the natural experiment they studied in Australia, Murray and Kippax (1977, 1978) obtained results for their No-TV, Low-TV (1 year's experience with the public channel of the Australian Broadcasting Corporation), and High-TV (2 years' experience with a commercial channel) that were strikingly similar to ours for total participation and sports. They also found that use of alternative media was affected, but the effects on social interaction were less clear. They attributed some of their results to the novelty of TV. Both their study and ours indicate that television displaces some leisure activities but not others. A team of researchers who conducted a time use study of sixth graders in California (Medrich, Roizin, Rubin, & Buckley, 1982) and another group who studied a natural experiment involving small groups of children in Scotland (Brown, Cramond, & Wilde, 1974) reached similar conclusions.

One interesting way to find out how TV use relates to other activities is to study people who were regular viewers but have temporarily lost the use of their set. As multiset households have become more common this possibility has diminished, but in 1976 to 1982, when Winick (1988) conducted such a study in New York City, only about half the homes in the United States had more than one set. The one-set families he interviewed reported considerable disruption in the 3 to 4 days after losing television reception, "even in many homes where viewing was minimal and there were many other ongoing activities" (Winick, 1988, p. 221). Over 80% reported moderate to severe dislocations during this period. Some form of readjustment tended to occur over the 5th to 8th days, and by the second week, "a move toward adaptation to the situation was common" (p. 222). Households in which the set was previously on longest tended to have the most difficulty.

> Households with a relatively high level of education were more likely than those with lower levels of education to handle the loss of the set with relative equanimity. Persons who belonged to a number of voluntary organizations and participated in activities outside the home were better able to adapt to the loss than those not so involved in the community. (p. 222)

Again, these findings are consistent with those we obtained in Notel, Unitel, and Multitel and point to the habitual nature of television use (as discussed by Robert Kubey, Chapter 7, this volume).

Conclusions Regarding Participation in Other Activities

The functional equivalence hypothesis was rejected by both Brown et al. (1974) and Murray and Kippax (1978); they argued instead that television affects the structure of leisure. Most of their results—and ours from Notel, Unitel, and Multitel—are consistent instead with the default hypothesis in which any effects of television are not due to a simple, straightforward, across-the-board displacement of other activities but to concurrent trade-offs in time use. As is the case for the functional equivalence hypothesis, these studies provide little support for "the more, the more" hypothesis.

Along with Medrich et al. (1982), we (Williams & Handford, 1986) have argued that the choice to watch television rather than to do any one of a myriad other activities, in the home or elsewhere, is often not as a conscious choice. The set is turned on out of habit or boredom; the experience of finding something else to do—"a game to play, something to make—has become alien" (Williams & Handford, 1986, p. 187). As I and others (e.g., Rosengren & Windahl, 1989; Wober, 1990) argue with regard to school achievement, a self-perpetuating upward or downward spiral may develop in which those who do other activities find enjoyment and reward in them and become less rather than more likely to turn to television. The responses of people who had lost the use of their TV set and were interviewed by Winick (1988) also are consistent with these notions.

Unfortunately, the opportunity and thus the choice to do many activities varies with socioeconomic status because they involve special equipment, lessons, or fees. And whereas children in some neighborhoods may play sports at little or no cost in their local park, for other children it may be safe only to be indoors, where finances again may limit the alternative choices.

General Conclusions

Under the summary and conclusion headings at the end of each of the main sections of this chapter, I've summarized the research findings and my conclusions regarding our knowledge of the role of television in relation to creativity and imagination, persistence, IQ, school achievement, and participation in other activities. Rather than reiterating those statements, I'd like to conclude this chapter by drawing your attention to some findings and patterns that seem to me to be particularly noteworthy or striking.

First, there is now considerable evidence that in a variety of areas (including imaginative play, persistence, and later school achievement), watching educational and informative programming intended for children in the preschool years has positive effects in keeping with the curriculum of the programs. Aletha Huston and John Wright (Chapter 2, this volume) discuss additional evidence of such effects. We should, therefore, do everything possible to increase the universal availability of educational and informative children's programming.

Second, there is some evidence that programming high in action and aggression has negative effects, not only on aggressive behavior, as Eric Dubow and Laurie Miller (Chapter 5, this volume) discuss, but also on other behaviors, such as imaginative or fantasy play and persistence. There also is some evidence that watching more entertainment and live action programming and watching less informative programming may be related to greater impulsivity, but the correlational nature of these studies does not permit causal inferences.

Third, there is evidence that children's use of television and other media varies with IQ, with lower-IQ students watching more television and using less print than higher IQ students. There also is some intriguing evidence that in the absence of TV, IQ scores are more independent of reading skill and print use than they are when TV is available.

Fourth, there is considerable evidence and agreement, even among researchers who otherwise differ in their assessment of the evidence regarding effects of television, that heavy viewing is detrimental for school achievement. There is less agreement about what qualifies as heavy, with a range from more than 2 to more than 6 hours per day.

Fifth, there is converging evidence from studies in several countries, especially longitudinal studies in which the same viewers are studied repeatedly at several age levels, that television use develops in relation to school achievement from the preschool years onward in what I and Wober (1991) have referred to as upward or downward spirals or what Rosengren and Windahl (1989) have called positive or vicious circles. It seems plausible to me that this may also be true for areas other than school achievement.

Sixth, socioeconomic status (SES) interacts with television use in its effects. When the range of alternative activities for children is limited, the effects of TV and, in particular, heavy viewing, are less negative than is true for more privileged children with many more potential alternative activities.

Reviews give us the opportunity to assess the current state of our knowledge and where that knowledge is lacking. In most of the research on the topics covered in this chapter the focus has been on normative analyses and statements that refer to groups or group comparisons. Even in longitudinal studies in which the same people have been studied at several points in their development, the typical approach is to group the findings and make statements that apply across individuals rather than to conduct idiographic analyses for each individual. As you have read, we have learned a great deal from longitudinal studies about the complex patterns that result from the interplay of the influences of television, parent practices, gender, and so forth. Such studies are enormously time-consuming and expensive, but they provide a much richer set of findings that take taboos into account the many relevant factors and their interactions. In my opinion, we would benefit not only from more studies of that nature but also from including more idiographic analyses and ethnographic studies. For example, I find myself wondering how some of the upward and downward spirals actually operate at the level of individuals and their families. The time seems ripe for some new approaches to flesh out some of the patterns revealed about the use and effects of television in this and the other chapters of this book.

Notes

1. For an interesting discussion of the history and politics of appointments to the Commission and its report, see Liebert and Sprafkin (1988), especially Chapters 5 and 6.

2. I am grateful to Mary Morrison for telling me about the town we came to call "Notel," and to the Canada Council (later, the Social Sciences and Humanities Research Council of Canada) for funding our research.

3. CBC is a public service network, publicly funded through a grant from parliament at arms length from the federal government in power in Canada.

4. This reference, all others beginning with Williams, T. M.; Corteen & Williams (1986); Harrison & Williams (1986); and Suedfeld et al.; refer to my former name, Tannis MacBeth Williams. I have recently reverted to Tannis M. MacBeth.

5. Before-and-after comparisons of the students who were assessed in both phases, first in Grades 4 and 7 and 2 years later in Grades 6 and 9, are called longitudinal comparisons because the same people were studied on more than one occasion.

6. Comparisons between students in Grades 4 and 7 in Phase 1 and those in Grades 4 and 7 in Phase 2 are called cross-sectional because they involve different people. Comparisons between the grades within each phase are also cross-sectional.

7. In Phase 1 the ideational fluency (total) and originality (uniqueness) scores were strongly related and the pattern of results was the same; Notel students had higher scores than those in both Unitel and Multitel, who did not differ. Scoring for originality is extremely time-consuming and funds were limited, so only total-idea scores were analyzed in Phase 2.

8. The median is the point above and below that which 50% of the students score.

9. If the proportion for Notel (40.4%) is compared with the proportion for Unitel and Multitel combined (27.6%), which is the predicted difference, the result, $\chi^2 (1) = 2.75$, has a significant probability ($p < .05$) with a one-tailed test in which the direction of difference is specified and a marginal probability of $p < .10$ if it is not specified. This is a new analysis I've calculated for this chapter. If the proportions for all three towns are compared, the pattern of difference is not significant with either a one- or two-tailed test (as was reported in Suedfeld et al., 1986).

10. In another report based on data for the same sample of children, Anderson, Field, Collins, Lorch, and Nathan (1985) discussed possible reasons for the discrepancy between the reports of parents in their study and the Nielsen figure of 27.8 hours per week for 2- to 5-year-olds during the same historical period. These include the possibilities that light viewers were overrepresented

in their sample and that viewing may be heavier during preannounced rating periods when many attractive programs are shown. Both possibilities strike me as likely. It also is important to note that video cameras were installed in these homes and that the weekly viewing estimates for the diary reports and video records corresponded closely, indicating that the low parental reports were accurate for the children in this sample.

11. In all three towns, students who reported watching more TV also reported more comic reading.

12. In this study children who did well on the WISC Vocabulary test in Phase 1 and were retested 2 years later also tended to do well then, $r(134) = .70, p < .001$, and this also was true for the WISC Block Design test, $r(134) = .55, p < .001$.

13. The data on this question that I reported earlier were based on IQ scores from the group tests (Williams & Boyes, 1986), whereas in this section I am now reporting WISC and other individual IQ test findings (Harrison & Williams, 1986).

14. The data for this portion of the study were collected by Mary Morrison and are reported with her permission.

15. Meta-analysis is a special technique for summarizing, in a statistical way, the findings of a set of studies, taking into account the size of each finding and the size of the sample on which it was based.

16. Wober (1991) also used the phrase "downward spiral" in discussing the impact of negative stereotypes and expectations regarding young, heavy television viewers on their school performance.

17. This was the only study in the project that involved a third phase of data collection, which we undertook because the Phase 2 scores for Unitel second graders were very low.

18. The Phase 2 pattern was complicated because of the anomalously low Unitel scores.

19. The correlations between IQ and fluent reading were as follows: Notel, Phase 1, $r(45) = .19$, n.s.; Unitel and Multitel combined, Phase 1, $r(136) = .44, p < .001$; Notel Phase 2, $r(73) = .36, p < .001$; Unitel and Multitel, $r(165) = .41, p < .001$.

20. The United States.

21. The Television Information Office of the (U.S.) National Association of Broadcasters in the United States.

22. I suspect that the relationship between the kinds of private activities we studied (e.g., knitting, hiking) and use and effects of TV is individualized and depends on each person's interests so that when individuals are grouped together the patterns wash out or cancel each other. This is what I have found in a different research area, and it is part of my motivation in calling, at the end of this chapter, for individual and ethnographic approaches as well as more longitudinal studies.

23. In the case of persistence, we did not study children and did not obtain information about participation in other activities for the particular adults who provided persistence data on the Duncker Candle and Nine-Dot Problems. For academic achievement, our main focus was on reading in the early elementary grades, whereas for participation in other activities, it was on older students (Grades 7 to 12) and adults.

References

Abelman, R. (1984). Television and the gifted child. *Roeper Review, 7*(2), 115-118.

Abelman, R. (1987). Child giftedness and its role in the parental mediation of television viewing. *Roeper Review, 9*(4), 217-220, 240.

Anderson, C., & Maguire, T. (1978). The effect of TV viewing on the educational performance of elementary school children. *Alberta Journal of Educational Research, 24,* 156-163.

Anderson, D., & Collins, P. (1988). *The impact on children's education: Television's influence on cognitive development* (Office of Research Working Paper No. 2). Washington, DC: U.S. Office of Education, Office of Educational Research and Improvement.

Anderson, D. R., Field, D. E., Collins, P. A., Lorch, E. P., & Nathan, J. G. (1985). Estimates of young children's time with television: A methodological comparison of parent reports with time-lapse video observation. *Child Development, 56,* 1345-1357.

Anderson, D. R., Levin, S. R., & Lorch, E. P. (1977). The effects of TV program pacing on the behavior of preschool children. *AV Communication Review, 25,* 154-166.

Anderson, R. C., Wilson, P. T., & Fielding, L. G. (1988). Growth in reading and how children spend their time outside of school. *Reading Research Quarterly, 23,* 285-303.

Ball, S., Palmer, P., & Millward, E. (1986). Television and its educational impact: A reconsideration. In J. Bryant & D. Zillmann (Eds.), *Perspectives on media effects* (pp. 129-142). Hillsdale, NJ: Lawrence Erlbaum.

Barker, R. G. (1968). *Ecological psychology: Concepts and methods for studying the environment of human behavior.* Stanford, CA: Stanford University Press.

Barker, R. G., & Gump, P. V. (1964). *Big school, small school.* Stanford, CA: Stanford University Press.

Barker, R. G., & Wright, H. R. (1971). *Midwest and its children.* Camden, CT: Archon Books. (Original work published in 1955)

Barron, N. F., & Harrington, D. M. (1981). Creativity, intelligence, and personality. *Annual Review of Psychology, 32,* 439-476.

Beentjes, J. W. J. (1989). Learning from television and books: A Dutch replication study based on Salomon's model. *Educational Technology Research and Development, 37,* 47-58.

Briller, B., & Miller, S. (1984). Assessing academic achievement. *Society, 21*(6), 6-9.

Brown, J., Cramond, D. J., & Wilde, R. (1974). Displacement effects of television and the child's functional orientation to media. In J. G. Blumler & E. Katz (Eds.), *The uses of mass communications* (pp. 93-112). Beverly Hills, CA: Sage.

California Assessment Program. (1981). *Student achievement in California schools. 1979-1980 annual report: Television and student achievement.* Sacramento: California State Department of Education. (ERIC Document Reproduction Service No. ED 195 559)

California Assessment Program. (1982). *Survey of sixth grade school achievement and television viewing habits.* Sacramento: California State Department of Education.

Chall, J. S. (1983). *Stages of reading development.* New York: McGraw-Hill.

Collins, P. A. (1991, April). *The impact of television on preschoolers' perseverance, impulsivity, and restlessness.* Paper presented at the biennial meeting of the Society for Research in Child Development, Seattle, WA.

Comstock, G. (1980). *Television in America.* Beverly Hills, CA: Sage.

Comstock, G. (1989). *The evolution of American television.* Newbury Park, CA: Sage.

Comstock, G., Chaffee, S., Katzman, N., McCombs, M., & Roberts, D. (1978). *Television and human behavior.* New York: Columbia University Press.

Comstock, G., & Paik, H. (1991). *Television and the American child.* San Diego, CA: Academic Press.

Comstock, G. A., & Rubinstein, E. A. (Eds.). (1972a). *Television and social behavior (Vol. 1), Media content and control.* Washington, DC: Government Printing Office.

Comstock, G. A., & Rubinstein, E. A. (Eds.). (1972b). *Television and social behavior (Vol. 3), Television and adolescent aggressiveness.* Washington, DC: Government Printing Office.

Comstock, G. A., Rubinstein, E. A., & Murray, J. P. (Eds.). (1972). *Television and social behavior (Vol. 5), Television's effects: Further explorations.* Washington, DC: Government Printing Office.

Corteen, R. S., & Williams, T. M. (1986). Television and reading skills. In T. M. Williams (Ed.), *The impact of television: A natural experiment in three communities* (pp. 39-86). Orlando, FL: Academic Press.

Desmond, R. J., Singer, J. L., & Singer, D. G. (1990). Family mediation: Parental communication patterns and the influences of television on children. In J. Bryant (Ed.), *Television and the American family* (pp. 293-309). Hillsdale, NJ: Lawrence Erlbaum.

Desmond, R. J., Singer, J. L., Singer, D. G., Calam, R., & Colimore, K. (1985). Family mediation patterns and television viewing: Young children's use and grasp of the medium. *Human Communication Research, 11,* 461-480.

Dornbusch, S. M., Ritter, P. L., Leiderman, P. H., Roberts, D. F., & Freleigh, M. J. (1987). The relationship of parenting style to adolescents' school performance. *Child Development, 58,* 1244-1257.

Dorr, A. (1986). *Television and children: A special medium for a special audience.* Newbury Park, CA: Sage.

Duncker, K. (1945). On problem solving. *Psychological Monographs, 58,* 270.

Dworetzky, J. P. (1982). *Psychology.* St. Paul, MN: West.

Friedrich, L. K., & Stein, A. H. (1973). Aggressive and prosocial television programs and the natural behavior of preschool children. *Monographs of the Society for Research in Child Development, 38*(Serial No. 151).

Furu, T. (1971). *The functions of television for children and adolescents.* Tokyo: Sophia University.

Gadberry, S. (1980). Effects of restricting first graders' TV viewing on leisure time use, IQ change, and cognitive style. *Journal of Applied Developmental Psychology, 1*(1), 45-57.

Gates, A. I., & McKillop, A. S. (1962). *Gates-McKillop Diagnostic Reading Tests.* New York: Teacher's College Press.

Gerbner, G., Gross, L., Morgan, M., & Signorielli, N. (1984). Facts, fantasies, and schools. *Society, 21*(6), 9-13.

Gibbons, J., Anderson, D. R., Smith, R., Field, D. E., & Fischer, C. (1986). Young children's recall and reconstruction of audio and audiovisual narratives. *Child Development, 57,* 1014-1023.

Greenfield, P. M., & Beagles-Roos, J. (1988). Radio versus television: Their cognitive impact on children of different socioeconomic and ethnic groups. *Journal of Communication, 38*(2), 71-92.

Greenfield, P. M., Bruzzone, L., Koyamatsu, K., Satuloff, W., Nixon, K., Brodie, M., & Kingsdale, D. (1987). What is rock music doing to the minds of our youth? A first experimental look at the effects of rock music lyrics and music videos. *Journal of Early Adolescence, 7,* 315-329.

Greenfield, P. M., Farrar, D., & Beagles-Roos, J. (1986). Is the medium the message? An experimental comparison of the effects of radio and television on imagination. *Journal of Applied Developmental Psychology, 7,* 201-218.

Greenfield, P., Geber, B., Beagles-Roos, J., Farrar, D., & Gat, I. (1981, April). *Television and radio experimentally compared: Effects of the medium on the imagination and transmission of content.* Paper presented at the biennial meeting of the Society for Research in Child Development, Boston, MA.

Greenfield, P. M., Yut, E., Chung, M., Land, D., Kreider, H., Pantoja, M., & Horsley, K. (1993). The program-length commercial: A study of the effects of television/toy tie-ins on imaginative play. In G. L. Berry & J. K. Asamen (Eds.), *Children and television: Images in a changing sociocultural world* (pp. 53-72). Newbury Park, CA: Sage.

Guilford, J. P. (1975). Creativity: A quarter century of progress. In I. A. Taylor & J. W. Getzels (Eds.), *Perspectives in creativity* (pp. 37-59). Chicago: Aldine.

Hall, E. R., Esty, E. T., & Fisch, S. M. (1990). Television and children's problem-solving behavior: A synopsis of an evaluation of the effects of *Square One TV. Journal of Mathematical Behavior, 9*(2), 161-174.

Harrison, L. F., & Williams, T. M. (1986). Television and cognitive development. In T. M. Williams (Ed.), *The impact of television: A natural experiment in three communities* (pp. 87-142). Orlando, FL: Academic Press.

Healy, J. (1990). Chaos on *Sesame Street. American Educator, 14*(4), 22-29.

Henggeler, S. W., Cohen, R., Edwards, J. J., Summerville, M. B., & Ray, G. E. (1991). Family stress as a link in the association between television viewing and achievement. *Child Study Journal, 21*(1), 1-10.

Hess, R. D., & Holloway, S. D. (1984). Family and school as educational institutions. In R. D. Parke (Ed.), *Review of child development research* (Vol. 7, pp. 179-222). Chicago: University of Chicago Press.

Hoff-Ginsberg, E., & Shatz, M. (1982). Linguistic input and the child's acquisition of language. *Psychological Bulletin, 92*, 3-26.

Hoffner, C., Cantor, J., & Thorson, E. (1988). Children's understanding of a televised narrative. *Communication Research, 15*, 227-245.

Hofmann, R. J., & Flook, M. A. (1980). An experimental investigation of the role of television in facilitating shape recognition. *Journal of Genetic Psychology, 136*, 305-306.

Hornik, R. (1978). Television access and the slowing of cognitive growth. *American Educational Research Journal, 15*(1), 1-15.

Hornik, R. (1981). Out of school television and schooling: Hypotheses and methods. *Review of Educational Research, 51*, 193-214.

Huston, A. C., Donnerstein, E., Fairchild, H., Feshbach, N. D., Katz, P. A., Murray, J. P., Rubinstein, E. A., Wilcox, B. L., & Zuckerman, D. (1992). *Big world, small screen: The role of television in American society*. Lincoln: University of Nebraska Press.

Jastak, J. F., & Wilkinson, G. S. (1984). *Wide-Range Achievement Test-Revised: Administration manual*. Willington, DE: Jastak.

Jönsson, A. (1986). TV: A threat or a complement to school? *Journal of Educational Television, 12*(1), 29-38.

Keys, W., & Foxman, D. (1989). *A world of differences*. Slough, UK: National Foundation for Educational Research.

Kubey, R., & Csikszentmihalyi, M. (1990). *Television and the quality of life: How viewing shapes everyday experience*. Hillsdale, NJ: Lawrence Erlbaum.

Langer, E. J., & Piper, A. (1988). Television from a mindful/mindless perspective. In S. Oskamp (Ed.), *Applied social psychology annual: Television as a social issue* (Vol. 8, pp. 247-260). Newbury Park, CA: Sage.

Lemish, D., & Rice, M. L. (1986). Television as a talking picture book: A prop for language acquisition. *Journal of Child Language, 13*, 251-274.

Liebert, R. M., & Sprafkin, J. (1988). *The early window: Effects of television on children and youth*. New York: Pergamon.

Lyle, J., & Hoffman, H. R. (1972). Children's use of television and other media. In E. A. Rubinstein, G. A. Comstock, & J. P. Murray (Eds.), *Television and social behavior (Vol. 4),*

Television in day-to-day life: Patterns of use (pp. 129-256). Washington, DC: Government Printing Office.

Maccoby, E. E. (1951). Television: Its impact on school children. *Public Opinion Quarterly, 15,* 421-444.

Medrich, E. A., Roizen, J. A., Rubin, V., & Buckley, S. (1982). *The serious business of growing up: A study of children's lives outside school.* Berkeley: University of California Press.

McLuhan, M. (1964). *Understanding media: The extensions of man.* New York: Singer.

Meline, C. W. (1976). Does the medium matter? *Journal of Communication, 26*(3), 81-89.

Messaris, P. (1994). Does TV belong in the classroom? Cognitive consequences of visual "literacy." In S. A. Deetz (Ed.), *Communication yearbook 17* (pp. 431-452). Thousand Oaks, CA: Sage.

Meyersohn, R. (1968). Television and the rest of leisure. *Public Opinion Quarterly, 32,* 102-112.

Mielke, K. W. (1994). On the relationship between television viewing and academic achievement. *Journal of Broadcasting and Electronic Media, 38*(3), 361-366.

Morgan, M., & Gross, L. (1982). Television and educational achievement and aspiration. In D. Pearl, L. Bouthilet, & J. Lazar (Eds.), *Television and behavior: Ten years of scientific progress and implications for the 80s* (Vol. 2). Rockville, MD: National Institute of Mental Health.

Murray, J. P. (1993). The developing child in a multimedia society. In G. L. Berry & J. K. Asamen (Eds.), *Children and television: Images in a changing sociocultural world* (pp. 9-22). Newbury Park, CA: Sage.

Murray, J. P., & Kippax, S. (1977). Television diffusion and social behavior in three communities: A field experiment. *Australian Journal of Psychology, 29*(1), 31-43.

Murray, J. P., & Kippax, S. (1978). Children's social behavior in three towns with differing television experience. *Journal of Communication, 30*(4), 19-29.

Murray, J. P., Rubinstein, E. A., & Comstock, G. A. (Eds.). (1972). *Television and social behavior (Vol. 2), Television and learning.* Washington, DC: Government Printing Office.

National Assessment of Educational Progress. (1986). *Television: What do national assessment results tell us?* Princeton, NJ: Educational Testing Service.

Neuman, S. B. (1986, April). *Television and reading: A research synthesis.* Paper presented at the annual meeting of the American Educational Research Association, San Francisco, CA.

Neuman, S. B. (1991). *Literacy in the television age: The myth of the TV effect.* Norwood, NJ: Ablex.

Office of Educational Research and Improvement. (Ed.). (1990). *National education longitudinal study of 1988: A profile of the American eighth grader. Research in brief* (Stock No. 065-000-00404-6). Washington, DC: Government Printing Office.

Office of Educational Research and Improvement. (1992). *Meeting goal 3: How well are we doing? Education research report.* Washington, DC: U.S. Department of Education, Research Reports, Outreach Office.

Peirce, K. (1983). Relation between time spent viewing television and children's writing skills. *Journalism Quarterly, 60*(3), 445-448.

Postman, N. (1979). First curriculum: Comparing school and television. *Phi Delta Kappan, 61,* 163-168.

Rice, M. L., Huston, A. C., Truglio, R., & Wright, J. (1990). Words from *Sesame Street:* Learning vocabulary while viewing. *Developmental Psychology, 26,* 421-428.

Roberts, D. F., Bachen, C. M., Hornby, M. C., & Hernandez-Ramos, P. (1984). Reading and television: Predictors of reading achievement at different age levels. *Communication Research, 11*(1), 9-49.

Robinson, J. P. (1981). Television and leisure time: A new scenario. *Journal of Communication, 31*(1), 120-130.
Rosengren, K. E., Roe, K., & Sonesson, E. (1983). *Finality and causality in adolescents' mass media use* (Media Panel Report No. 24 [Mimeo]). Lund, Sweden: University of Lund.
Rosengren, K. E., & Windahl, S. (1989). *Media matter: TV use in childhood and adolescence.* Norwood, NJ: Ablex.
Rubinstein, E. A., Comstock, G. A., & Murray, J. P. (Eds.). (1972). *Television and social behavior (Vol. 4), Television in day-to-day life: Patterns of use.* Washington, DC: Government Printing Office.
Runco, M. A., & Pezdek, K. (1984). The effect of television and radio on children's creativity. *Human Communication Research, 11*(1), 109-120.
Salomon, G. (1983). Television watching and mental effort: A social psychological review. In J. Bryant & D. R. Anderson (Eds.), *Children's understanding of television: Research on attention and comprehension* (pp. 181-198). New York: Academic Press.
Salomon, G. (1984). Television is "easy" and print is "tough": The differential investment of mental effort as a function of perceptions and attributions. *Journal of Educational Psychology, 76,* 647-658.
Schramm, W., Lyle, J., & Parker, E. B. (1961). *Television in the lives of our children.* Stanford, CA: Stanford University Press.
Searls, D. T., Mead, N. A., & Ward, B. (1985). The relationship of students' reading skills to TV watching, leisure time reading, and homework. *Journal of Reading, 29,* 158-162.
Selnow, G. W., & Reynolds, H. (1984). Some opportunity costs of television viewing. *Journal of Broadcasting, 28*(3), 315-322.
Singer, D. G. (1982). Television and the developing imagination of the child. In D. Pearl, L. Bouthilet, & J. Lazar (Eds.), *Television and behavior: Ten years of scientific progress and implications for the 80s* (DHHS Publication No. ADM82-1196, pp. 39-52). Washington, DC: Government Printing Office.
Singer, D. G. (1993). Creativity of children in a television world. In G. L. Berry & J. K. Asamen (Eds.), *Children and television: Images in a changing sociocultural world* (pp. 73-88). Newbury Park, CA: Sage.
Singer, D. G., & Singer, J. L. (1990). *The house of make-believe.* Cambridge, MA: Harvard University Press.
Singer, J. L., & Singer, D. G. (1981). *Television, imagination, and aggression: A study of preschoolers' play.* Hillsdale, NJ: Lawrence Erlbaum.
Singer, J. L., & Singer, D. G. (1983). Implications of childhood television viewing for cognition, imagination, and emotion. In J. Bryant & D. R. Anderson (Eds.), *Children's understanding of television: Images in a changing sociocultural world* (pp. 265-296). New York: Academic Press.
Singer, J. L., Singer, D. G., & Rapaczynski, W. S. (1984). Family patterns and television viewing as predictors of children's beliefs and aggression. *Journal of Communication, 34*(2), 73-89.
Singer, J. L., & Singer, D. T. (1986). Family experiences and television viewing as predictors of children's imagination, restlessness, and aggression. *Journal of Social Issues, 42*(3), 107-124.
Stevenson, D. L., & Baker, D. P. (1987). The family-school relation and the child's school performance. *Child Development, 58,* 1348-1357.
Suedfeld, P., Little, B. R., Rank, A. D., Rank, D. S., & Ballard, E. J. (1986). Television and adults: Thinking, personality, and attitudes. In T. M. Williams (Ed.), *The impact of television: A natural experiment in three communities* (pp. 361-394). Orlando, FL: Academic Press.

Swerdlow, J. (1981). What is television doing to real people? *Today's Education, 70*(3), 50-57.

Thomas, A., & Chess, S. (1977). *Temperament and development.* New York: Brunner/Mazel.

Torrance, E. P. (1974). *Torrance tests of creative thinking.* Lexington, MA: Personnel Press.

Tower, R. B., Singer, D. G., Singer, J. L., & Biggs, A. (1979). Differential effects of television programming on preschoolers' cognition, imagination, and social play. *American Journal of Orthopsychiatry, 49*(2), 265-281.

U.S. Department of Education. (1991, November). *Trends in academic progress* (Report No. 21-T-01). Washington, DC: Author.

van der Voort, T. H. A., & Valkenburg, P. M. (1994). Television's impact on fantasy play: A review of research. *Developmental Review, 14*(1), 27-51.

van der Voort, T. H. A., & Vooijs, M. W. (1990). Validity of children's direct estimates of time spent television viewing. *Journal of Broadcasting and Electronic Media, 34,* 93-99.

von Feilitzen, C. (1976). The functions served by the media. In R. Brown (Ed.), *Children and television* (pp. 90-115). Beverly Hills, CA: Sage.

Wade, S. E. (1971). Adolescence, creativity, and media. *American Behavioral Scientist, 14,* 341-351.

Wallach, M. A., & Kogan, N. (1965). *Modes of thinking in young children.* New York: Holt, Rinehart & Winston.

Wartella, E., Alexander, A., & Lemish, D. (1979). The mass media environment of children. *American Behavioral Scientist, 23*(1), 33-52.

Watkins, B. (1988). Children's representations of television and real-life stories. *Communication Research, 15*(2), 159-185.

Williams, P. A., Haertel, E. H., Haertel, G. D., & Walberg, H. J. (1982). The impact of leisure time television on school learning: A research synthesis. *American Educational Research Journal, 19*(1), 19-50.

Williams, T. M. (1981). How and what do children learn from television? *Human Communication Research, 7*(2), 180-192.

Williams, T. M. (1986a). Background and overview. In T. M. Williams (Ed.), *The impact of television: A natural experiment in three communities* (pp. 1-37). Orlando, FL: Academic Press.

Williams, T. M. (1986b). *The impact of television: A natural experiment in three communities.* Orlando, FL: Academic Press.

Williams, T. M. (1986c). Summary, conclusions, and implications. In T. M. Williams (Ed.), *The impact of television: A natural experiment in three communities* (pp. 395-430). Orlando, FL: Academic Press.

Williams, T. M., & Boyes, M. C. (1986). Television viewing patterns and use of other media. In T. M. Williams (Ed.), *The impact of television: A natural experiment in three communities* (pp. 215-264). Orlando, FL: Academic Press.

Williams, T. M., & Handford, A. G. (1986). Television and other leisure activities. In T. M. Williams (Ed.), *The impact of television: A natural experiment in three communities* (pp. 143-214). Orlando, FL: Academic Press.

Winick, C. (1988). The functions of television: Life without the big box. In S. Oskamp (Ed.), *Applied social psychology annual: Television as a social issue* (Vol. 8, pp. 217-237). Newbury Park, CA: Sage.

Winn, M. (1985). *The plug-in drug.* New York: Penguin.

Wober, J. M. (1990). Never mind the picture, sense the screen. *Journal of Educational Television, 16*(2), 87-93.

Wober, J. M. (1991). Light and heavy television viewers: Their pictures in the public mind. *Journal of Educational Television, 17*(2), 101-108.

Wober, J. M. (1992). Text in a texture of television: Children's homework experience. *Journal of Educational Television, 18*(1), 23-24.

Wright, J. C. (1995, March). Effects of viewing *Sesame Street:* A longitudinal study of media and time use. In J. Holz (Chair), *Sesame Street: The experiment continues.* Symposium conducted at the biennial meeting of the Society for Research in Child Development, Indianapolis, IN.

Zuckerman, D. M., Singer, D. G., & Singer, J. L. (1980). Television viewing, children's reading, and related classroom behavior. *Journal of Communication, 30*(1), 166-174.

BIZARRO
By DAN PIRARO

7

Television Dependence, Diagnosis, and Prevention
With Commentary on Video Games, Pornography, and Media Education

Robert W. Kubey

In this chapter, I first examine what is known about psychological dependence on television, applying the psychiatric criteria used in diagnosing substance dependencies to viewing habits. The chapter then turns to concerns about how people can gain greater control over their viewing, with specific attention to the concerns of those responsible for children.

Because media violence is so often the focus of society's concerns about the nondiscriminant and unsupervised use of television by children, I also offer observations and suggestions on this topic. The chapter next considers the positive potentials posed by video and computer games but also why use of these new media can be habit forming. Finally, the long-standing controversy over the effects of pornography is addressed, as is the question of whether

AUTHOR'S NOTE: Portions of this chapter were originally presented at the 98th annual meeting of the American Psychological Association, Boston, August 1990. At that time, diagnostic criteria as covered in *DSM-III-R* were applied. I wish to thank Hartmut Mokros, Ph.D. and James Hutchinson, M.D., for their helpful suggestions on elements of this chapter.

there is such a thing as pornography addiction. New concerns about interactive erotica are raised. In light of the foregoing, at the conclusion of the chapter I briefly consider the value of formal media education.

Television Dependence

Many people today believe that television viewing can be addictive. Although only 2% and 12.5% of adults in two separate surveys believed that they were addicted, 65% to 70% believed that others were addicted (McIlwraith, 1990; McIlwraith, Jacobvitz, Kubey, & Alexander, 1991; Smith, 1986).

Although it is tempting to use the term *addiction* when referring to individuals who report upward of 60 hours of viewing each week, the term connotes different things to different people. It seems likely that less confusion will result if we are more careful in the words we choose.

Indeed, the primary diagnostic manual used by psychotherapists throughout North America, the American Psychiatric Association's (1994) *Diagnostic and Statistical Manual of Mental Disorders* (4th ed.) *(DSM-IV),* does not use the term addiction, nor did its previous edition published in 1987. Instead, the committees that wrote the *DSM* preferred the term *substance dependence* to conceptualize what others might call addiction. Still, there remain researchers and clinicians who use the term addiction, especially with regard to pornography. As a result, in the pages ahead I will use that term from time to time.

How the Viewing Habit Is Formed

Before launching into a more general discussion of television dependence, I want to recount some of the relevant findings I have reported in earlier research using the experience sampling method (ESM). Since the mid-1970s, my colleagues and I have used this method to study how people use and experience television, as well as other media.

The ESM involves having research subjects report what they are doing and how they are feeling each time they are signaled with a radio-controlled beeper. Typically, each respondent is signaled six to eight times each day, from morning till night, for a week. The timing of the signals is predetermined by the research team to occur at random intervals, and participants do not know when to expect a signal. The research has enabled us to study television viewing along with other daily activities as they naturally occur.

In addition to the beepers, participants also carry a small booklet of self-report forms. After each signal, the individual stops to fill out a short report form telling us how he or she felt on a number of standard psychological measures of mood and mental activity. The ESM has already proved useful in the diagnosis and understanding of psychopathologies such as the eating disorders bulimia and anorexia (Johnson & Larson, 1982; Larson & Johnson, 1981), drug and alcohol abuse (Larson, Csikszentmihalyi, & Freeman, 1984), schizophrenia (deVries, 1987), and multiple personality disorder (Lowenstein, Hamilton, Alagna, Reid, & deVries, 1987).

With the ESM we have found that television viewing typically involves less concentration and alertness, and is experienced more passively, than almost all other daily activities, except when people report "doing nothing" (Csikszentmihalyi & Kubey, 1981; Kubey, 1984; Kubey & Csikszentmihalyi, 1990a). These very basic findings have held up for people from ages 10 to 82 and from people studied in the United States, Canada, West Germany, and Italy.

The main positive experience people report when viewing is relaxation, but the relaxed and passive bodily and mental states associated with viewing may also make it difficult for many people to turn the set off. Furthermore, the passive viewing state doesn't stop once people turn off the set, it can "spill over" into how they feel afterward. Most viewers continue to feel relaxed regardless of how long they view, but some report less satisfaction and greater difficulty concentrating the longer they view (Kubey, 1984; Kubey & Csikszentmihalyi, 1990a).

The spillover effect suggests that viewing can inculcate passivity in some viewers, at least in the short term, and it appears that many viewers find it more difficult to turn off the set the longer they view. Activities that might have seemed simple to do at 6:00 p.m. begin to appear more formidable as the viewer becomes accustomed to spending time passively.[1]

The mood modulating and psychological coping features of television use are evidenced in ESM studies by the fact that people who report feeling significantly worse early in the afternoon are more likely to report later the same day that they watched a lot of television, whereas people who report feeling better in the afternoon are more likely later that day to report a light night of viewing (Kubey, 1984; Kubey & Csikszentmihalyi, 1990b). That people use television to escape negative and unpleasant moods has been shown by others as well (Schallow & McIlwraith, 1986-1987; Steiner, 1963). In fact, adults who called themselves "TV addicts" were also significantly more likely than "nonaddicted" viewers to report using television to cope with negative moods, such as loneliness, sadness, anxiety, and anger (McIlwraith, 1990).

Television has been found to distract viewers from the negative thinking and rumination that can contribute to unpleasant mood states (Bryant & Zillmann, 1984; McIlwraith & Schallow, 1983; Singer, 1980; Singer & Singer, 1983). Also, viewing appears to be particularly effective in reducing normal stress and mild tension (Milkman & Sunderwirth, 1987). The distraction function of TV has even been found to reduce patients' reports of pain during dental procedures (Seyrek, Corah, & Pace, 1984).

Self-labeled addicts say they are particularly likely to use television when they have nothing to do and to fill open time (McIlwraith, 1990). By comparison with light viewers who watch less than 2 hours a day, heavy viewers (more than 4 hours) generally report feeling worse when alone and when in unstructured situations, such as waiting in line or when "between" activities (Kubey, 1986).

These findings suggest a possible dependence on the medium for filling the voids that accompany solitude or open time. Sensation-seeking and avoidance of unpleasant thoughts, memories, and emotions have also been theorized to be at play. Eysenck (1978), for example, theorized that extroverts would become dependent on television because of a low tolerance for boredom and a need to increase arousal.

One interpretation is that viewing is simply symptomatic, that is, people who feel anxious when alone or in unstructured situations will gravitate to television to feel less anxious and alone and more psychologically structured. Put another way, people use television to distract themselves from their negative ruminations and mood states by letting the medium help structure their attention. In one way, the effect may not be very different from the immediate, positive change in mood observed in an infant when his or her attention is suddenly structured by the sound and sight of a shaking rattle.

In both the United States (Smith, 1986) and Canada (McIlwraith, 1990) researchers have studied self-labeled TV addicts. In both studies they scored significantly higher than viewers who described themselves as "nonaddicted" on measures of mind wandering, distractibility, boredom, and unfocused daydreaming (from the Poor Attentional Control Scale of the Short Imaginal Processes Inventory, a relatively simple paper-and-pencil psychological measurement instrument). This suggests the possibility of a vicious circle wherein the experience of negative moods and thoughts when alone and when unstructured may interact with the ease with which people can quickly escape these feelings by viewing (Kubey, 1986). As a result of many hours spent viewing television over many years, some people may become unpracticed in spending time alone, entertaining themselves, or even in directing their own attention (Harrison & Williams, 1986; Kubey, 1986, 1990a; Singer & Singer, 1983).

Many hours spent watching television each day over many years may also decrease tolerance of the self. Conceivably, lonely people who are generally more inclined to use television in the first place may, in turn, become even more uncomfortable when alone and left without the quasi-social experience the medium offers. As Harrison and Williams (1986) put it, constant use of television "seems unlikely to encourage the ability to tolerate aloneness with one's thoughts and ideas" (p. 125). Heavy viewers do tend to have more time on their hands, typically spending more time alone than light viewers. Among the demographic groups with more heavy viewers in their ranks are the old, the unemployed, and persons recently divorced or separated (Huston et al., 1992; Kubey, 1980; Kubey & Csikszentmihalyi, 1990a; Smith, 1986; Steiner, 1963; Williams, 1986).

In short, a television viewing habit may be self-perpetuating. Viewing may lead to more viewing and may elicit what has been called "attentional inertia," that is, "the longer people look at television, the greater is the probability that they will continue to look" (Anderson, Alwitt, Lorch, & Levin, 1979, p. 339). Discomfort in noncommitted, or solitary, time can lead to viewing, but after years of such behavior and a thousand hours or more of viewing each year, it seems quite possible that an ingrained television habit could cause some people to feel uncomfortable when left with "nothing to do" or alone and not viewing (Kubey, 1986).

Not only does television viewing relax people, anecdotal reports indicate that it relaxes them quickly. Within moments of sitting or lying down and pushing a TV set's power button, many viewers report feeling more relaxed than they did before. Also, because the reinforcement of relaxation occurs quickly, people readily learn to associate viewing with relaxation. The association is then repeatedly reinforced (operant conditioning) because although the quality of other emotional and mental states may deteriorate somewhat, viewers remain relaxed throughout viewing (Kubey, 1984; Kubey & Csikszentmihalyi, 1990a). The habit is readily formed but can be very difficult to break (Daley, 1978; Winick, 1988).

Let's consider drug use for a possible analogy. "The attribute of a drug that most contributes to its *abuse liability* is not its ability to produce tolerance or physical dependence but rather its ability to reinforce the drug-taking behaviors" (Swonger & Constantine, 1976, p. 235). This is why both the speed of a drug's effect and how quickly it leaves the body can be critical factors as to whether or not dependence occurs. It's important to note that reinforcement needn't be experienced consciously for it to be effective.

It may prove instructive to consider the induction of relaxation with two common tranquilizers (benzodiazepines), Valium (diazepam) and Tranxene (clorazepate). The time it takes for Valium to take effect and actually reduce anxiety is shorter than for Tranxene. It is in part because of the fast relief from tension provided by Valium that some people are at greater risk of developing a substance dependence with it than with Tranxene. Some physicians prescribe Tranxene precisely for this reason. In other words, if a person is rewarded with a significant change in mood shortly after taking a substance, it is more likely that the person will use the substance frequently than if it were slower acting.

By the same token, some tranquilizers and antidepressants whose "half-lives" are very short (the drug leaves the body rapidly relative to other drugs) can also be more habit forming precisely because the patient is more likely to be aware that the drug's effects are wearing off. When the return to feeling bad is rapid, the tendency to turn to the drug for relief once again can be greater than if its effects were to wear off more gradually.

Returning to television's effects, the relaxation effect appears to be most noticeable when the viewer is viewing, not afterward; we found little evidence that people feel better or more relaxed after viewing (Kubey, 1984; Kubey & Csikszentmihalyi, 1990a). Thus, the change in mood that one experiences from the time of viewing to when one suddenly stops viewing may be abrupt, perhaps more comparable to the effect of drugs that wear off quickly than slowly. These principles may be involved in the development of some television dependencies.

Viewing also begets more viewing because one must generally keep watching to keep feeling relaxed (Kubey, 1984; Kubey & Csikszentmihalyi, 1990a). A kind of psychological and physical inertia may develop. Although paying the bills might not have seemed difficult immediately after dinner, after 2 or 3 hours spent with TV, viewers become accustomed to having their experience effortlessly and passively structured. Getting up and taking on a more demanding task may begin to seem more formidable.[2]

Relative to the other possible means available to bring about distraction and relaxation, television is among the quickest and certainly among the cheapest. Also, in contrast to conversation or games, one does not need anyone else to watch TV. Indeed, in many Western, developed nations television is readily and instantly available 24 hours a day. Nowadays, with well over 30 cable channels available to most North American households, one can almost always find something of interest to view. Self-control over one's viewing may have become more of a challenge for many than it was in the not so distant past (Kubey, 1990a).

Applying DSM-IV
Substance Dependence Criteria

Using the American Psychiatric Association's (1994) diagnostic and statistical manual *(DSM-IV)* as a guide for making a diagnosis of television dependence is instructive. Indeed, Dr. Allen J. Frances, who oversaw the most recent revision of the manual, concluded that "Under the broader definition, many kinds of compulsive behavior could be considered addictive, including obsessive sex or *compulsive television viewing* [italics added]" (Goleman, 1990, p. C8).

DSM-IV lists seven possible criteria for making a diagnosis of substance dependence (pp. 176-181). Three must apply to make a diagnosis of dependence. Diagnosis also involves a time dimension: *DSM-IV* states that "dependence is defined as a cluster of three or more of the symptoms listed next occurring at any time in the same 12-month period" (p. 176).

In considering these criteria and the relevant literature on television viewing, five of the seven diagnostic criteria would appear to be applicable to television viewing and its concomitant behaviors and effects. The two

DSM-IV criteria that I believe do not readily apply to television viewing habits, or are less applicable, are reported first.

Less Applicable Criteria

1. Number 1 in *DSM:* "Tolerance, as defined by either of the following: (a) a need for markedly increased amounts of the substance to achieve intoxication or desired effect" or "(b) markedly diminished effect with continued use of the same amount of the substance" (p. 181).

Even here, however, it is noteworthy that we have found that viewers obtain the benefit of relaxation only when they are viewing. For this reason, among others, we have hypothesized that viewing often continues for as long as it does. Heavier viewers also enjoy their viewing less on average than do light viewers (Kubey, 1984; Kubey & Csikszentmihalyi, 1990a).

2. Number 7 in *DSM:* "The substance use is continued despite knowledge of having a persistent or recurrent physical or psychological problem that is likely to have been caused or exacerbated by the substance" (p. 181).

As will be noted later, there may be a small percentage of people for whom this criterion could be applied, but the use of the word *knowledge* demands awareness, and awareness of having a significant physical or psychological problem due to TV use is probably rare. Still, it is almost certainly the case that some individuals recognize that their television viewing habit interferes with their social relations, level of physical exercise, or work habits. In these instances, television could be seen as exacerbating physical or psychological problems.

There is evidence that children and adolescents who view a great deal of television tend to be more obese than those who view less (Dietz & Gortmaker, 1985; Taras, Sallis, Patterson, Nader, & Nelson, 1989).[3] There is also new research suggesting that a child's metabolism slows down when watching television. Furthermore, consumption of "junk food" among adult self-labeled TV addicts is higher than for nonaddicts (McIlwraith, 1990). Some people also report feeling more passive after viewing than before they began, and this passivity may decrease the likelihood that viewers will become involved in more active and potentially rewarding activities (Kubey, 1984, 1990a; Kubey & Csikszentmihalyi, 1990a).

Applicable Criteria

Now let us turn to the more relevant diagnostic criteria. As with those mentioned earlier, I have used the exact language of *DSM-IV*. Each criterion is followed by observations regarding how known television behaviors are related.

> 1. Number 3 in *DSM*: "The substance is often taken in larger amounts or over a longer period than was intended" (p. 181).

It is common for viewers of all ages to report sitting down to watch just one program but to end up watching much more than planned. So this diagnostic criterion may fit many viewers.

In a Gallup Poll, 42% of the 1,241 U.S. adults who were surveyed reported that they "spent too much time watching television" (Gallup & Newport, 1990). Mander (1978) reported that some of the typical viewers he interviewed said things such as, "If a television is on, I just can't keep my eyes off it" and "I don't want to watch as much as I do but I can't help it. It makes me watch it" (p. 158). Renowned psychologists Milton Rosenberg (1978) and Percy Tannenbaum (1980) have each reported on the strong attraction and hold of television in their own lives (for a discussion see Kubey & Csikszentmihalyi, 1990a, p. 38; also Winick, 1988).

Indeed, the viewing habit is so entrenched in many people that the choice to view is made almost automatically (Kubey, 1990a; Williams & Handford, 1986). Once dinner is done or the dishes are washed, many individuals sit down to watch television regardless of what programs are on.

> 2. Number 4 in *DSM*: "There is a persistent desire or unsuccessful efforts to cut down or control substance use" (p. 181).

As noted previously, it is common for people to report that they believe they spend too much time viewing. This belief itself appears to be on the rise. The percentage of adults in the United States who felt that they watched too much television in the late 1970s was 31%, 11 points lower than the 1990 figure of 42% (Gallup & Newport, 1990).

It is also relatively common for people to report that they feel powerless to stop viewing on their own without abandoning the set altogether or interfering with it electronically (Daley, 1978). Some people have told me that they have given up their cable subscriptions precisely so that they have less choice and will thereby watch less. Also, as stated in the *DSM-IV*, technically one need only have a "persistent desire . . . to cut down or control substance use" (American Psychiatric Association, 1994, p. 181) for the criterion to apply. Presumably, some of the Gallup Poll respondents would qualify.

>   3. Number 5 in *DSM:* "A great deal of time is spent in activities necessary to obtain the substance . . . , use the substance (e.g., chain smoking), or recover from its effects" (p. 181).

Clearly, with the vast majority of Americans spending 2 to 4 hours daily with television, or over half of all their leisure time, a great deal of time is spent using television.

>   4. Number 6 in *DSM:* "Important social, occupational, or recreational activities are given up or reduced because of substance use" (p. 181). "The individual may withdraw from family activities and hobbies in order to use the substance in private" (p. 178).

There is a good deal of research that shows that television can bring family members together but also that it can reduce familial contact (Bronfenbrenner, 1973; Huston & Wright, Chapter 2, this volume; Kubey, 1990b, 1990c; Maccoby, 1951; National Institute of Mental Health [NIMH], 1982). Not a few adults feel neglected by their partners who use television heavily (e.g., so called "football widows"). People have reported to me that they feel that they must regularly compete with television personalities for the attention of family members (Kubey, 1994).

Many people also use television (not to mention other media) purposely to avoid contact with their family. Particularly disturbing is the suggestion that some children may be emotionally, and perhaps even physically, neglected because their caregivers are too engaged in television programs to attend to their needs (Desmond, Singer, & Singer, 1988; Shanahan & Morgan, 1989).

With regard to recreation, some viewers will necessarily engage less in other activities if they are spending 3, 4, or more hours each day watching television. For example, Williams and Handford (1986) found that adolescents and adults participated much less in community activities and sports when TV was available than when it was not (see MacBeth, Chapter 1, this volume).

As for occupational activities, there undoubtedly are people who bring work home from the office but do not do as much (or perhaps a lower-quality job) than they might because of a television habit that is not under control.

5. Number 2 in *DSM:* "withdrawal, as manifested by either of the following: (a) the characteristic withdrawal syndrome for the substance" or "(b) the same (or a closely related) substance is taken to relieve or avoid withdrawal symptoms" (p. 181). Withdrawal includes "a maladaptive behavioral change" and it is noted that "withdrawal symptoms vary greatly" (p. 178).

This criterion is a bit more difficult to apply to television viewing behaviors because we are largely limited to anecdotal reports and a small number of social science studies of withdrawal-like symptoms.[4] Still, such reports are not hard to find.

Steiner (1963), for example, presents individuals' reports of a variety of behaviors of psychological interest that occurred following the loss of a television set due to a technological malfunction. Here are three examples: " 'The family walked around like a chicken without a head.' 'It was terrible. We did nothing, my husband and I talked.' 'Screamed constantly. Children bothered me and my nerves were on edge. Tried to interest them in games, but impossible. TV is part of them' " (p. 99). In her informal interviews, Winn (1977, pp. 21-22) has presented many similar anecdotes.

Today, such reports are less frequent, in part because most homes have more than one set. To be completely without a television set today is unusual, which is perhaps still another sign of how entrenched television viewing has become.

Nonetheless, Winick (1988) offers a valuable review of studies of families whose television sets were in repair. He writes,

The first 3 or 4 days for most persons were the worst, even in many homes where viewing was minimal and where there were other ongoing activities. In over half of all the households, during these first few days of loss, the regular routines were disrupted, family members had difficulties in dealing with the newly available time, anxiety and aggressions were expressed, and established expectations for the behavior of other household members were not met. People living alone tended to be bored and irritated. Over four-fifths of the respondents reported moderate to severe dislocations during this period. . . . The fifth to eighth day represented, in many cases, some form of readjustment to the new situation. By the second week, a move toward adaptation to the situation was common. (pp. 221-222)

Daley (1978, pp. 147-148) offers a similar account of his family's difficulties stopping viewing and how easily the habit reformed itself after 6 months of abstinence.

A number of newspapers, in the United States and abroad, have offered money as an incentive to get individuals or families to stop viewing television for some limited period of time, often a week or a month (reviewed in Condry, 1989; Kubey & Csikszentmihalyi, 1990a; Winick, 1988). Increased tension between family members has been described and many families could not complete the period of abstinence agreed on (Ryan, 1974). In a German study it was reported that there was increased verbal and physical fighting after viewing stopped.

If a family has been spending the lion's share of its free time together over a period of years watching television, as is the case for many families today, it may take some days or weeks, or longer, for the family to reconfigure itself around a new set of activities. Particularly because watching television is so easy to do, family members may have become less imaginative about other ways to spend their time together.

In sum, although there is not a great deal of hard empirical evidence, it does seem likely that some individuals, and perhaps entire families, go through something akin to withdrawal if television suddenly disappears. Furthermore, in congruence with Section B of this criterion, other enjoyable leisure and media activities are typically used to supplant TV viewing for those trying to give it up. It is also interesting to note that television is sometimes used by individuals seeking to withdraw from drugs such as heroin, cocaine, and alcohol as a less harmful means of escape and distraction (Dyznskyi, personal communication, October 20, 1994; Kubey & Csikszentmihalyi, 1990a, p. 184-185).

As can be seen, when *DSM-IV*'s diagnostic criteria are applied to television viewing habits, a diagnosis of substance dependence can be made for many people. The key missing feature, it would seem, is that we are not accustomed to thinking of television as a substance: It is neither a liquid (alcohol), nor a solid (a pill). Still, the viewing of television does, in some way, involve taking something into the body, even if that something is only light and sound and even if no residue of the substance can be later found in the body. Although it may not be a substance, millions of people nonetheless believe that they, or people they know, need to gain better control of their use of the medium. To that end, we next turn our attention.

Controlling the Television Habit

Although methods to diagnose television dependence have not been established, there are ways that individuals or families can achieve better control of their viewing habits. A few suggestions follow, but I must note that these are commonsense measures and although some have been tried by individuals, none, to my knowledge, has been put to a controlled, empirical test. One exception is the introduction of a behavioral approach employing a "token economy" wherein children earn tokens by engaging in non-TV activities that parents wish to encourage. The tokens can then be used to "buy" television time. In one early test, only very limited success in curbing heavy television use among children was achieved (Jason, 1987).

But such an approach raises a new problem. Does making television the reward or making removal of TV the punishment simply increase the general sense among children and adults that television is among the most preferred of activities?

As with other habits and dependencies that people wish to change, it may be most helpful initially for people simply to recognize how much they are viewing and how frequently or infrequently television provides the rewards and benefits they want to obtain. One way to do this is to keep a diary for a week of all programs viewed. For many, adding up the hours at the end of the week can be quite sobering. Some people may also be assisted by rating the quality of their experience with TV or how much they enjoyed or learned from various programs. Again, at the end of a week, such a diary may prove illuminating.

Taking stock of how much TV we watch may be especially striking when we consider that North Americans have an average of 5.5 hours of free time each day (Robinson, 1989) and typically view TV for more than 3 hours each day. In short, for most people, more than half of all free time is spent watching television.

Or we could do a little arithmetic. If a person lives to age 75 and typically sleeps about 8 hours a night, he or she will have lived 50 "waking" years. If viewing television consumes 4 hours each day, or 25% of each 16 hour waking day, one can then conclude that 12.5 years of the person's 50 waking years will be spent watching television. This may be how some people wish to spend their time, but few people have assessed their viewing habit in these terms.

But it is rarely enough merely to raise awareness of how much we are viewing. It is also important to exercise willpower and to find other activities to supplant the time with television.

With regard to "will," it may not be quite as difficult as it sometimes seems simply to turn off the set. Viewers often know that a particular program or movie of the week is not very good within the first few minutes, but instead of switching off the set, they view for the full 2 hours, perhaps with some minor interest in whether it was the yogurt store manager or the aerobics instructor who committed the murder, and then feel cheated and contemptuous of themselves for having "wasted" their time.

We may be able to effectively reduce our viewing by becoming more cognizant early on that sometimes we are not really missing so much after all. Five or 10 minutes after turning off an only somewhat gripping mystery story, we rarely care any longer what was going to happen.[5]

As for supplanting television viewing with other activities, generating a list of enjoyable activities, constructive activities, or both, that can be done in or around the home may prove helpful. The list might be posted on the refrigerator or even on the TV set. Using such a list of enjoyable leisure activities has proved effective for patients suffering from mild depressive episodes (Lewinsohn, 1974).

Instead of reflexively going to the television as soon as dinner is done, those interested in reducing their viewing can go to the list to help remind themselves of other activities—calling a friend, writing a letter, reading, playing cards or a board game, paying the bills, working on a computer, polishing shoes—that might be done instead of watching TV. The idea is to break the repetitive, habitual, and self-perpetuating nature of the habit.

Of course, it must be noted that television producers are masters at finding clever ways to get people to view longer than they had originally intended. New stories are "teased" in the preceding hours with titillating suggestions that spike viewer interest and increase the possibility that we will view beyond the single program that we may have planned to watch.

Using a television guide can also be helpful in cutting down on TV viewing. We can choose which programs to watch ahead of time and then watch only those programs preselected, slotting other activities between the shows we don't want to miss. A VCR can also be effective in time-shifting. (Actually, many viewers never return to some of the material they've taped, which is itself an indication that viewing those programs was not so critical after all.) The VCR also permits viewers to speed search through unwanted material.

One viewer who likes sketch comedy reports that by taping his favorite comedy program, *Saturday Night Live,* and by then eliminating the opening monologue, the musical guests, all of the ads, and the sketches that he can tell aren't gelling from their inception, he can reduce what was once a 90-minute experience to one that takes as little as 20 minutes.

Or for a small charge ($8-$12), anyone can set up their own "mini" film festival at home, renting films by a favorite director, thereby making the experience a more personally active one by stopping and studying particular scenes. Such a use of the VCR might actually increase one's total time with TV, while making a much more discriminating and rewarding viewing experience possible.

Altering viewing habits can be particularly difficult in families because, as with so many other features of family life, television viewing is often systemic in nature. As with couples who smoke and wish to quit, reduction of television viewing is likely to go more smoothly if family members work together and decide jointly to get their habit under control.

One frequent choice of those wishing to reduce their viewing is to go "cold turkey." Indeed, the fact that many people choose this approach is another way in which television dependency is similar to substance dependencies. Quite a few people have told me that if they own a television, viewing soon begins to dominate family life and that the only way they can get things under control is to remove the set altogether or to cancel their cable subscription.

Daley's (1978, pp. 147-148) experiences in trying to curtail his family's viewing may prove interesting for some readers. There is also a book on the subject, *Breaking the TV Habit* by Joan Wilkins (1982). There are now special electronic switches that can be attached to a television set permitting only those members of the household who have a code number or combination to "unlock" the set. Some people consider this to be an extreme approach. Others find it an easy way for parents to control their children's viewing.

Nowadays, many new television sets include design features that make it possible to block out particular channels. In early 1996, President Clinton and members of the U.S. Congress and Senate required the development of a "v-chip," a microchip built in to new television sets, that would permit caregivers to block the reception of any program with a high violence rating. Of course, such a development is contingent on the television industry rating such programs and encoding them with the appropriate readable violence code.

In sum, I have suggested a number of approaches that individuals and parents may wish to consider when trying to change their television viewing habits or dependencies. My suggestions are not based on systematic research designed to assess the effectiveness of different approaches, however, as there has been so little research on this topic.

Parental Responsibility, Children, and Violence

In making decisions and judgments about what is in the best interests of a child, and especially about children and media, it is critical to remember that every child is simultaneously unique and changing, often rapidly. Furthermore, every medium is different, and TV shows, video games, movies, and books offer an enormous range in content, form, and style. Still, there are some similarities across most children at different ages and across media and different programs, games, and stories. So although idiosyncratic judgments with regard to each child are critical, there are also some general observations that can be made.

Today, we probably have more children at risk for developing a dependency on television than ever before. I have observed, as have others (James Hutchinson, M.D., personal communication, April, 1994), that a substantial number of parents do not believe that they can, or should, control their children's viewing. Some believe that there is no potential harm in anything that a child might watch. They believe that children can negotiate the television text on their own.

Many parents have reported to me that it is beyond their ability to limit their children's viewing. None of us wants to be a dictator, but in my opinion, parents should not back down when making decisions about what their children may view on television. If parents are not in reasonable control of their households, and of their children and their activities, we might conclude that the socialization process is, at best, undergoing change. At worst, one might expect all manner of social problems to ensue (Kubey, 1994).

Parental monitoring of children's viewing is important because I believe that certain kinds of programs and material are unsuitable for some children, young children in particular. I am especially concerned about "reality programming" and news programs that often engender unnecessary and substantial fear. Indeed, I am as concerned about the fear-induction effects of violence as I am about the potential modeling effects (Kubey, 1987); and

Joanne Cantor (Chapter 4, this volume) clearly documents such fear-induction effects.

In short, children sometimes need to be supervised in their use of television, video games, computers, and other media, just as they sometimes need supervision when carving a pumpkin, walking down stairs, or riding a bicycle on the street.

As with any activity, too much of the same thing may not always be best, especially for a developing child. If other activities and experiences are not occurring with the frequency that a caregiver or parent deems to be appropriate because of a television or video game habit, then, in my opinion it is the right and responsibility of the caregiver to limit such activities. Children ought to get outside now and then, they ought to sleep a reasonable number of hours, and when they're old enough they ought to read and do their homework. The reader might turn to MacBeth (Chapter 6, this volume) for a review of the extensive literature relating children's use of television to their academic achievement.

Just as we would not permit children to eat all the candy they collect on Halloween or permit a child to read at night with poor light until his or her eyes are strained, so too must caregivers make similar judgments about the use of television and video games.

Simultaneously, we must also encourage children to develop their own internal self-monitoring abilities so that they can increasingly make these determinations for themselves.

Much of what I have just written will strike many readers as obvious. I have made these points for two reasons. The first is that some media analysts, most often those allied with the "cultural studies" approach to media studies, an approach that has made many important contributions to our understanding of how audiences experience and understand the media, believe that parents ought never to censor or prohibit a child from partaking in any medium or story that they might wish to experience. For some, it is a presumptuous and arrogant act for a parent to intrude on or censor the media experience of a child.

For theoretical, political, and pedagogical reasons, some theorists have concluded that the media are a different kind of phenomenon from things such as fire, "dangerous strangers," candy, and unguarded cliffs and stairs. Television shows, books, and video games are all cultural products and can be actively "negotiated" by audience members. Notably, much of the research on such negotiations, or "readings," of media texts has been done with adolescents and adults, not children. Nevertheless, some cultural studies advocates have criticized developmental psychologists for being too proscriptive in their views about appropriate media content for children (Buckingham & Sefton-Green, 1996; Seiter, in press).

My second reason for emphasizing the need for caregivers to supervise children's media use is that many parents report that they were not restricted in their own viewing when they were young, yet they often watched a lot of violence on television. Insofar as they believe they were not psychologically harmed in any way, they now believe that they can safely permit their children to watch whatever they like.

When confronted by the idea that contemporary adults were not at all harmed by the violence they viewed as children and that, consequently, there is no need to monitor a contemporary child's viewing, I would suggest consideration be given to the five ideas that follow.

First, perhaps such parents have been affected but are not aware of the effect(s)—perhaps many of us have become desensitized to violence in the media in ways that we do not even recognize.

Second, many of today's movies that later find their way to television are far more graphically violent than depictions experienced in film or television 15 or 20 years ago. For example, people's bodies and heads are sometimes blown apart, in slow motion and in convincing and disturbing detail (Kubey, 1987); women in some movies are pursued by mass murderers with the camera taking the point of view of the stalker, helping to enhance the sense that the viewer is doing the stalking.

Third, increasingly of late, television news programs show much more than they once did of the graphic results of violence on humans. Young children are particularly likely to be frightened by this kind of material and older children and adolescents fear that it may happen to them (Cantor, Chapter 4, this volume). The recent media frenzy over the abduction and killing of Polly Klass in California and over Susan Smith's murder of her two young sons in South Carolina have upset tens of thousands of children—unnecessarily so in my view. In fact, quite a few adults tell me that they themselves are increasingly being disturbed and frightened by the news they see on television.

Fourth, although many television programs and video games are both fun and educational, there also are many other things that we want our children to do. Sometimes television viewing and video game play get in the way. Less structured activities may also offer children more opportunities to develop their imagination and creativity than the often structured nature of media activities.

Fifth, today no one who cares for children and who monitors their TV viewing can be assured that the child won't suddenly be confronted with a message that is frightening, inappropriate, or both. Indeed, polls have shown that more parents now than in the past feel compelled to suddenly turn the set off when some frightening or problematic event is being presented. Nowadays, many parents make sure that the remote control is nearby whenever they view with their children.

My older son was 6 when he first watched *The Wizard of Oz* on TV, a favorite movie of mine that my wife and I concluded was now appropriate for his viewing, even though it contains frightening scenes of monkeys flying and witches melting. During one commercial break, CBS promoted a story to be shown a few days later on its popular program *60 Minutes*. The ad included both a voice-over and words on screen promoting a story titled "Kids Killing Kids?" The promotion was dominated by news footage of a child being rushed into a hospital emergency room on a stretcher, wrapped in gauze and bleeding. My son was frightened by what he had seen and heard. He wanted to know whether or not kids really killed kids. We talked about it for a while, even though it meant missing Dorothy's initial meeting with the Cowardly Lion.

I am not recommending that children be constantly supervised, only that for many children today, television's current offerings demand more vigilance on the part of parents than was the case 30 or 40 years ago. I believe that we need to become more savvy about violence in the media and the different forms it takes because I believe that some forms of violence are much more problematic for children than others—an issue to which I turn next.

Media Violence Versus Fairy Tale Violence

Some parents report to me that they are worried that their child has developed an obsession with a particular favorite videotape and worry that there's something awry. Although I know of no research on the subject, it's my strong hunch that this is a fairly normal phenomenon, at least in statistical terms owing to the number of parents who inquire about it, but also because children have long had favorite storybooks or fairy tales that they want read to them over and over again.

In the recent past, few parents worried much if their toddler carried a worn copy of *Sleeping Beauty* everywhere she or he went. But the sight of a young child carrying about the VHS version of *Aladdin* seems to some like another thing altogether. I'm not sure that it is.

The late Bruno Bettelheim (1976) had it right, I think, in claiming in his book, *The Uses of Enchantment,* that fairy tales are often used by children to deal with common anxieties and concerns. By having the same story read over and over, the child gains a kind of psychological mastery over material that may have been initially upsetting.

Just as we adults will try to gain a similar mastery over difficult material by rereading the same gut-wrenching paragraph in a novel where the protagonist is suddenly attacked or killed or finds out that she is really the child of someone else, so too will some children take comfort in hearing the same story over and over again.

To be sure, if the child wants to watch wrestling every night, this is a different matter and there are different questions at play because in this case the violence is graphic, realistic, and in the here and now. The great thing about fairy tales, and many other children's stories, is that the story almost invariably occurs "long, long ago and far, far away."

Unlike TV news and a great deal of other televised content, which gives every appearance of being immediate, real, and urgent, the early exposition in children's fairy tales typically distances the child from the potentially threatening events of the story in both time and place. This is the genius of such stories and Bettelheim hypothesized that they had evolved this way and had been handed down through the ages precisely because of these characteristics. The other reason that they have survived is that they are thought to deal effectively with what Bettelheim and many other child psychologists believe to be the common problems and fears of children concerning abandonment, sibling rivalry, self-control, and identity: "Am I really their child? Was I adopted?" and so on.

When the fairy tale is being read to the child, the child is also physically close to the parent or caregiver, often sitting on a lap. The caregiver is able to sensitively monitor the child's reactions and tell whether the story is too much. If the child's body suddenly stiffens, the reader knows it. Of course, by being physically close to a parent or other familiar caregiver, the young child is, almost by definition, in a secure, safe, and familiar setting when the fairy tale is being read. In marked contrast, all too many frightening stories on television are experienced by the child when alone or when only with other children; hence, there is little or no adult monitoring of both content and reaction.

As noted, much contemporary television material is seemingly "live," as with news and "reality" programs that purport to be real, although they are often reenactments and always carefully, and often intentionally, edited for optimal impact and fear induction. Two professional wrestlers committing mayhem on one another gives every appearance to the child of being real, graphic, frightening, and occurring in the here and now. It is a far different story from *Hansel and Gretel*, a fairy tale often cited for its particularly violent elements, albeit ones that are set far enough away and long enough ago and in a fanciful enough manner that most children can readily handle the story.

I might add that I have also been asked whether it is wise for children to watch themselves over and over again on a videotape. One parent asked whether it was OK for his young daughter to watch herself have a bath each night on videotape. This kind of question is very difficult to answer. I would be somewhat concerned about overfeeding the child's healthy narcissism and would probably limit the viewing of such a tape if it were my own child, especially if the child rarely took a "real" bath, but as with so many parental judgments, individual parents must use their best sense of their child's vulnerabilities and strengths to decide what's best for that child.

Viewing With Children

Experts on children and media generally advise parents to frequently watch TV with their children to help them understand what they are viewing and for children to learn from their parent's reactions. If a parent sees someone, real or fictional, on television doing something they find unacceptable there is nothing wrong, in my opinion, with expressing disapproval. Perhaps better yet, one might ask what the child thinks or feels about what the person did. Just as parents let their children know on occasion that the child's behavior needs improvement or that some adult or child in real life is doing something wrong, so too may they want to point these things out on television.

Just as important, we should also point to behaviors that we believe are exemplary and deserving of replication. All too often, we tell children what we don't want them to do rather than what we want them to do. Positive reinforcement is generally more effective than punishment.

This is not to say that we should overburden children with constant instructive talk during television viewing. That would be a mistake, too. I am arguing only that parents can use television as a learning tool in the home.

Parents also need to be wary of severely criticizing certain programs that their children enjoy. Clearly, as noted earlier, if you believe a program is not appropriate for your child you have the right to turn it off or make a comment. If, however, your child loves, say, *Mister Rogers' Neighborhood* or *Barney,* and even if you find these programs childish and occasionally silly, I recommend that you not show disrespect for your child's developing tastes and predilections by laughing at or deriding his or her favorite program. Recognize that these programs are designed for very young children, not for you! That's why they seem childish. Every child's program cannot be *Sesame Street,* a program that often appeals to both adults and children. I'll have more to say about more formal media education at the conclusion of this chapter, but let us first turn our attention to video and computer games.

Video Games and Computer Games

Today, media psychologists are asked as often about computer games and video games as about children's television habits, and with video games the term addiction comes up even more often. There has, unfortunately, been much less research on video games, but it is not difficult to apply many of the explanations offered earlier regarding how television dependence may develop to explain in part the newer phenomenon of people's affinity for these games. As with television, the games offer the player a kind of escape, and as with television, players learn quickly that they momentarily feel better when playing computer games; hence, a kind of psychological reinforcement develops.

But video and computer games also have particular characteristics that make children and adults especially likely to report that they are "addicted" to them. There is the general challenge posed by the game and the wish to overcome it and succeed, and there is the critical characteristic that the games are designed to minutely increase in challenge and difficulty along with the increasing ability of the player.

In being programmed to constantly challenge players at their current ability, video and computer games offer a nearly perfect level of difficulty for the player who enjoys such challenges. Many of us are never quite as exhilarated as when we have harnessed our abilities and set them against a difficult but surmountable challenge (Csikszentmihalyi, 1990). Video and computer games can offer children and adults such a challenge.

Indeed, as we have written elsewhere, computer and video games offer all the essential features that we know are likely to result in a "flow" experience of intense and enjoyable involvement and a high level of concentration: closely matched skills and challenges in the activity and rapid feedback regarding one's performance (Kubey & Csikszentmihalyi, 1990a). The games give the player nearly instantaneous feedback as to whether the last activity (shot, jump, run, or whatever) was successful. In computer play, as with sports, musical performance, and many hobbies, the feedback is quick and clear, and insofar as it is often occurring at the height of one's own personal level of performance, it's no wonder the games are extremely engaging and, perhaps, "addictive."

It should be noted that there have been a few cases reported in the news in recent years in North America and in Britain indicating that a very small number of children have exhibited symptoms of epilepsy in response to the flashing colors and other stimuli in the games. Video game manufacturers have not denied that this can occur and some have warned adults to be on the lookout for such problems.

Through watching my own son and his friends play video and computer games, I have observed that children exhibit different levels of eye and mental fatigue in response to different games. My son can play some games for 45 minutes straight with no evidence of such symptoms. But in other, very intense games I have observed that after only 10 or 15 minutes his eyes begin to blink rapidly and mental fatigue seems to set in. Indeed, I have my own variable visual (and auditory) tolerance for different games.

Parents have reported to me that long hours of uninterrupted video game play have occasionally left a child feeling nauseated or listless. Before I learned more about such effects, I once let my son play too long and after about 90 minutes he was complaining of slight nausea and fatigue. Even if you love video games and encourage children to play them, it might some-times be the case, as with other activities, that too much of a good thing is not so good.

How can you limit children's video game or computer play? One obvious and effective technique is to tell a child, and his or her friends, that they may play only for some specific period. This might be 20 to 40 minutes depending on the game, who the children are, the time of day, the weather outside, how much mental and physical energy they have left, and yes, perhaps even whether you can stand to hear the Super Mario Brothers music one more time before losing your sanity.

To enforce the limit, I have found it very effective to use a kitchen timer and to set it to the time I have deemed appropriate. I do not generally advise putting the ticking timer right on top of the TV or computer, lest we make too much of it. I leave mine in the kitchen near where my son and his buddies play their games and when it rings, they know to stop. And they do!

Were I to suddenly come in and tell them that 20 minutes were up, they would try to negotiate with me for more time. The timer seems to externalize responsibility, I happen to think in an acceptable way in this instance, and the children believe in its authority. Can I get the behavior I seek with my own voice? I can. But it is by my authority that the timer is set in the first place and it generally works better.

Dependence on Pornography

We have not yet paid attention to a type of media content that has also often been claimed to be addictive, one that has always been controversial and will surely remain so in the years ahead. Indeed, with the advent of interactive pornography available via CD-ROM, the debate over the value or harm of pornography is sure to heat up once again. In the concluding pages of this chapter, I will review some of the alleged effects of traditional pornography available via magazines and video and their alleged potential for habit formation. I will then turn my attention to new concerns that I believe are raised by the delivery of interactive erotica.

Research and reporting on pornography's effects has long been politicized and, consequently, it can be especially difficult to weigh the validity and veracity of some contributions to this literature. As with other media effects debates, it is very difficult to disentangle cause from effect. Still, a number of researchers and clinicians report both negative effects and evidence for dependence or in their words, "addiction," with regard to the use of pornography. Indeed, as will be seen, some of these negative effects are thought to be inevitably intertwined with "pornography addiction."

There is the frequent claim, for example, that large, private pornography collections are often found by authorities in the residences of persons arrested for sexual crimes (Cline, 1994; Reed, 1994), especially pedophiles (Lanning

& Burgess, 1989). [There is also evidence indicating that some rapists and child molesters use sexually explicit materials both before and during some sexual assaults (Marshall, 1988).] At a minimum we must say that a relationship between the frequent use of pornography and problematic sexual disorders exists for some individuals. Whether the pornography is merely symptomatic of the disorder or plays a causal role is much more difficult to establish.

Still, for some, there is little doubt that both negative effects and pornography addiction do indeed occur. Reed (1994), a practicing psychiatrist, is explicit in his presentation of specific criteria that he believes would constitute an addiction to pornography (pp. 251-252). He notes that the *DSM* itself recognizes that many paraphilias (compulsive sexual deviances) frequently involve the use and collection of pornography. Reed lists 13 paraphilias and how they are related to the use of pornography.

Cline (1994), a clinical psychologist who has treated hundreds of people with sexual disorders, describes a four-step process in the involvement of his patients with pornography. First described is an "addiction effect" wherein the person comes back repeatedly for more material because it provides "a very powerful sexual stimulant or aphrodisiac effect followed by sexual release most often through masturbation" (p. 233).

Cline goes on to describe an "escalation effect" in which there is an "increasing need for more of the stimulant to get the same effect" obtained initially (p. 233). Third, he observes "desensitization" in which things that might have once seemed shocking become less so and are thereby legitimized. Fourth, Cline claims that there is an "increasing tendency to act out sexually the behaviors viewed in the pornography" (p. 234).

A number of psychological and physiological mechanisms have been posited for how pornography addiction might develop. Among the most common is that sexual gratification is a powerful reinforcer (Lyons, Anderson, & Larson, 1994). This is the "addiction effect" described previously by Cline wherein learning is made all the more powerful by virtue of the sexual release that attends pornography's use. Here, Cline draws on McGaugh's (1983) memory research that suggests that experiences that co-occur with high emotional arousal may be better remembered. Reed (1994) suggests the possibility that some such learning might be occurring on the biological as well as the psychological level when he points out that "the neurotransmitters that are activated by pornography use may trigger similar neural pathways as cocaine or heroin" (p. 265).

I earlier applied an operant conditioning approach to the role relaxation plays in the development of the television viewing habit. It certainly makes sense that the pleasure accompanying orgasm may increase the potential for a habit to develop for some users of pornography, especially those who have few or no other outlets for sexual gratification. The early literature on sexual behavior points to strong associations developing between the particular ways in which first or early sexual gratifications were obtained and the object or means of that gratification (Ellis, 1906/1936). If one's primary means of sexual gratification at an early and impressionable age is via a particular technique or a particular object of desire, then there may be a kind of fixation on that technique, object, or both.

Cline (1994) argues further that if sexual problems can be alleviated in sex-counseling clinics with the use of sexual films, books, and videos as tools in therapy, then one must suspect that exposure to pornography can also have an effect. For Cline, and for many other observers, pornography provides powerful occasions in which modeling and imitative learning can occur.

Zillmann and Bryant (1988b) have made an important experimental contribution to the addiction hypothesis in showing that prolonged exposure to pornography can decrease some people's level of satisfaction with their partners and with the quality of their sex lives. Zillmann (1994) has gone on to propose that in many instances, "initial sexual dissatisfaction drives exposure to pornography" and a vicious circle then ensues. With consumption of pornography, the dissatisfaction grows stronger and draws the person into further consumption. For Zillmann, consumption of pornography invites comparisons that help drive dissatisfaction: "Consumers compare what they have, by way of sexual intimacy, with what pornography tells them they might and should have" (p. 210).

I have similarly proposed that the frequent exposure of highly romanticized and sexually arousing material on television, and elsewhere in our mainstream contemporary media, may fuel similar dissatisfactions and a propensity toward invidious comparison in a much broader spectrum of the population than was previously the case (Kubey, 1994; see also Bryant & Rockwell, 1994).

Other effects of pornography, aside from dependence, addiction, and modeling, have been studied and merit comment. Weaver (1994) has reviewed evidence indicating that exposure to pornography increases "sexual callousness" toward women. This callousness includes increased aggressivity toward women and a desensitization to the injury that violence or sexual assault causes.

Zillmann and Bryant (1988a, 1988b) have been interested in the degree to which "family values" may be on a collision course with pornography, and they again offer experimental evidence. These studies (see Zillmann, 1994 for a review) typically expose an experimental group of adults to pornographic videos over a number of weeks (often 6). Then, a week after the exposure, the groups' answers to survey questions are compared with those of a control group that was not exposed.[6]

The researchers' studies show that experimentally produced prolonged exposure to pornography results in a greater acceptance of both male and female promiscuity, and that as promiscuity is presumed to be more natural, adults also begin to assume that faithfulness between sexual intimates is less common than is assumed by those in the control group. The participants also report being more accepting of nonexclusive sexual intimacy for themselves.

In one study, when asked, "Do you feel that the institution of marriage is essential to the well functioning of society?" 60% of the control group agreed, but this was true for only 38.8% of the group exposed to pornography. Zillmann and Bryant (1988a) have also reported that exposure to pornography reduced the desire of their research participants, male and female, student and nonstudent, to want to have children. Zillmann (1994) suggests that this finding may,

> Support the contention that prolonged consumption of pornography makes having children and raising a family appear an unnecessary inconvenience, presumably because pornography continually projects easy access to superlative sexual gratification, these gratifications being attainable without emotional investment, without social confinements, without economic obligations, and without sacrifices of time and effort. (p. 208)

In this regard, the immediate gratification that commercial television so frequently offers and promotes may in its own right be in conflict with the values of constancy and commitment so necessary to the healthy functioning of family life (Kubey, 1994).

It is important to point out that the VCR has led to an explosion in pornographic videos and that such materials are today far more accessible to people, including children and adolescents, than they have ever been before. Also, if a pornography habit, or addiction, can indeed develop, it would seem more likely to develop if pornographic materials can be easily obtained and if the use of such materials is socially sanctioned.

It is not difficult to imagine how young people can come into contact with such materials. Even if a 12-year-old boy cannot rent a pornographic video on his own, it may well be that his friend's older brother who is 16, but looks 18, can. Of course, an increasing number of parents own such materials and keep them in their homes. Pornography is also now available via television cable systems.

Although I by no means frown on all uses of pornography, I do believe that it is not to be recommended for certain audiences. Again, I believe it is unwise for a 12-year-old boy to experience hard-core pornography, especially because it is likely to be one of the child's very first exposures to sexual intimacy and because as already noted, early intense sexual experiences may constitute particularly powerful early occasions for learning and impression formation.

Zillmann and Bryant's (1988a, 1988b) work suggests that such materials might also prove detrimental in the formation of a boy's impressions of female sexuality insofar as most such pornography depicts women as sexual objects whose primary goal is to serve the sexual desires of men. An occasional viewing of such materials by a pubescent or prepubescent boy might not have any deleterious or strong effects. When we recognize, however, that some boys may view such material every few days or even more often, and if we add that the boy typically seeks and obtains sexual release on viewing, I believe we raise the possibility that not only may a strong habit develop, it may be one that we would not want to encourage. This is especially true when we consider that this same boy is likely to begin having his first real sexual experiences with a girl or young woman in the not so distant future.

These concerns are multiplied when we consider the current advent of interactive, CD-ROM driven erotica. Typical of this new technological innovation are products such as "Virtual Valerie." This product presents movie quality images of young women who take their clothes off at the command of the viewer. Women on the screen can also be programmed at the touch of a button to say arousing things to the viewer and to perform a variety of sexually suggestive acts before the viewer's eyes. The CD-ROM technology and software for interactive erotica are developing rapidly and this is already believed to be one of the leading applications of CD-ROM, interactive media.

Let's return again to our 12-year-old boy. Imagine that he has obtained copies of a couple of interactive video products such as Virtual Valerie. Imagine that he interacts with them while masturbating a number of times a week, typically spending 10 to 30 minutes in each encounter, off and on for 3 years; then, at age 15, he goes on his first date with a "real" young woman his same age. Might his expectations of how she will act and how he should act if they become intimate have been altered by the many hours spent with his interactive pornography disks?

As yet, we do not know the answer. Conceivably there may be salutary benefits. Perhaps this form of pornography will help some people fantasize and obtain sexual release in such a way that there is a reduction in the commission of sexual crimes (see Linz & Malamuth, 1993, for a review of research on the positive cathartic effect of traditional pornography). Still, combining common sense with what we know about the learning of sexual behavior, I must say that I am concerned about young people, and some adults, overusing, and perhaps becoming dependent on, such a form of entertainment.

On Media Regulation and Media Education

The growth in media in this century has been nothing short of phenomenal. The electronic media, from radio and television to video games and computers, have revolutionized the ways in which we are entertained and receive information and how we perceive the world around us. The development of these media technologies and media content can be partly credited to the economic and political freedoms that we enjoy. It is hard to imagine so much material being developed or new technologies being invented and proliferating so quickly were it not for free markets and the profit motive.

At the same time, unbridled development in the media industries, as with many industries, can also bring problems. Just as unregulated manufacturing industries can pollute the land, air, and water that sustain life, so too can irresponsible, profit-driven media production pollute the public mind and experience of a culture. The commercialization of news may foster competition and the quick dissemination of breaking stories, but it may also lead to sensationalism and carelessness in the preparation of information for public consumption.

The commercialization of entertainment has brought about ever more media materials, many of them charming, educational, and inspiring. But much material of questionable value is also available, and from a regulatory point of view, one of the prime differences between the electronic media and what came before in print is that radio, television, and computer communications come directly into the home, often by the touch of a single button by children as young as 12 months.

Increasingly, it seems, many citizens have come to the conclusion that the media are making available ideas and practices that are at odds with the very values that they would wish the society to uphold. To my mind, more often than not, such media excesses are both initiated and encouraged by the commercial underpinning of media production and the delivery systems we have adopted as a society. This is not easily changed.

The Federal Communications Commission (FCC) in the United States could surely threaten license revocation with greater frequency than it currently does (almost never) and actually revoke licenses from time to time when stations and networks are clearly not fulfilling their public service requirements. I also think it is appropriate for the public, through its local, state, and federal governments, to put pressure on the media industries to operate in the public interest. Consumer boycotts are a sensible means of advocacy and public protest. After all, the founding of the United States was marked by a consumer boycott of tea.

Rather than cut the funding of the Corporation for Public Broadcasting and PBS, as has been advocated by the new leaders of the U.S. Congress, in my view, more government funding for public broadcasting is called for. A comparison of other countries' public broadcasting expenditures against the annual $1.09 per capita expenditure in the United States is striking. Current comparable spending for public broadcasting in the United Kingdom is $38.56, in Canada $32.15, and in Japan $17.71, this according to a Tom Shales's *Washington Post* column from February 1995. That's a ratio of nearly 30 to 1 in Canada and over 35 to 1 in England!

What could be done with increased funding? How about a commercially free public broadcasting service dedicated completely to the interests and needs of children and parents? Such a development is especially important nowadays for less economically advantaged children who generally do not have access to cable or to the more valuable video selections made by parents who can afford VCRs and videotape rentals and purchases. As a result, the only remaining television programming available for poor children in the United States that is not governed by the whims of the marketplace is PBS.

Ideally, media producers would self-govern, because it is very problematic for a free society to engage in official censorship. Because, however, I do not expect Hollywood to reform itself along the lines that I might like and because

I do not expect governments to intervene substantially, nor am I entirely comfortable with them doing so, I have long since come to the conclusion that one of the best possible responses to the media environment in which we now live is media education.

As a culture, we need to become much more media savvy. Adults need to help children become more knowledgeable about the media—more media literate if you will—and I believe we need to develop formal media education in the schools. Tens of millions of children spend upward of 4 hours daily in contact with the electronic media, and they almost certainly will do so as adults as well. A great percentage of our political and commercial discourse occurs in the media. That most of our schools provide no formal training in how these media are produced, and in how they communicate and persuade, is shortsighted at best.

Much media education focuses on helping students engage in more critical readings and evaluations of the media products they encounter. This is ideally augmented by direct, hands-on experience in producing the media, because media educators worldwide agree that creating media helps students develop their critical faculties much more rapidly and effectively than almost any other educational practice. In many schools, students also study how different groups of people interpret the same media product differently.

Readers new to the field might ask themselves why studying audiences has any relevance to basic education. The answer coming from media educators is that it can be critical, increasingly so as we advance multicultural approaches to education. In this approach to media education students come to learn, early on, that different people and different groups often understand and interpret the same texts and communication acts differently. One way to advance and teach tolerance, then, is to encourage students from very early on to understand that the person next to them in school or on the street or in the living room may be having an altogether different response to what people say and do, as well as to the same picture, story, or television program.

I have seen this approach to media education being developed very effectively around the world. In Israel, children as young as 5 and 6 pick out favorite pictures from magazines at home and bring them into school. The children then talk or, at older ages (I watched 9-year-olds for example), write about what they see in these pictures. They are asked to tell or write a story about the picture. Of course, what they see and tell varies. As a result, in these very early years of formal schooling, children begin to learn how their schoolmates from different backgrounds see, interpret, and create differently.

Another exercise has the teacher expose only a small portion of a set of magazine pictures chosen in advance. The students than examine the exposed portions and try to guess what's going on in the hidden part of the picture. Children (and adults) have great fun with this and see different things. Here again, we have a way to get people at very young ages to engage in imaginative thinking and also appreciate how people think and respond differently.

On a site visit to a school outside London a few years ago, I had the opportunity to see a media education exercise being piloted under the auspices of the British Film Institute. Here, kindergartners were given still cameras to take on a walk about their school and to a nearby park. They took photos of the school's immediate environs. Later, working with their teachers, the students worked on a group story with the developed pictures and then they chose and set music behind the pictures for a multimedia show about their school, where it is, and what goes on about it.

In this extraordinarily well-devised exercise students learn not only how to use a camera but also that the camera sees only so much and that, therefore, there are editing decisions being made from the very beginning of the media production about what viewers will see. Students experience the editing process again later as they storyboard their photos and see how some pictures help tell the story better than others, how some pictures end up on the kindergarten room (editing room) floor, and then how different musical choices enhance and set different moods. By the end of the project, the children have learned a lot about media production through an engaging hands-on experience. Interested readers can find more complete discussions of similar exercises in my edited book, *Media Literacy in the Information Age* (Kubey, 1996).

It should be mentioned that most media education does not involve a direct emphasis on reducing the student's consumption of television or other media, although some teachers in the United States do attempt this goal. Many of the leading innovators in media education believe it is wrong to try actively to dissuade students from enjoying the stories they like so much from the movies or on TV. Bashing the programs and stories that students love generally runs counter to the ideals of most media educators, which are to develop a deeper appreciation and critical stance with regard to the media. Ideally this involves students becoming more discriminating in their media use, but it is generally thought to be unwise to force a view on students that television will harm them.

A somewhat more indirect approach that might strike the fancy of those who would like children to view less has its basis in an approach to getting control of the television habit discussed earlier in this chapter. Here, each child or student in a classroom is asked to keep a television log of all his or her viewing for a week; or the child can try to encourage the whole family to keep a log. The results of these logs can be analyzed individually or in class. I have seen whole classes apply their math skills to calculating average viewing rates of different programs for the whole class and so on.

In this way, children begin to see how much viewing is going on and how much time is being absorbed. If, as a result of this exercise, the child chooses to view less, so be it. But at least the choice came from the child and was not forced.

I am also generally supportive of people or families voluntarily trying a TV-free week. This is often very instructive because people, adults as much as children, come to see how deeply interwoven and habitual television use has become in their lives. Again, as a result of such an experiment some families or children choose to watch less, but the decision is made autonomously and freely, and this is ideal from my point of view.

With regard to formal media education, I do want to be clear that I do not advocate an end to traditional training in literature and the print media. Far from it. Rather, I advocate educational inclusion of the other media that occupy our attention and thoughts in the modern world (Kubey, 1991). Good media education involves lots of writing, including criticism, as well as preparation for media production itself.

The idea still promulgated by some educational traditionalists, that we should not teach about film or television because they are not in the same league with great literature is, to my mind, an antiquated and demonstrably false notion. In the first place, we don't study texts, art, and literature only to come into contact with what some people have deemed as the very best. Indeed, I would argue that we can often learn more about what makes for an excellent short story or film or piece of music by looking and listening to stories, films, and music that did not come out so very well.

Second, there are film and television productions every bit as important, artful, and valuable for interpretation and discussion as traditional literature. Films and television programs such as Welles's *Citizen Kane,* Capra's *It's a Wonderful Life,* or Burns's *The Civil War* are as evocative, as artfully told, and as quintessentially "American" as any of the print literature that is often deemed appropriate for English (or history) classes. Furthermore, critical pedagogy demands that we study the world and environment around us, the weather, the buildings, the people, the cities. Certainly the constantly changing media world in which we all now live is also worthy of study.

The prime reason that students do not formally study film and television stories is because most educational systems haven't adjusted to modern modes of storytelling, because teachers have not been trained to teach about film and television, and because our society assumes that popular and commercial entertainment is not worthy of study. In time this will change. After all, critics who say that we should not use popular, commercial materials in the contemporary classroom seem unaware that many of both Twain's and Dickens's original works were first read in the popular, commercial magazines and newspapers of their day.

To be sure, formal media education is rapidly developing in many countries around the world. Australia recently mandated media education for virtually 100% of its students from kindergarten to Grade 12. Since 1987, Ontario, with roughly one third of Canada's population, has mandated media literacy instruction in English classes for all students from Grades 7 through 12. In 1995 in England, it is expected that some 6,000 to 7,000 students will take one of their advanced level examinations for university admission in media studies. Scotland and South Africa can also boast substantially more formal development of media education than can the United States, leaving the very country that produces more of the world's media product than any other as the least developed media educator in the English-speaking world. How this has come about is one of the subjects of my current research.

But change is afoot in the United States. In 1992, the Communications and Society Program of the Aspen Institute held a National Leadership Conference on Media Literacy. Their *Forum Report* (Aufderheide, 1992) summarizes the conclusions they drew and the definition of a "media-literate person" as one who "can decode, evaluate, analyze, and produce both print and electronic media" (p. 1).[7] The first major media literacy conference in the United States occurred in September 1995 in North Carolina, and in the last few years, intensive institutes and seminars for teachers have been offered at an increasing rate.

Although the future for media education in the United States is growing brighter with each passing year, the obstacles to widespread acceptance remain substantial. For one thing, the United States makes almost no federal educational policy, and only a couple of states have mandated any expertise in communications generally. Nor is there adequate training of teachers to do media education. Also, with all the other demands on teachers, and tighter and tighter school budgets, it will be years before the United States begins to catch up significantly with Australia, the United Kingdom, or Canada.

Meanwhile, there's nothing to stop the interested parent or caregiver from encouraging analysis at home or from contacting the various organizations in the United States and Canada that offer media education materials.[8]

Notes

1. This is not to say that viewers don't also view television in a more active frame of mind, from time to time, but our research shows that viewers generally report feeling passive when viewing. For most viewers, active viewing moments are infrequent by comparison (Csikszentmihalyi & Kubey, 1981; Kubey, in press). Some researchers conclude that viewers, especially young children, are not passive when they view and that children do not adopt the "zombielike" expression often described by parents and depicted in comics. Much of this research, however, is done in laboratories where people may well engage in a more active form of viewing than in the comfort and familiarity of their own homes. The experimental viewer often anticipates that they will be tested after viewing, and they often are. The same problem of distorting results can occur when people are asked by researchers to carefully describe what a particular program means to them or why they watch it. As pointed out by Ang (1985) and others, it is possible that in both experimental and field research, the phenomenon under study, audience activity or a retrospective assessment of one's thinking processes during viewing, is confounded by the very methods used. Because ESM studies have not singled television out from other daily activities and because we ask only for very simple affective and cognitive assessments, we believe that the distorting influences of methodology do not pertain to the same extent as in laboratory studies.

2. Indeed, research going back nearly three decades in the United States, England, and Japan has demonstrated that TV viewing passivity often is associated with mild feelings of guilt and self-contempt (Bower, 1973; Furu, 1971; Himmelweit & Swift, 1976; Steiner, 1963), especially among more affluent and educated viewers.

3. According to Robinson et al. (1993), however, in some cases this relationship may be extremely weak at best, and causal inferences may not be warranted.

4. It is interesting to note that there are very few reports of patients' television viewing habits in the clinical literature, yet some psychotherapists have told me that difficulty limiting viewing (or more frequently, limiting their partner's or children's viewing) is sometimes raised by patients in therapy. More frequently, patients in psychotherapy compare their own experiences, feelings, and ideas to those of particular characters in television programs they watch. This is particularly likely to occur at moments of intense emotion in therapy (James Hutchinson, M.D., personal communication, February 1994). Such a phenomenon may be rather benign, but it may also indicate externalization, that is, avoiding and defending against fully experiencing and taking ownership of uncomfortable thoughts, feelings, and behaviors.

5. Tannenbaum (1980), however, showed that suspense plots can indeed be gripping. Under experimental conditions he found that some viewers will go to considerable lengths to see how a suspenseful story turns out.

6. People in both groups are randomly assigned to these two treatment conditions. Most of this research has been done with college students, but the researchers have also occasionally expanded their research to community samples.

7. Aufderheide's (1992) report will also soon be republished in a book edited by Kubey (1996).

8. In the United States, readers might wish to contact the National Telemedia Council, 120 E. Wilson St., Madison, WI 53703, (608) 257-7712, or the Center for Media Literacy, 4727 Wilshire Blvd. #403, Los Angeles, CA 90010, (213) 931-4177. In Canada, try the Association for Media Literacy, 300-47 Ranleigh Avenue, Toronto, Ontario M4N 1X2, Canada, (416) 488-7280.

References

American Psychiatric Association. (1994). *Diagnostic and statistical manual of mental disorders* (4th ed.). Washington, DC: Author.

Anderson, D. R., Alwitt, L. F., Lorch E. P., & Levin, S. T. (1979). Watching children watch television. In G. Hale & M. Lewis (Eds.), *Attention and the development of cognitive skills* (pp. 331-361). New York: Plenum.

Ang, I. (1985). *Watching* Dallas: *Soap opera and the melodramatic imagination.* London: Methuen.

Aufderheide, P. (1992). *Media literacy: A report on the National Leadership Conference on Media Literacy.* Washington, DC: Aspen Institute.

Bettelheim, B. (1976). *The uses of enchantment: The meaning and importance of fairy tales.* New York: Knopf.

Bower, R. T. (1973). *Television and the public.* New York: Holt, Rinehart & Winston.

Bronfenbrenner, U. (1973). Television and the family. In A. Clayre (Ed.), *The impact of broadcasting* (p. 20). London: Compton Russell.

Bryant, J., & Rockwell, S. C. (1994). Effects of massive exposure to sexually oriented prime-time television programming on adolescent moral judgment. In D. Zillmann, J. Bryant, & A. C. Huston (Eds.), *Media, children, and the family: Social scientific, psychodynamic, and clinical perspectives* (pp. 183-195). Hillsdale, NJ: Lawrence Erlbaum.

Bryant, J., & Zillmann, D. (1984). Using television to alleviate boredom and stress: Selective exposure as a function of induced excitational states. *Journal of Broadcasting and Electronic Media, 28*(1), 1-20.

Buckingham, D., & Sefton-Green, J. (1996). Multimedia education: A curriculum for the future? In R. Kubey (Ed.). *Media literacy in the information age. Information and behavior, Vol. 6.* New Brunswick, NJ: Transaction Publishing.

Cline, V. B. (1994). Pornography effects: Empirical and clinical evidence. In D. Zillmann, J. Bryant, & A. C. Huston (Eds.), *Media, children, and the family: Social scientific, psychodynamic, and clinical perspectives* (pp. 229-247). Hillsdale, NJ: Lawrence Erlbaum.

Condry, J. (1989). *The psychology of television.* Hillsdale, NJ: Lawrence Erlbaum.

Csikszentmihalyi, M. (1990). *Flow: The psychology of optimal experience.* New York: Harper & Row.

Csikszentmihalyi, M., & Kubey, R. W. (1981). Television and the rest of life: A systematic comparison of subjective experience. *Public Opinion Quarterly, 45,* 317-328.

Daley, E. A. (1978). *Father feelings.* New York: William Morrow.

Desmond, R. J., Singer, J. C., & Singer, D. G. (1988). Family mediation and children's cognition, aggression, and comprehension of television: A longitudinal study. *Journal of Applied Developmental Psychology, 9,* 329-347.

deVries, M. W. (1987). Investigating mental disorders in their natural settings. *Journal of Nervous and Mental Disease, 175*(9), 509-513.

Dietz, W., & Gortmaker, S. L. (1985). Do we fatten our children at the television set: Obesity and television viewing in children and adolescents. *Pediatric, 75,* 807-812.

Ellis, H. (1936). *Studies in the psychology of sex, Vol. II.* New York: Random House. (Original work published in 1906)

Eysenck, H. (1978). *Sex, violence, and the media.* London: Maurice-Temple-Smith.

Furu, T. (1971). *The function of television for children and adolescents.* Tokyo: Sophia University Press.

Gallup, G., & Newport, F. (1990, October 10). Americans love—and hate—their TVs. *San Francisco Chronicle,* p. B3.

Goleman, D. (1990, October 16). How viewers grow addicted to television. *New York Times,* p. C1.

Harrison, L. F., & Williams, T. M. (1986). Television and cognitive development. In T. M. Williams (Ed.), *The impact of television* (pp. 87-142). New York: Academic Press.

Himmelweit, H., & Swift, B. (1976). Continuities and discontinuities in media usage and taste: A longitudinal study. *Journal of Social Issues, 32,* 133-156.

Huston, A. C., Donnerstein, E., Fairchild, H., Feshbach, N. D., Katz, P. A., Murray, J. P., Rubinstein, E. A., Wilcox, B. L., & Zuckerman, D. (1992). *Big world, small screen: The role of television in American society.* Lincoln, NE: University of Nebraska Press.

Jason, L. A. (1987). Reducing children's excessive television viewing and assessing secondary changes. *Journal of Clinical and Child Psychology, 16,* 245-250.

Johnson, C., & Larson, R. (1982). Bulimia: An analysis of moods and behavior. *Psychosomatic Medicine, 44,* 341-351.

Kubey, R. W. (1980). Television and aging: Past, present, and future. *The Gerontologist, 20*(1), 16-35.

Kubey, R. W. (1984). *Leisure, television, and subjective experience.* Unpublished doctoral dissertation, University of Chicago.

Kubey, R. W. (1986). Television use in everyday life: Coping with unstructured time. *Journal of Communication, 36*(3), 108-123.

Kubey, R. (1987). *Testimony before the Subcommittee on Antitrust, Monopolies, and Business Rights of the Committee on the Judiciary, U.S. Senate, on a Television Violence Antitrust Exemption, June 25* (Serial No. J-100027). Washington, DC: Government Printing Office.

Kubey, R. (1990a, August 5). A body at rest tends to stay on the couch. *New York Times,* Section 2, p. 27.

Kubey, R. (1990b). Television and family harmony among children, adolescents, and adults: Results from the experience sampling method. In J. Bryant (Ed.), *Television and the American family* (pp. 73-88). Hillsdale, NJ: Lawrence Erlbaum.

Kubey, R. (1990c). Television and the quality of family life. *Communication Quarterly, 38,* 312-324.

Kubey, R. (1991, March 6). The case for media education. *Education Week, 10,* p. 27.

Kubey, R. (1994). Media implications for the quality of family life. In D. Zillmann, J. Bryant, & A. C. Huston (Eds.), *Media, children, and the family: Social scientific, psychodynamic, and clinical perspectives* (pp. 183-195). Hillsdale, NJ: Lawrence Erlbaum.

Kubey, R. (Ed.). (1996). *Media literacy in the information age: Current perspectives. Information and Behavior, Vol. 6.* New Brunswick, NJ: Transaction Publishing.

Kubey, R. (in press). On not finding media effects: Conceptual problems in the notion of an "active" audience (with a reply to Elihu Katz). In L. Grossberg, J. Hay, & E. Wartella (Eds.), *Toward a comprehensive theory of the audience.* Boulder, CO: Westview.

Kubey, R., & Csikszentmihalyi, M. (1990a). *Television and the quality of life: How viewing shapes everyday experience.* Hillsdale, NJ: Lawrence Erlbaum.

Kubey, R., & Csikszentmihalyi, M. (1990b). Television as escape: Subjective experience before an evening of heavy viewing. *Communication Reports, 3*(2), 92-100.

Lanning, K., & Burgess, A. (1989). Child pornography and sex rings. In D. Zillmann & J. Bryant (Eds.), *Pornography: Research advances and policy considerations* (pp. 235-255). Hillsdale, NJ: Lawrence Erlbaum.

Larson, R., Csikszentmihalyi, M., & Freeman, M. (1984). Alcohol and marijuana use in adolescents' daily lives: A random sample of experiences. *International Journal of Addictions, 19,* 367-381.

Larson, R., & Johnson, C. (1981). Anorexia nervosa in the context of daily experience. *Journal of Youth and Adolescence, 10,* 341-351.

Lewinsohn, P. M. (1974). Behavioral approach to depression. In R. J. Friedman & M. M. Katz (Eds.), *The psychology of depression: Contemporary theory and research* (pp. 157-185). New York: John Wiley.

Linz, D., & Malamuth, N. (1993). *Pornography.* Newbury Park, CA: Sage.

Lowenstein, R. J., Hamilton, J., Alagna, S., Reid, N., & deVries, M. (1987). Experiential sampling in the study of multiple personality disorder. *American Journal of Psychiatry, 144*(1), 19-24.

Lyons, J. S., Anderson, R. L., & Larson, D. B. (1994). A systematic review of the effects of aggressive and nonaggressive pornography. In D. Zillmann, J. Bryant, & A. C. Huston (Eds.), *Media, children, and the family: Social scientific, psychodynamic, and clinical perspectives* (pp. 271-310). Hillsdale, NJ: Lawrence Erlbaum.

Maccoby, E. (1951). Television: Its impact on school children. *Public Opinion Quarterly, 15,* 421-444.

Mander, J. (1978). *Four arguments for the elimination of television.* New York: Morrow Quill.

Marshall, W. L. (1988). The use of explicit sexual stimuli by rapists, child molesters, and nonoffender males. *Journal of Sex Research, 25,* 267-288.

McGaugh, J. L. (1983). Preserving the presence of the past. *American Psychologist, 38,* 161.

McIlwraith, R. D. (1990, August). *Theories of television addiction.* Paper presented at the annual meeting of the American Psychological Association, Boston, MA.

McIlwraith, R. D., Jacobvitz, R. S., Kubey, R., & Alexander, A. (1991). Television addiction: Theories and data behind the ubiquitous metaphor. *American Behavioral Scientist, 35*(2), 104-121.

McIlwraith, R. D., & Schallow, J. R. (1983). Adult fantasy life and patterns of media use. *Journal of Communication, 33*(1), 78-91.

Milkman, H., & Sunderwirth, S. (1987). *Craving for ecstasy: The consciousness and chemistry of escape.* Toronto: Lexington Books.

National Institute of Mental Health. (1982). *Television and behavior: Ten years of scientific progress and implications for the eighties* (Vol. 1). Rockville, MD: U.S. Department of Health and Human Services.

Reed, M. D. (1994). Pornography addiction and compulsive sexual behavior. In D. Zillmann, J. Bryant, & A. C. Huston (Eds.), *Media, children, and the family: Social scientific, psychodynamic, and clinical perspectives* (pp. 249-269). Hillsdale, NJ: Lawrence Erlbaum.

Robinson, J. (1989, April). Time for work. *American Demographics,* p. 68.

Robinson, T. N., Hammer, L. D., Killen, J. D., Kraemer, H. C., Wilson, D. M., Hayward, C., & Taylor, C. B. (1993). Does television viewing increase obesity and reduce physical activity? Cross-sectional and longitudinal analyses among adolescent girls. *Pediatrics, 91,* 273-280.

Rosenberg, M. (1978). *Television and its viewers* [Radio broadcast of Conversations at Chicago]. Chicago: University of Chicago.

Ryan, B. H. (1974, June 9). Would you free your children from the monster? *Denver Post.*

Schallow, J., & McIlwraith, R. (1986-1987). Is television viewing really bad for your imagination: Content and process of TV viewing and imaginal styles. *Imagination, Cognition, and Personality, 6*(10), 25-42.

Seiter, E. (in press). How parents view their children's television viewing. In L. Grossberg, J. Hay, & E. Wartella (Eds.), *Toward a comprehensive theory of the audience.* Boulder, CO: Westview.

Seyrek, S. K., Corah, N. L., & Pace, L. F. (1984). Comparison of three distraction techniques in reducing stress in dental patients. *Journal of the American Dental Association, 108,* 327-329.

Shales, T. (1995, February 27). Misguided missiles aimed at public TV. *The Washington Post,* p. B1.

Shanahan, J., & Morgan, M. (1989). Television as a diagnostic indicator in child therapy: An exploratory study. *Child and Adolescent Social Work, 6,* 175-191.

Singer, J. (1980). The power and limitations of television: A cognitive-affective analysis. In P. Tannenbaum (Ed.), *The entertainment functions of television* (pp. 31-65). Hillsdale, NJ: Lawrence Erlbaum.

Singer, J., & Singer, D. (1983). Implications of childhood television viewing for cognition, imagination, and emotion. In J. Bryant & D. Anderson (Eds.), *Children's understanding of television: Research on attention and comprehension* (pp. 265-296). New York: Academic Press.

Smith, R. (1986). Television addiction. In J. Bryant & D. Anderson (Eds.), *Perspectives on media effects* (pp. 109-128). Hillsdale, NJ: Lawrence Erlbaum.

Steiner, G. (1963). *The people look at television.* New York: Knopf.

Swonger, A. K., & Constantine, L. L. (1976). *Drugs and therapy: A psychotherapists handbook of psychotropic drugs.* Boston: Little, Brown.

Tannenbaum, P. (1980). Entertainment as vicarious emotional experience. In P. Tannenbaum (Ed.), *The entertainment functions of television* (pp. 107-131). Hillsdale, NJ: Lawrence Erlbaum.

Taras, H. L., Sallis, J. F., Patterson, T. L., Nader, P. R., & Nelson, J. A. (1989). Television's influence on children's diet and physical activity. *Journal of Developmental and Behavioral Pediatrics, 10,* 176-180.

Weaver, J. B. (1994). Pornography and sexual callousness: The perceptual and behavioral consequences of exposure to pornography. In D. Zillmann, J. Bryant, & A. C. Huston (Eds.), *Media, children, and the family: Social scientific, psychodynamic, and clinical perspectives* (pp. 215-228). Hillsdale, NJ: Lawrence Erlbaum.

Wilkins, J. A. (1982). *Breaking the TV habit.* New York: Scribner.

Williams, T. M. (Ed.). (1986). *The impact of television: A natural experiment in three communities.* New York: Academic Press.

Williams, T. M., & Handford, A. G. (1986). Television and other leisure activities. In T. M. Williams (Ed.), *The impact of television* (pp. 143-213). New York: Academic Press.

Winick, C. (1988). The functions of television: Life without the big box. In S. Oskamp (Ed.), *Television as a social issue* (pp. 217-237). Newbury Park, CA: Sage.

Winn, M. (1977). *The plug-in drug.* New York: Viking.

Zillmann, D. (1994). Erotica and family values. In D. Zillmann, J. Bryant, & A. C. Huston (Eds.), *Media, children, and the family: Social scientific, psychodynamic, and clinical perspectives* (pp. 199-213). Hillsdale, NJ: Lawrence Erlbaum.

Zillmann, D., & Bryant, J. (1988a). Effects of prolonged consumption of pornography on family values. *Journal of Family Issues, 9,* 518-544.

Zillmann, D., & Bryant, J. (1988b). Pornography's impact on sexual satisfaction. *Journal of Applied Social Psychology, 18,* 438-453.

Author Index

261

Subject Index

About the Editor

Tannis M. MacBeth, Ph.D., formerly Tannis MacBeth Williams, is a developmental psychologist in the Department of Psychology at the University of British Columbia in Vancouver, B.C., Canada. The common thread underlying her research has been her focus on social issues. Her research on the content and effects of television began with her discovery in 1973 of a town without television. Currently, she is analyzing portrayals of gender, racial-ethnic groups, aggression, emotion, and so forth in informative and noninformative children's TV programs. In another current research project, she is studying the role of stereotypes in beliefs and attitudes regarding mood and other fluctuations over the menstrual, lunar, and day-of-week cycles. She also is studying parent-child attachment relationships and the adult attachment relationships of twins. She has written many journal articles and numerous chapters and is author of *The Impact of Television: A Natural Experiment in Three Communities* (1986).

About the Authors

Joanne Cantor, Ph.D., is Professor of Communication Arts at the University of Wisconsin—Madison, where she has worked since receiving her Ph.D. from Indiana University in 1974. She has published more than 60 scholarly articles and chapters on the impact of the mass media on children, adolescents, and adults. Her main interests are focused on television and children, particularly children's emotional reactions to television. She has received funding from the National Institute of Mental Health, the National Science Foundation, and the H. F. Guggenheim Foundation. She is a member of the research team for the National Television Violence Study, funded by the National Cable Television Association and coordinated by the Los Angeles-based nonprofit group Mediascope. She is also a consultant and research adviser to Wisconsin Public Television for their award-winning children's series *Get Real!* and she is contributing to a Guggenheim-funded book on the attractions of violence.

Eric F. Dubow, Ph.D., is Professor in the Department of Psychology at Bowling Green State University in Bowling Green, Ohio. His research interests include the development of aggression in children, the identification of risk and protective factors in children's adjustment, the development and evaluation of school-based primary prevention programs to promote resilience in children, and child clinical psychology. His recent publications include journal articles and book chapters.

Sherryl Browne Graves, Ph.D., is Associate Professor and Chairperson in the Department of Educational Foundations and Counseling Programs in the

Division of Programs in Education at Hunter College of the City University of New York. She received her Ph.D. from Harvard University in clinical psychology and public practice. Before coming to Hunter College, she taught at New York University and the University of Rafael Urdaneta in Maracaibo, Venezuela. Her research interests include the impact of media and technology on children, the nature of racial and ethnic attitude development in children and youths, and the role of women from underrepresented groups in higher education. She is actively involved in the area of multicultural education. In addition to writing on the topic, she has conducted workshops addressing issues of diversity in a variety of educational settings. She has served as a consultant to a variety of television broadcast and production groups, including the Children's Television Workshop, Lancit Media, WGBH, ITVS (Independent Television Service), and the Corporation for Public Broadcasting. She has served as a research consultant or evaluator for a variety of projects, including the computer equity expert project of the Women's Action Alliance and the American Social History Project of the Hunter College Center for Media and Learning. Currently, she is coproject director for the DeWitt Wallace Readers' Digest, Pathways to Teaching minority teacher recruitment and training grant.

Aletha C. Huston, Ph.D., is University Distinguished Professor of Human Development and Codirector of the Center for Research on the Influences of Television on Children at the University of Kansas. She is Past President of the Developmental Psychology Division of the American Psychological Association and the recipient of the Irvin Youngberg Award for Outstanding Achievement in Applied Sciences. She is author of *Big World, Small Screen: The Role of Television in American Society* and winner of the Award for Distinguished Contribution to Psychology and the Media from the Division of Media Psychology of the American Psychological Association. She has conducted research on television and children since 1970 when she carried out a ground-breaking field experiment investigating the effects of prosocial television and violent programs for the Surgeon General's Scientific Advisory Committee on Television and Social Behavior. In collaboration with John Wright, she has published numerous articles and chapters on children's reactions to the forms and content of television with particular emphasis on learning about how television can enhance children's development.

Robert W. Kubey, Ph.D., is Associate Professor of Communication in the School of Communication, Information, and Library Studies at Rutgers University, New Brunswick, New Jersey; and Research Director of the Media Education Laboratory in the Department of Visual and Performing Arts at Rutgers, Newark, New Jersey. Trained as a developmental psychologist at the University of Chicago, he has been an Annenberg Scholar in Media Literacy at the University of Pennsylvania, a National Institute of Mental Health postdoctoral research fellow in the Program in Social Ecology at the University of California at Irvine, a research fellow of the Gerontological Society of America, and a fellow of Rutgers' Center for the Critical Analysis of Contemporary Culture. He has also been Visiting Professor at Stanford University and has served as a faculty member of the Institute on Media Education at Harvard University. He is coauthor, with Mihaly Csikszentmihalyi, of *Television and the Quality of Life: How Viewing Shapes Everyday Experience* (1990); is currently completing *Creating Television: Then and Now,* a book about the creative decision-making process in Hollywood; and is the editor of *Media Literacy in the Information Age: Current Perspectives, Information and Behavior, Vol. 6* (1996).

Laurie S. Miller, Ph.D., is Assistant Professor of Clinical Psychology in the Department of Psychiatry at Columbia University College of Physicians and Surgeons. She is also Director of the Disruptive Behavior Disorder Clinic in Pediatric Psychiatry at Columbia Presbyterian Medical Center. Her research interests include the development, prevention, and treatment of childhood conduct problems and antisocial behavior. She has developed a multisystemic early intervention program for inner-city preschoolers who are at high risk for behavior problems. She is currently conducting a study to test the efficacy of this program. She is also involved in a number of longitudinal studies that examine the role of individual factors (e.g., intelligence, social-cognition), family factors (e.g., parenting practices, parental psychopathology), and community factors (e.g., witnessing community violence) in the development of disruptive behavior in children and adolescents. Her recent publications include several journal articles.

John C. Wright, Ph.D., completed his Ph.D. in psychology at Stanford in 1960. From 1960 to 1968 he served on the faculty of the University of

Minnesota; from 1968 to the present he has been Professor in the Department of Human Development at the University of Kansas, where together with his spouse, Aletha C. Huston, he directs the Center for Research on the Influences of Television on Children (CRITC). His research has focused on the cognitive development of children, especially the development of attention and information-getting skills, curiosity, exploration, and search. He studied cognitive style and is the author of the Kansas Reflection-Impulsivity Scale for Preschoolers (KRISP). With Professor Huston he has received more than $3 million in research grant support from government and foundations. He has published more than 100 articles, chapters, and books on children's understanding of television and its long-term effects on their intellectual development. Currently, he is studying children's processing of form and content, reality-factuality and imagery of TV, and the contrasting effects of educational and entertainment programming on young children. This research has been presented at numerous conferences, including a special conference at the White House in 1995 and a variety of programs ranging from NBC's *Today Show* to NPR's *Talk of the Nation.*